Meanings and situations

International Library of Sociology

Founded by Karl Mannheim

Editor : John Rex, University of Warwick

Arbor Scientate
Arbor Vitae

A catalogue of the books available in the **International Library of Sociology**, and new books in preparation for the Library, will be found at the end of this volume.

Meanings and situations

Arthur Brittan

Routledge & Kegan Paul
London and Boston

First published 1973
by Routledge & Kegan Paul Ltd
Broadway House, 68–74 Carter Lane,
London EC4V 5EL and
9 Park Street,
Boston, Mass. 02108, USA
Printed in Great Britain by
Clarke, Doble & Brendon Ltd
Plymouth
© Arthur Brittan 1973

ISBN 0 7100 7509 X (c)
ISBN 0 7100 7551 0 (p)
Library of Congress Catalogue Card No. 72-90009

Contents

For my Mother

Introduction

There is a great deal of presumption involved in attempting to write a book on aspects of sociological thought. In a sense, every sociologist is a theorist of sorts. Even the most committed empiricist employs an 'anti-theory' which in itself, on inspection, turns out to be a theoretical statement.

The conscious attempt, therefore, to deliberately write about theory is not to be seen as an exercise in word magic. If every sociologist is his own theorist, then the justification for theory must surely lie in the fact that theorizing is a crucial sociological activity. It is an activity which is not divorced from the everyday activities of 'bread-and-butter sociologists'. In this sense, therefore, theory is a process which is not to be confused with the endless elaboration of conceptual models. It is part and parcel of being sociologically alive.

Of course, it might be asserted that one's presumption lies in attempting to tread in the hallowed footsteps of the 'nineteenth-century giants', or slavishly emulating the 'contemporary gurus' of the sociological establishment. Indeed, it must be admitted that all too often sociological thought seems to boil down to a debate with Marx's ghost or an attack on Parsons. This leads to the absurd situation in which sociological theory is conducted in terms of a confrontation between the 'conflict' and 'consensus' models of society.

In this confrontation there seems to be no room for alternative perspectives. Possible alternatives are relegated to the sphere of ideology, or are regarded as being sociologically irrelevant. An interest in 'social phenomenology', ethnomethodology or even 'structuralism' is seen as merely being the preoccupation of a species of intellectual mavericks. There is, undoubtedly, an element of truth in the notion that sociologists are frequently seduced by

1

intellectual fashions derived from the philosophical *avant-garde*, without paying due regard to the context in which these ideas are relevant, yet the same can be said for other members of the 'self-styled' intellectual élite.

In addition, the fantastic claims that are made every few years for a new liberating concept of perspective, leads one to the conclusion that sociologists are involved in their own millenarian movement. Such claims have been made for role theory, action theory, cybernetics, systems theory, information theory, games theory, etc., etc. It is essential to realize that this proliferation of concepts, models and theories never represents points of arrival – they merely indicate the essential open-ended and processual nature of the sociological enterprise. There is no theoretical certainty in sociology. The polarization of sociology into two armed and antagonistic theoretical camps obviously completely distorts social reality – it also ignores the possibility that 'millenarianism' often has a transforming quality.

Conceptual purity

The way in which some practitioners approach their subject-matter may force the cynic into thinking that sociologists spend a great proportion of their creative lives in coining neologisms in order to legitimate their continuous employment as sociologists. This is not an attack on sociological millenarianism as such. Criticisms of this sort usually derive either from humanists who are shocked by the sociologists' rape of language, or from natural scientists who believe that science is something that goes on in laboratories. It is not surprising, therefore, that sociologists over-react by an almost obsessive sensitivity to the need for conceptual clarity on one hand, and an irrational ritualistic emulation of appropriate methodological procedures of the natural sciences on the other hand. This leads, inevitably, to a concern with conceptual purity, and eventually to the hope that sociology will eventually aspire to the condition of economics, just as all art is supposed to aspire to the condition of music.

In Britain, this aspiration is illustrated by the way in which sociologists seem unwilling to formulate conceptual schemes without some sort of deference to linguistic philosophy. There is always a metaphorical linguistic philosopher looking over the theorist's shoulder before he summons up enough enthusiasm to commit himself to any level of abstraction. The key word is clarity, at least, this is the internalized injunction and ideal. But this lucidity is never achieved, except perhaps in the work of such diverse theorists as Homans and Merton. Also, the traditional British involvement in grass-root empiricism usually means that theory is regarded with an excessive degree of suspicion, particularly when this theory has its origins in 'dubious' continental philosophies or turgid 'American dogma'.

What Glaser and Strauss call the 'rhetoric of verification'[1] is, I think, still the unofficial orthodoxy of the British sociological establishment, in spite of the inroads that other viewpoints have made among younger sociologists. It is still true to say that British sociology has not produced a substantive theoretical perspective of its own. It borrows ideas and concepts from everybody else but for various reasons, particularly those relating to the peculiar status that sociology enjoys *vis-à-vis* other academic disciplines, an indigenous home-grown theory seems as far away now as it was fifty years ago. The theoretical perspectives that British sociology uses derive from Durkheim as transmitted through social anthropology, and to a lesser extent from Weberian interpretative sociology. Also some British sociologists have labelled themselves Marxist without necessarily allowing their Marxism to influence their research designs. These theoretical concerns have never been central, but somehow have been used as legitimations of research, rather than arising from the actual empirical situation. It is in this context that the rhetoric of verification and the falsification thesis have come to provide (so it is argued) British sociologists with a mechanism which avoids the apparent pitfalls that their continental colleagues have fallen into, that is, the pitfalls associated with speculative theorizing.

Modelmania

It is not my intention to get involved in the endless debate about what constitutes a theory or a model. Certainly in sociology it would seem to be highly unlikely that we can speak of theories in the same way that natural scientists do. Nor for that matter is the current interest in model building and conceptual analysis necessarily indicative of sociology's coming of age. If the status of a discipline is measured by the number of times certain ideas and concepts are aired, then sociology should certainly be standing at the pyramid of academic respectability. However, the generation of concepts does not necessarily entail academic status. This is not to deny the need for a distinctive sociological language, which marks off, and symbolizes, a selected group of social phenomena. Unfortunately there is a tendency for language in sociology and other social sciences sometimes to achieve an autonomy of its own. In particular, this is true when sociologists embark upon their philosophy of science obsession.

Sociologists tend to encapsulate social reality in a network of constructs which they often label 'theory'. More often than not,

3

these constructs are borrowed from other disciplines. There is nothing intrinsically wrong with borrowing provided one realizes that the translation from one frame of reference to another is only valid when the translation is recognized as denoting similarity, not absolute correspondence. To use the organic metaphor, or the computer analogue is one thing, but to construe society as an organism or a computer is another. This certainly has happened with respect to a number of key concepts utilized in the natural sciences and translated into the social sciences.

Recently, for example, the term model has become highly fashionable amongst various social scientists. No sociologist worth his salt can apparently afford to neglect at least one reference to a model at some stage of his research. Once he does this, then presumably his research needs no further justification.[2]

> Those scientists who speak of their work as model building often give the impression that such an endeavour is the only true begetter of scientific knowledge and that the construction and testing of models is itself the very model of modern scientific activity. They do so especially in behavioural science, and the emphasis on models is a characteristic feature of those schools or approaches to which the label behavioural science is applied in a narrow and distinctive sense, in contrast to what are regarded as more belletristic studies of man and his works. In short models – to play on another meaning of the word – are much in fashion, though to say so is by no means to prejudge their scientific significance and worth. The words model and mode have indeed the same root; today, model building is science à la mode.

To be in the fashion is all very well, but fashion is no substitute for genuine sociological inquiry. There is a danger that the obsession with models and model building will lead to a new form of spurious scientism. A decade or two ago, before the development of the philosophy of science psychosis, there seemed to be no need for a prolonged discussion on the nature of models and theories. Today this has changed. The use of a model somehow legitimates a piece of research.

In addition, the term model is used in a highly ambiguous manner. It is not always clear as to whether model and theory are being used interchangeably. In sociology, it could be argued that this confusion is probably due to the fact that what is usually designated as a theory is, in actuality, a model. One could go so far as to argue that there are no genuine sociological theories – that all we have in sociology is an abundance of models. If this is the case, then by no stretch of the imagination could we speak of symbolic interaction-

4

ism as constituting a theory, yet it is conceivable that there are a number of models embedded in the symbolic interactionist framework, which somehow give the impression that we are talking about a theory. However, it must be remembered that we are considering theory from the perspective of the 'rhetoric of verification', and this does not necessarily exhaust the possible alternatives implicit in the idea of a 'theory'.

Defensive sociology

It is not only modelmania which pinpoints the philosophy of science obsession amongst large sections of the sociological community. Rather, it is the whole question of playing the theory game in terms of rules deriving from the natural sciences. The painstaking analysis of propositions which purport to be theory often assumes the aspect of the logic-games of scholastic philosophers. More time is spent on conceptual hair-splitting than in actually doing theory. Indeed, by the time one comes to the real meat of the theory, it is probably qualified out of existence. The failure of nerve that sociologists exhibit when they theorize is partly explainable by the continuous hostility of public spokesmen in other disciplines who demand that sociology conforms to the criteria which they demand for their own disciplines. Unfortunately, this means that sociological theory often seems to adopt a defensive stance. It becomes rooted in a posture which is non-sociological. Systems theory, for example, makes all kinds of scientific claims for sociology, stating that sociology can be a science, provided it pays lip-service to the canons of equilibrium and homeostasis. This is purely defensive. It assumes that sociology cannot, and does not, generate its own concepts and models. The hope that academic respectability can be gained by the use of analogies and concepts originally located in other universes of discourse is, I think, an admission that sociology has no subject-matter, and that ultimately it must rely on explanations and theories which are not sociological.

Moreover, this abdication of responsibility has the consequence that reductionism is given a completely free hand. If there are no genuine sociological explanations, then we must look to psychology, or economics, or even to biology for our concepts. Homans, as we know, champions a non-sociological sociology. Whether or not there are any general sociological propositions seems to me to be beside the point when theorists persist in looking for hidden forces behind the phenomenal social world. It is all very well saying that the only first-order propositions in sociology derive from elementary stimulus–response psychology. The search for these propositions and their possible establishment leaves out the central core of human

5

experience – the experience and negotiation of meaning. Assuming that we are ever in a position to confirm Homans's hope for a behaviourally located sociology and social science, then what we are left with is a purely formal behavioural system without any reference to culture or meaning. Similarly, the attempt to confine sociology to residual categories or leftovers from other social sciences ignores any commitment to a social level of analysis. The flight from sociology by some of its practitioners is not very surprising because there is nothing more difficult to sustain than the sociological vision. Harold Fallding puts it this way: [3]

> The difficulty of studying social realities is not the way they may require masses of data that only a team can muster. For some problems this may well be necessary but you can view a social fact in a single person. Part of the reason for regressing from sociology into psychology, in particular, may be that we have our own subjectivity to witness to the reality of the things psychology studies. On the other hand, the sociological facts of which we are the vehicles are often things of which we are barely conscious. But the main reason why the study of social facts is difficult is that the sociological point of view is difficult to sustain. Sociological vision comes by training. Yet without this vision we are blind to powerful forces. It should be understood why anybody calls attention to the separate existence of social facts: it is not that they are more important than the facts reported by other disciplines, but that other disciplines do not touch them. We do not deny, say, psychology to establish sociology. It is just that when the psychology of a situation has been given the whole tale is not told. Our aim is to complete knowledge.

Of course, it is precisely the attempt to establish the social sphere that leads to so many difficulties. It is not as self-evident as Durkheim supposed it to be, nor, for that matter, is it easy to construct genuine social theory. Paradoxically, what is often labelled sociological theory, is more often than not a defensive metaphor borrowed from non-sociological sources. Certainly the great sociological themes like anomie, alienation, community etc., are fundamentally sociological, yet their application is often anything but sociological. Thus, 'anomie', for example, appears in some of its contemporary manifestations as an appendage to psychiatric analysis with all sorts of mental health connotations attached.

Behavioural ideology and sociological dualism

Sociological theorizing, it follows, is beset by a tendency to construe the social world in non-sociological categories. No doubt the social can be considered to be epiphenomenal – a mere disguise behind which other forces are at work. It is extremely difficult to escape economic, psychological and biological reductionism. The way out for a number of sociologists is to go over to the other side and join the enemy ranks. Sociology then becomes transformed into a behavioural science with all the attendant paraphernalia of the verification principle. Once the behavioural ideology is substituted for the traditional social science identity, it is then possible to view all social behaviour in terms of the strictest scientific criteria. Watsonian behaviourism might be dead, but it is surely resuscitated both in the letter and the spirit of the 'behavioural science label'.

The attempt to erect a behavioural edifice mediated through simulation techniques, information theory, systems and game theory, obviously lends itself to the mathematization of sociology and, perhaps also, to its aim of academic acceptance by older and more 'respectable' disciplines. Nothing is more disturbing to the behavioural lobby than the spectacle of some of the ways in which *other* sociologists conduct their sociological lives. The notion of sociological commitment and radicalism seems an abject surrender to 'subjectivism' and an abandonment of objective standards. Now it cannot be denied that 'behavioural science' does seem to pay off in terms of inventories and empirical generalizations, as evidenced by Berelson's and Steiner's[4] compendium of behavioural research findings. It is not my intention to denigrate this kind of activity. My concern is with the question of whether 'behavioural science' is equivalent to, or is a substitute for, the image of sociology as a social or a cultural science. In other words, has the behavioural ideology replaced the social science identity?

This is not a new issue. In fact it is a theme that has a hoary history. The arguments, for and against, have been stated many times under different labels. However, the arguments were often couched in the language of philosophic discourse and, to a certain extent, reflect the polarities implicit in Western thought as a whole. A long line of German thinkers from Kant onwards were much aware of the special problems relating to the distinction between natural and cultural sciences. Rickert, Dilthey and Weber pointed to the state of tension and confrontation between these polarities. This has led to a fundamental dualism in sociology. The claim that sociology is a science is countered by the claim that it is a humanity.

The scientific claim assumes that sociology is subject to the same empirical procedures as other scientific disciplines. In principle, it is believed that sociology should pursue the same ideals of measurement and quantification, although it is admitted that, in practice, this might not be so feasible. But in general, this difficulty is, as it was seen to be, a matter attributable to the complexity of the subject-matter, rather than its inassessibility. Ultimately, the object of scientific sociology is to approximate to the experimental condition. Of course, it is recognized that this is only possible in a limited number of cases. For instance, most introductory texts in sociology usually start off with a chapter on the nature of sociology as a science. Invariably, they invoke the rhetoric of scientific method without denying the special nature of the sociological perspective. All are optimistic. There is no reason to doubt, they all seem to argue, that although sociology is in its infancy – in its embryonic stage – there is a royal road to the creation of a science of society. Given time, sociology will arrive at its destination of scientific respectability. In the meantime, there is a lot of preliminary groundwork to be covered, but eventually this will be replaced by an explanatory theory. Although nobody reads Comte now, and Positivism is supposed to be old hat, I think it is not too far-fetched to say that a goodly proportion of contemporary Western sociologists are unconsciously fixated on the Comtean ideal, in spite of 'The Structure of Social Action'.

It is unfortunate that the plaintive cry for a scientific sociology is invariably accompanied by the necessity for the introduction of some form of reductionist explanation. The general propositions that Homans so eloquently champions, would clear the way for the premature demise of sociology and its replacement by the behavioural identity. Perhaps this has already happened, in spite of the mushrooming of the newer critical sociology in both Europe and the USA. As I have implied, these points of issue are part of the historical debate about the nature of sociology. Most sociologists go about their sociological work without necessarily getting too upset about the status of their discipline as a science. But in everyday practice, there is every indication that the operational procedures used in the frontline of research assume an uncompromising behavioural stance. In doing this, sociologists are lending credence to the claim that sociology is fundamentally dualistic in nature – or even more extremely, that sociology is in reality, two separate but parallel disciplines.

Charles Bolton believes that the behavioural science identity had taken over sociology's public image and theoretical structure virtually without anybody noticing. He writes: [5]

The Behavioural Science identity is not merely a name but also an ideology. The ideology involves the substitution of a methodological rationale for a theoretical one in identifying sociology. From the viewpoint of Behavioural Science, the unity of various behavioural sciences lies in their common method; the differentiation among them becomes one of a division of labour, not a difference in a point of view. A sociologist is defined as a person who has been trained in applying the scientific method to a particular kind of behaving system: social systems. For some years, of course, hardly anyone has questioned the desirability of the field's becoming more scientific. But certain implications of the logic of the Behavioural science ideology may prove enervating to the long run development of sociology . . . sociology is just not concerned with behaviour in the strict sense. In the sense appropriate to the methodological presuppositions of Behavioural Science, behaviour is a physical movement or change of internal state of an organism – such as the movement of an arm through space, the physiological changes we call blushing, the movement of an organism closer to or away from a stimulus. Sociology is not concerned with these things, per se. Sociology is concerned with social acts or interactions, which always involve the meaningful aspect of human phenomena that is relative to a symbolic context.

Behaving systems and conceptual neutrality

The emphasis on behaviour in sociology is not primarily focused on the behaving individual but rather on the behaviour of systems. It is systems that 'behave' and 'act'. It is the social system which is in a state of equilibrium or disequilibrium – it is the system which has needs and objects. Therefore, it is the system which must be studied as an empirical whole.

Whatever the advantages of studying sociology in terms of systemic concepts, it leads directly into the behavioural orientation. In this respect, it is no accident that systems analysis has fitted in so nicely with the 'social engineering' approach to policy formulation. More recently, some of the traditional structural-functional systems models have been replaced by highly sophisticated simulation conceptualizations. Systems programming has come to serve as a highly fashionable substitute for traditional functionalism, while, at the same time, providing a convenient crutch for the marriage of methodology and theory. At these lofty heights, many sociologists convince themselves that they at last have found a way of handling social phenomena in an appropriate framework which does justice to both the scientific and cultural aspects of the discipline. Walter Buckley, for instance, after demolishing both Parsons and Homans devotes his entire book to the construction of a 'New Systems Model' which he believes avoids the pitfalls of psychological reductionism on the one hand, and sociological imperialism on the other.[6] Systems are seen as the basic theoretical tool of any science – and, as such, are completely neutral. They are also believed to serve the cause of interdisciplinary cohesion and co-operation from which a number of multi-variate propositions may be derived. Therefore, on the face of it, systems analysis seems to have a lot going for it. But it is arguable whether it is really neutral. Certainly, if employed heuristically, the systems concept seems to generate an aura of neutrality, especially in the context of the study of organizations, but it generally tends to be compounded of holistic and equilibrium assumptions. No matter what claims are made for the systems concept in other domains, when utilized in sociology, it assumes a behavioural posture. This is in spite of its apparent concern with 'consciousness'. What is termed and believed to be an objective conceptual tool becomes blatant ideology. Sociologists, like most other human beings, are seduced by the reification of words. Proponents of systems analysis are very much addicted to word magic – a charge which, we all know, is generally levelled at sociology as a whole, but which is especially pertinent when the holy name of science is used to legitimate methodological commitments.

Again, I must emphasize that it is not scientific sociology which is under scrutiny here, but some rather dubious assumptions and procedures which ultimately lead to the very negation of the sociological enterprise. My quarrel is with those theorists who have given up sociological inquiry for the attractions of a parsimonious reductionism. Like Homans,[7] I subscribe to the ideal of explanation in social theory, but unlike Homans I do not believe that these explanatory propositions necessarily derive from a profit–loss account or some reward–punishment schedule. If it is argued that the most general propositions are always non-sociological, and that second-order propositions are only conceivable in terms of some deductive scheme which uses psychological and behavioural starting-points, and if this constitutes 'science' in sociology, then I believe I belong to the humanist camp.

The alternative to the behavioural identity is not simply to be conceived of as humanism. Peter Berger[8] has elegantly argued for a humanistic sociology but this in itself is not a negation of the role of science in sociology. A humanistic sociology is premised on a concern with the central core of human living – namely man as a creator of his own symbolic and value systems. While interested in the study of collectivities in their patterns of emergence and repetition, humanistic sociology never loses sight of the fact that it has a prior commitment to man's quest for self-knowledge. This self-knowledge is not only a sociological concern, but is part of the broader philosophical anthropology that has characterized European thought ever since Plato.

Broadly speaking, this involvement in the search for self-knowledge is centred on the assumption that perhaps the most important concept in the social sciences is the concept of consciousness. Without an attempt to come to grips with this problem, the sociologist is not genuinely sociological in his feeling for the social sphere. To deny consciousness is to claim that sociology is a behavioural science. The humanistic perspective is firmly rooted in the assumption that men can comment on their own behaviour, that they can make indications to themselves, that they can construct alternative behaviours in given situations. It is also firmly rooted in the idea that human behaviour is meaningful and that meaning is, in its basic constituent forms, an interactive and social process.

To be conscious, therefore, presupposes a social origin of that consciousness. To possess a self presupposes encounters with others possessing selves. To be a sociologist presupposes that the sociologist 'qua sociologist' is a conscious being and that sociology is a form of consciousness. To be Marxist in approach to the social, presupposes a commitment to the centrality of consciousness. Indeed, without some form of construct to denote consciousness or the self concept, it is highly probable that sociology would sink without trace into the behavioural sea. The description and understanding of social conduct can only be mediated through some form of symbolic process which is located in consciousness. From the perspective of humanistic sociology, the greatest problem is the admitted difficulty of an adequate methodology to tease out the subtleties of consciousness. The method of 'Verstehen' has been associated with cultural and interpretative sociology as constituting the most important way of attacking social phenomena. Unfortunately, 'Verstehen' has been misunderstood by its critics and abused by its practitioners. It does not have to act as a substitute for intuition, nor does it imply the relegation of empirical methods to a secondary role.

Humanistic sociology and the interpretative method

When Weber says that understanding at the level of meaning is the property most appropriate to sociological theorizing, he is making statements about human intentions. Weber defines intention as the meaning that the behaviour has to the acting individual, or how the individual defines the situation. But Weber never ignores causal explanations. An adequate discussion of a social process included both types of explanation. Many of Weber's detractors seem to forget that he insisted that interpretation at the level of meaning must be supplemented by a causally adequate explanation.

He never claims that 'Verstehen' stands by itself.[9] It is interesting to note that he has been called to task by some critics for his insistence that only both types of explanation give us a complete account of the social sphere. For example, Winch believes that causal adequacy is not necessary for a complete understanding of behaviour: [10]

> I want to question Weber's implied suggestion that Verstehen is something which is logically incomplete and needs supplementing by a different method altogether, namely the collection of statistics. Against this, I want to insist that if a proffered interpretation is wrong, statistics though they may suggest this is so, are not the decisive and ultimate court of appeal for the validity of sociological interpretations in the way Weber suggests. What is then needed is a better interpretation, not something different in kind.

Here we come to the heart of the matter. Because, if it is argued, like Winch does, that it is a question of formulating better interpretations rather than the testing of hypotheses by means of the methods of statistics, then we are claiming that the social sciences are not of the same order as the natural sciences, that they are not subject to the same methodological procedures, and that by definition they are not sciences at all. If one assents to this argument, then one is saying that the social sciences should conform to the methods and procedures current in the humanities. The German neo-Kantians made the fundamental distinction between 'Geistenwissenschaften' and 'Naturwissenschaften'. Dilthey thought the former were those studies which could only be understood in terms of interpretative understanding ('Verstehen'), whereas the latter were subject to the test of the scientific approach. In other words, culture could only be understood in cultural terms. It could only be understood in cultural terms by the application of appropriate symbolic and non-positivistic procedures. Ideally, interpretation in the cultural sciences should be modelled on well-trodden methods of classical scholarship.

The interpretation of classical texts, and also contemporary works of fiction or art, is conducted as an exercise in imaginary reconstruction of motive and intention. It is not enough to comment on the style and form of a work of art; one must also get at the intention of the author or artist. In other words, interpretation involves arriving at the meaning of the text both from the point of view of the interpreter, and that of the author.[11]

> In interpreting a text, what essentially we are trying to do is to identify a meaning, an idea, to which the text in question is designed to give expression. In other words, interpretation is a

method of comparative study by means of which we are attempting to establish a relation between an observable event (a readable text) and an idea which existed in a human mind prior to the writing of the text, and to which the latter is designed to give expression. The object of our study is therefore to establish a degree of correspondence between a phenomenon and an idea.

The method of interpretation was not only confined to the explication of textual criticism, but also to the study of history and social conduct. In the hands of Dilthey, and in a different context Rickert, the cultural sciences, which included both history and sociology, were seen as being particularly amenable to this type of analysis. The cultural sciences were not considered in the same way as the natural sciences, they dealt with a qualitatively different set of phenomena, namely those phenomena which were expressive of human valuation and choice. As such, they were absolutely antithetical to a natural science framework. What was needed was not statistics and measurement but an almost empathic ability to identify with the object of study.

Now, in its extreme form, this can lead to an untenable idealism in which the objects of perception are seen as mere extensions of one's idiosyncratic interpretations and preferences. But this does not necessarily follow. After all, there are very rigorous standards employed by literary and art critics. The historian or sociologist who follows this mode of analysis does not operate in an area of formless intuition. He can and does use critical standards, although they are not the standards of behavioural science.

We might admit that this kind of analysis is perfectly feasible when considering aesthetic objects or texts, but is questionable when examining social structures. Societies may, or may not be, works of art, but there is no need to assume that they can be understood purely in terms of an interpretative leap. This, I might add, is not the position of interpretative sociology. The method of 'Verstehen' is no substitute for empirical work in the social sciences. In Weber's view, it complements scientific work, it does not replace it.

However, 'Verstehen' operates in the everyday world. It is not a process which is switched on and off for the benefit of sociologists. This everyday world 'existed before our birth, experienced and interpreted by others. Now it is given to our experiences and interpretations.'[12]

In other words, these everyday experiences are the 'facts' of the social sciences. The social scientist's facts are always the subjective intentions, feelings, attitudes, definitions of the situation and acts of human beings. These facts are interpretations of reality which

13

are real for the people in the situation, whether they are based on a wrong interpretation of the situation or not. The manual worker who identifies with a middle-class life-style may be victim of 'false consciousness', but this identification is a social fact, and must be understood as such. Acts of interpretation are themselves interpretations of other people's interpretations. In stressing the Weberian interpretative position, we are in fact stressing the essential duality of sociology. Whatever the deficiencies of the method of interpretation, there can be no gainsaying this duality. An acceptance of the ambiguities at the heart of the sociological enterprise would do away with the interminable discussions that sociologists engage in about sociology's scientific status. As Warren Dunham writes:[13]

> The problem as to whether sociology can become a science in the true sense of the word or must be content to remain a point of view and an approach to social life may not be an important issue, in the long run. What is important is that we should continue to add to our information and knowledge about the structure and function of societies throughout the world. Perhaps the man hours that have gone into the attempt to construct sociology as one of the natural sciences represents a certain kind of futility and loses sight of the main thrust of the sociological enterprise, which is to create for man a sophisticated awareness of the history, nature and consequence of his involvement and identification with the social life of his times.

In a sense, it is conceivable that the tensions induced by the confrontation between the proponents of the behavioural ideology and supporters of the humanistic approach are, in reality, the means whereby new concepts and ideas are generated. However, at a more realistic level, this fundamental cleavage, whether expressed in terms of positivism *v.* idealism or process *v.* structure, or the countless other dichotomies which polarize the sociological perspective, is in fact regarded as constituting an either/or situation. There is always the hope that final victory for one position or the other is just around the corner, in spite of the evidence that the history of sociology can be construed as a funeral pyre for outmoded models and general theories of society.

The committed sociologist

Certainly, there is no final victory for the notion of sociology as a science in the behavioural mode. What we can say is that the tensions within the discipline are forcing sociologists to search out their own root assumptions. Granted that a morbid introspective analysis of sociology, under its various masks, might possibly develop into an occupational disease, it seems to be a step in the right direction. The images that sociologists grandly present of themselves to the general public are too often premised on borrowed identities. And the most damaging image or presentation of self is that associated with the role of the sociologist as priest, or priest masquerading as scientist.[14]

> The scientist as priest is committed to an end that he defines as both truth and good and of itself. The truth and the good are, as with all faiths that have moved our world, institutionalized within a highly dedicated culture or subculture and involve a specialized frame of discourse, common symbols, an elaborate communal ethic, a complete hierarchical organization, and a variety of other features commonly found in the churches of our day. Physicist Harold Schilling (1958) has argued that science also has its creeds and that the way they come into being, and the role they have played in science subsequently, are essentially the same as those of religious creeds.

The priestly mode in sociology assumes that laymen need the mediation of experts to explain the social world to them. The sociologist becomes a purveyor of truth. As a priest he performs his appropriate rituals in the language of science. He develops techniques of mystification and a highly elaborate sub-culture. At all costs he must remain objective while the common mass of humanity wallows around in a morass of subjectivity. Role-distance must be maintained in spite of the sociologist's commitment to his subject-matter. At these exalted levels only the sociologist understands social reality; he therefore divides the world into categories – experts and laymen – scientific knowledge on the one hand and folk wisdom on the other. Unfortunately (fortunately for sociology), this self image is not confirmed by others; it is certainly not confirmed by other social sciences, nor by the lay public. If anything, the response to this image is downright hostile. The charge of arrogance is made with a great deal of justification, particularly when the sociologist employs the priestly mode to rationalize his attempts to become a social engineer. Strangely, when many natural scientists have long ago openly declared the metaphysical underpinnings of some of their assumptions, a number of sociologists have continued to labour under the illusion that sociology is an 'objective' science.

The subjective–objective dichotomy

Basically, the demand for objectivity in sociology is premised on the belief that a natural science of society is both possible and desirable.

Until the natural sciences broke with speculative metaphysics and became experimental, they were limited by the continuous intrusion of bias and subjectivity. It follows, so it is usually argued, that if this was true for the natural sciences, then it must apply with even more force in the social sciences, where human intentions often provide the essential locus of interest. Thus, the demand for operationalization of all hypothetical constructs denoting interior states or motives and intentions, is a cardinal strategy of 'behavioural science'. Presumably, when this is done we should be in a position to speak of an objective sociology. We could, of course, get bogged down in a long and protracted discussion about objectivity. However, for sociology, there are two important points to be made.

First, what is defined as objective will depend very much on *who* is doing the defining. It also depends on *when* and *where* the defining takes place. The definition of sociology as aspiring to, and in fact constituting, an 'objective science' is dependent on the state of play in the scientific community at large in a particular social and historical context. Thus, conceivably there might be different versions of what constitutes the objective. Obviously the version which is accepted by one group of scientists might not necessarily be accepted by another group. The objectivity of Marxism is different from the objectivity of academic social science.

Second, the distinction between the objective and the subjective is based on a false dichotomy. The notion that the 'inside' and 'outside' worlds are qualitatively different, and are therefore opposed, is a hangover from the Cartesian dualism which informed European philosophy for a very long time. To assume that there are two parallel ways of knowing is a gross over-simplification. The objective and the subjective are opposite sides of the same coin. There is no subjective without the objective and vice versa. The interior world is an interactive world which is continuously in interplay with the exterior world. As Berger has argued, the social is a dialectical process involving the interchange between man's externalization of his subjectivity, its objectification in symbolic form, and finally, its re-entry into his consciousness by the process of internalization.[15] In other words, man produces himself – he creates his own social objects, and in so doing is not a passive spectator – he is by his very social nature forced into an interactive relationship with the world. Of course, the outside world exists independently of man as a socius, yet its significance for man is one which he himself brings to it.

What about the canons of proof and the maxim of inter-subjectivity? Isn't this what science is really about? Isn't this what is meant by the demonstration of the objective nature of scientific method? What about logic and hypothetico-deductive method? Don't they constitute the minimum requirements for any scientific approach to the problem of objectivity? The answer to these questions must be yes, provided one accepts without question the metaphysical assumptions that are implicit in this particular view of the world. I am no philosopher of science, but it is very clear to me that science cannot be interpreted to be the exclusive property of those practitioners who believe that their adherence to the standards of a specific cognitive mode or method is devoid of the contamination of subjectivity. This contamination cannot be avoided. Even the commitment to logical procedures does not allow one to claim that, in this respect at least, one is moving in a completely neutral area. The fact that scientific knowledge is never certain but is subject to the laws of probability indicates that 'scientific objectivity' is related to human decisions about the levels of confidence that are acceptable for the purposes of research. It is these human decisions that generate doubts about the claim of a purely objective science and, even more so, a purely objective social science. Similarly, there is no reason to believe that a logical tradition which traces its origins back to Aristotle is the only possible logic. To quote Friedrichs again: [16]

> there is no ultimately self-validating mathematics or other logic that could take from man the necessity of *choosing* his axioms, selecting his logical models, and *accepting responsibility* for the particular grammar he chooses to apply to the problem confronting him. Even mathematical logic – the ultimate image of rationality – is wed to the same uncertainty that demands commitment in each of the other avenues of man's creativity . . .
>
> Mathematics, then, has taught us recently that logic is not one thing but a potentially infinite variety of axiomatic systems derived from man's fertile imagination. Even when one has *chosen* a particular logic, he operates within a system that remains dependent ultimately for its consistency on aspects of man's comprehension that lie outside the tautologies of symbolic logic and are more clearly expressive of man's existential nature.

Humanistic sociology and the autonomy of social facts

Reverting to the theme about the essential dualism of sociology, it would seem highly probable that a great part of the controversy surrounding the opposition of the humanistic image to the behavioural ideology, is based on differing views on the nature of the social world. A humanistic sociology does not entail identifying sociology with one of the traditional academic humanities (although it does share a great deal in common with history and criticism). By humanistic sociology is implied a concern with the social world in terms of categories relating to valuation, choice, intention, meaning, understanding, etc. It involves an acknowledgment that sociology is not neutral or value-free, but is deeply committed to the object of study. In other words, it must never be forgotten that the study of social interaction, whether at the level of the dyad, or at the level of the collectivity, can only be pursued in terms of the assumption that social actors are not necessarily playthings of forces that act on them. Certainly society can be regarded as a prison, it can be said to be overwhelmingly present, but men are not completely helpless in this situation. They can construct alternative societies and imagine alternative futures. Society is never 'given' in spite of the worst excesses of socialization theory. It always has to be reconfirmed with each new generation. Granted that social facts can be viewed as having a limited autonomy of their own, it must never be forgotten that this autonomy is only relevant within the context of the significance and meaning that men attach to those facts. Even brute force is never mediated directly. It always has some symbolic element which has meaning for those who are exposed to force. The social facts that sociology is concerned with are symbolic facts. They can only be studied, by acknowledging, that the objective world is largely man-made, and that the immediacy of the empirical world is saturated with the meaning that men attribute to objects.

To say all this is not to say that sociology is not a science and that empirical methods are not appropriate to the study of social interaction. What is singularly inappropriate is the assumption that social behaviour or conduct is only explainable at levels of analysis which are absolutely empty of human content. To do this, is, as we have argued, to claim that sociology is an exact behavioural science. *Methodology is a servant of sociology, not its master.* The most sophisticated use of simulation techniques, mathematical models and research designs do not by themselves guarantee that what one is studying is in fact the empirical world of social facts. Methods which are successful in economics, or psychology are not necessarily useful in sociology. What is absolutely essential is that the sociologist really knows what sort of facts he is looking for. He is obviously not looking for biological facts, he is not looking for psychological facts, he is not looking for economic facts, he is looking for social facts. The specification of these facts is the problem that gives most researchers and theorists their biggest headache. The empirical world which sociologists study is the world of symbols, meanings and consciousness. To examine this world one cannot do violence to it by proceeding as if it is something else. I agree with Herbert Blumer when he writes: [17]

18

most research enquiry – is not designed to develop a close and reasonably full familiarity with the area of life under study. There is no demand on the research scholar to do a lot of free exploration in the area, getting close to the people involved in it, seeing it in a variety of situations they meet, noting their problems and observing how they handle them, being party to their conversations and watching their life as it flows along. In place of such exploration and flexible pursuit of intimate contact with what is going on, reliance is put on starting with a theory or a model, posing the problem in terms of a model, setting a hypothesis with regard to the problem, outlining a mode of inquiry to test that hypothesis, using standardized instruments to get precise data, and so forth. I merely wish to reassert here that current designs of proper research procedure do not encourage or provide for the development of first-hand acquaintance with the sphere of life under study. . . . If one is going to respect the social, one's problems, guiding conceptions, data, schemes of relationship and ideas of interpretation have to be faithful to that empirical world. This is especially true in the case of human group life because of the persistent tendency of human beings in their collective life to build up separate worlds, marked by an operating milieu of different life situations and by the possession of different beliefs and conceptions for handling these situations.

This extended quotation gets to the heart of the matter. An adequate and relevant sociology respects the social world – the empirical reality with which it is engaged. This empirical reality does not consist of the beautifully elegant constructions of contemporary research methodology, but of the actual living life of men in the course of their everyday interaction. This everyday life cannot be reduced to the level of pointer readings on measuring instruments, nor can it be described in terms of pushes, urges, stimuli, responses and the inevitability of historical forces. It can only be understood in its own terms. And this understanding involves the ability to recognize the human world for what it is – an interactive symbolic world where men are capable of interpreting their own conduct, as well as interpreting other people's conduct. This does not mean to say that other forces do not influence social behaviour. The social world does not exist in a vacuum. However, in the final analysis, the social world is not explainable as the end product of the interplay of economic and biological factors, but, primarily, as the world in which men act towards each other in meaningful terms. Without culture, without meaning, we cannot speak of the discipline of sociology. I know that I am repeating the obvious, but the obvious is in continuous need of restatement.

The forces that act on men are never direct, but are filtered through the social worlds that men have constructed. There is no such thing as a pure economic system. There is no isomorphic correlation between economic exchange and human interaction. Similarly, there is no pure psychological system which is un-contaminated by the social. It is not a question of rendering unto Caesar the things that are Caesar's. The social sciences which study men do not proceed in competing, but parallel directions; they interpenetrate each other, nevertheless this interpenetration is not equivalent to complete submergence.

Social conduct then can only be grasped when one admits that the very 'stuff' of the sociologist's subject-matter is the common-place, the trivial, the tacit definitions of the situation, the language of everyday usage. There can be no macro-sociology without an adequate conceptualization of the nature of social interaction, and this conceptualization must be understandable at both the level of meaning and at the level of statistical probability. Weber's injunc-tion is just as relevant now as it was when he first stated it a number of decades ago.[18] There is in other words, both an objective and a subjective element in sociology.

The contrived tension between the objective and subjective is, as we have indicated, endemic to the sociological enterprise – it consti-tutes its dualistic heritage, especially when the objective is identified with the behavioural and the subjective is identified with the intuitive and non-scientific.

The definition and nature of the social

Recently, Walter Wallace[19] has argued that the confusion apparent in so much contemporary sociological theory is due to the failure of sociologists to distinguish between what he calls the 'Newtonian' (objective and behavioural) and the Weberian (subjective) definitions of the social. In actuality, most sociologists, whether they realize it or not, utilize both definitions, although frequently ranging them-selves on one side or the other. The trouble starts when they begin the task of sociological explanation. If they try to explain social phenomena from opposite perspectives, then they are forced into mutual areas of misunderstanding. Starting from completely differ-ent premises of what constitutes the social, they engage in interminable disputes about the relevance of their sociological explanations, while forgetting that their prior images of the social bear no relationship to each other at all. In the end, the disputes tend to completely ignore, or deny, the validity of the alternative viewpoint. Thus, the behaviourally orientated sociologist finds it difficult to speak in terms of values, attitudes, consciousness etc., while the 'Humanist' finds it impossible to entertain a view of conduct which relegates man to a natural object on which other forces impinge. The confusion, therefore, lies not so much in the explanations themselves, but in the way in which the prior definitions of the social tend to shape the explanations. If, for example, it is asserted that delinquency is explained by defective hereditary antecedents, then an alternative hypothesis which construes delinquent behaviour in terms of 'learning', or the acquisition of deviant norms, is a completely different type of account. The same 'social phenomenon' – delinquent conduct – is given different explanations based on differing notions of the nature of the social. These two viewpoints do not complement each other – they are mutually exclusive and contradictory. A sociological account which defines the social in terms of self-indication is qualitatively different from an account which employs a stimulus–response model. Similarly, a biological explanation is not complementary to an 'interactionist' explanation. They cannot be said to be complementary unless one is saying that they complement each other at different levels of analysis, that is, they complement each other vertically, rather than horizontally. They are not *additive* but *competing* explanations employing different root images about the nature of man and the 'idea' of the social. This is not to say that objective and subjective theories in sociology are diametrically opposed to each other. We have already stated that the objective and the subjective are aspects of the same continuum, but at the same time, to talk of complementary standpoints is only possible when there is some sort of consensus as to the nature of the 'social'.

We cannot focus on complementarities when, in fact, we are committed to either the 'behavioural ideology' or the 'humanistic identity'. It follows that, when objective and subjective theories are complementary, this implies that they are referring to the same social facts. Minimally, it would seem to me that the definition of the social relates to the study of human conduct in interaction. The word conduct implies both action and intention, and is therefore preferable to behaviour which has specific connotations. When one speaks of the complementary relationship of different theoretical positions, one is not speaking of an either/or stance in which sociology is defined as *either* being a behavioural science *or* a humanistic discipline. If one does take up such an extreme stand, then this means that we are really asserting that there are two disciplines under discussion, each referring to a different level of analysis, each claiming to be the real sociology. To me this seems to be an untenable position. While subscribing to the view that sociology is fundamentally an interpretative discipline, this does not mean that one is thereby committed to some form of intuitive methodology.

The essential dualism of sociology is not reflected in the dichotomy of behaviour *v.* interpretation, but rather in the interplay of idealism and realism, or in the tension between designated objective theories as against designated subjective theories. This dualism is evident in all the seminal theoretical perspectives. Certainly it is present in Durkheim, it is crucial to Weber, and it is squarely at the centre of Parsons's theoretical concerns (to this day I do not think that Parsons has completely resolved the relationship between voluntarism and positivism). The same tensions are very much to the fore in contemporary discussions of Marx, where consciousness has been promoted from being a mere epiphenomenon to a far more dynamic role. At a different level, the confrontation between so-called structural theories and process theories turns out to be, on further inspection, an alternative version of this pivotal dualism. There is no reason to suppose that the definition of the social can be pushed into an exclusive structural strait-jacket at the expense of process or vice versa. When this happens we are left with an overwhelming sociological determinism which leaves the human dimension completely out altogether, or we are left with micro-processes which are often construed as basic building bricks for the construction of a macro-sociology. No theory of society can be derived from the encounter of two individuals.

Symbolic reality and social interaction

Furthermore, there can be no theory of society without a definition of the social which is intrinsically true to empirical reality, and this, as we have seen, is essentially a symbolic reality. In order to understand this reality the sociologist has to merge his own subjectivity with the subjectivity of others. In other words, he submits his own interpretations to the test of inspection of other committed sociologists. But what he puts to the test is not only the pristine observation of behaviour, it is his interpretation of that behaviour which, in itself, is not divorced from the actor's definition of the situation. The sociologist cannot be a recording instrument, he cannot be a camera, because by definition he not only takes snapshots, he also processes them. This processing is not a private concern of the individual sociologist. The symbols and concepts which he uses are in common parlance, they can be conveyed to, and understood by, other sociologists. He uses a common sociological language which is meaningful to the sociological community. In a sense, this language is specialized and technical – at times it becomes mathematical – but ultimately the language employed derives from the common everyday world. It cannot be too far removed from this world because, if it is, it then violates the essential empirical world in which men interact. The principles of sociation cannot be described or explained except in terms of the actual empirical world in which men live.

Some sociologists like Simmel have attempted to come to grips with this social world by constructing and discovering a grammar of sociation or interaction. This grammar is discoverable, so it is believed, by the examination of typical instances of typical everyday encounters. In other words, the structure of interaction can only be understood by first establishing the rules which inform the formal element of human conduct. These rules of sociation constitute a social grammar on which it is believed all socio-cultural systems are built. Today this viewpoint is shared by a number of different theorists. Homans,[20] for example, has argued very persuasively for a *formal* social science, premised on the principles of exchange theory. Once these exchange relationships are discovered, we are on the way to explaining social behaviour. In a different context Kenneth Burke[21] and Hugh Duncan[22] have made out a strong case for a sociology of style versus the traditional emphasis on content. It is the claim of these theorists that in the past sociology has attempted to build its generalizations on criteria deriving from the contents of sociation, without taking into account the ground-rules and forms.[23]

It will be argued . . . that a sociological theory of social action can only be created if we show how forms, as well as contents, of symbolic expression are used to create and sustain social order. Following Simmel we argue that the study of society is the study of forms of sociation. But we argue further – and here our clue is supplied by Mead and Burke – that the data of sociation exist in the various kinds of symbolic expressions men use to enact their social roles in communication with one another. It is not enough to invoke ritual, play, ceremony, festivals, games or drama as analogies for society unless we make clear how these become, and continue to be, social forms.

Nobody would deny that to attempt to create a sociology of forms or style has proved to be a very difficult task. It must be admitted from the very outset that the grammar that one is talking about is not to be considered in the same manner as traditional grammar. The grammar of a particular language system is not equivalent to social grammar. However, this confusion is compounded of the fact that interaction itself is basically a symbolic process, it is expressed in language, or in the symbolic interplay of gestures. In a sense, therefore, language is constitutive of social

23

action but is not determinative (to claim that it is determinative is to be guilty of another form of reductionism). More crucially, what is intrinsic to social grammar, is the negotiation of meaning between two or more actors. This negotiation is never fixed for all time but is always open to some kind of reinterpretation. Interaction is not a closed system but is subject to novelty. It is in this sense that some form of 'interpretative humanism' seems to me to be most relevant to the attempt to construct a social grammar.

Of course, one can become the mindless slave of a particular theoretical commitment. This is the danger in any statement of allegiance to a conceptual system but, as against this, I would like to argue that commitment depends very much on the root images that one has of one's discipline. The root images are intimately related to the self image of the sociologist *qua* sociologist. Moreover, to a great extent the ideas and theories that attract particular sociologists are very much part and parcel of the way in which they define their own role as sociologists. Ultimately, these roles are aspects of the biography of the individual sociologist – they reflect his involvement in the world – they also reflect his socially produced values. It is impossible to argue that one theorizes in a particular way because one has arrived at one's position on purely logical and objective grounds. This is not to say that a social theory is merely a hodge-podge of personal interpretations about the social objects in the sociologist's environment, but it is to say that the choice of perspective is not a random process, it is intimately connected to the sociologist's life-situation. Some of the internecine debate in sociology can only be understood when it is remembered that a particular point of view is being maintained with such vehemence because it is also saturated with the ego-involvements and group attachments of its adherents.

Therefore, for me to say that I find the interpretative framework as being the one for which I have the most sympathy is merely to state a preference for a position which views man as being essentially a being with a degree of self-consciousness – this quality being the one which defines his actual humanity. But I go a bit further than this. It seems to me to be absolutely imperative that the social world be studied at a level which does justice to the empirical world. And this empirical world is best studied in terms of the symbolic worlds that men construct for themselves. This, to me, seems to define the humanistic perspective in sociology. It also seems to cover the broad spectrum of theories which can be identified with the interpretative stance of cultural sociology as exemplified in the European sociological tradition.

Credo and assumptions

I therefore make a number of assumptions about interpretative sociology which I will now attempt to summarize.

(1)   Sociology is essentially dualistic. It is both an interpretative and empirical discipline. It is not, in my view at least, a science in the classic mechanistic mould.

(2)   Because of this dualism, it readily lends itself to ideological commitment. There is a continuous state of tension between Realism and Idealism, between Positivism and Voluntarism and between various other polarities.

(3)   It is not a behavioural science. One of the consequences of this dualism in the recent past has been the tendency to push sociology into a methodological stance in which all social action is construed in terms of inputs and outputs, rewards and punishments etc. At one level the unit of analysis is the behaving system, at another it is the behaving individual. While this type of approach certainly pays dividends from the point of view of methodological efficiency, it cannot be said to resolve some of the critical problems at the heart of the sociological enterprise, namely, problems relating to human intentions.

(4)   It is not a humanity, at least, it cannot be regarded in the same way as traditional humanities. It *is* humanistic, which is to say, its focus of interest lies in the symbolic and meaningful aspects of social interaction. It therefore accepts that the inner world of intention, motive, attitude, etc., is the proper subject-matter of sociology – it constitutes the reservoir of social facts. A humanistic sociology does not imply the rejection of empirical methods. All it asks is that sociology should not lose itself in its methodology.

(5)   Sociology is basically an interpretative discipline. By this is implied the tradition deriving from Weber and others, and also certain aspects of symbolic interactionism and social phenomenology. Interpretation is taken to mean the active commitment of the sociologist to the symbolic reconstruction of the 'actor's world'.

(6)   Sociology should not be placed in the false situation in which the objective and the subjective are seen as constituting polar opposites. This dichotomy is at the heart of the trouble that sociologists have in approaching the social world. There is no such thing as the pure and pristine observer who is uncontaminated by his subject-matter. In this context, Hampden-Turner writing about existentialism makes a pertinent point.[24]

It is often assumed that existentialism is wholly subjective – an error which springs from a Cartesian frame of mind unable to suspend its structures. From here the conclusion is drawn that only objectivity can be validated. But most existentialists regard objectivity as nothing more than a consensus among investigators as to how a phenomenon is to be regarded and measured. Hence calls for objectivity are like calls for consensus politics – they affirm the most obvious and the least controversial.

The call for objectivity, while it might provide a useful warning against the pitfalls of bias etc., is often couched in the language of the knower, the sage or the priest. The priestly mode in sociology lends itself to the most arrogant assumption of the potency of the sociologist's role as social engineer and diagnostician.

(7)   The heart of the sociological enterprise is the negotiation of meaning between the self and the other. Interaction is conceived in terms of this self–other relationship. Collectivities are seen as inter-linkages between networks of self–other relationships.

(8)   Both the individual and society are regarded as different phases of the same basic social process, namely symbolic inter-action. Both are twin-born – each cannot exist without the other. The solitary self does not exist except in the imagination of the mystic. The opposition between the individual and society is not a natural one, but is rather a function of a false dichotomy between the subjective and the objective.

(9)   The empirical world which sociology investigates is a sym-bolic one. In a sense, the most important social fact is the fact of language. It is both constitutive and functional. It is constitutive in the sense that symbolic interaction creates and maintains social structure; it is functional in the sense that it serves as a mechanism of integration. However, this is not to say that there is no flesh behind the symbol – Wrong's[25] warning about the dangers attending an over-socialized conception of human behaviour must constantly be borne in mind.

(10)   Sociology is not only concerned with the establishment of generalizations about the contents of the social, it is also concerned with the generation of a social grammar or sociology of forms. In other words, style is just as important as content in discussions of social processes. When Simmel advocated a formal sociology, a great deal of the confusion that this advocacy seems to have caused was due to the assumption that 'formal' was to be taken as imply-ing the scaffolding on which social structure was erected. Nothing could be further from Simmel's intention. Style is not invariable, but subject to continuous change and innovation.

(11)   In a sense, therefore, sociology employs a number of humanistic metaphors. Society may not be a work of art, but there is a great deal of evidence to suppose that it is dramatic. The dramaturgical perspective has its critics, but I believe that some

form of dramaturgical approach is essential to the understanding of society as both style and content. I would go so far as to say that the drama is modelled on society and not the other way round. Goffman, Burke, Duncan and others have spelt out this commitment to the dramatic metaphor but have been grossly misrepresented by their critics. Its cogency derives from the fact that, as a metaphor, it is not dependent upon other discursive domains, but is right at the centre of the social domain. The notion of 'masks' and 'identities' is thus crucial to the understanding of social conduct.

(12)   The type of theory most appropriate to sociological thought is essentially processual in the sense that all social behaviour is constantly in a state of flux. Social structure is constantly being renegotiated through the ebb and flow of social processes. Thus, sociology is historical as well as being 'immediate'. The phenomenological present interacts with phenomenological past in creating and sustaining social relationships. Although men are for ever creating new meanings for themselves, these meanings are intimately tied to the historical past. Not only is theory in sociology best served by the processual approach, but the very act of theory construction is basically processual. In doing sociology, one is not standing apart from the world like the proverbial observer from Mars, one is dynamically a part of that world.

(13)   The research process itself is basically an interactive self–other relationship. It is not a subject–object relationship in which the researcher manipulates his variables as if he were completely abstracted from the process.[26]

> the very act of engaging in social research must be seen as a process of symbolic interaction, that being a scientist reflects a continual attempt to lift ones own idiosyncratic experiences to the level of consensual and the shared meaning. It is in this context that the research method becomes the major means of acting on the symbolic environment and making those actions consensual in the broader community of sociologists.

(14)   In his encounter with the social world the sociologist is faced with the self-fulfilling prophecy. The discovery of a generalization often leads to the withering away of that generalization, making prediction a very difficult task. The very statement of a sociological generalization at the public level has a habit of being reflexive and self-defeating, because the sociologist, by definition, has altered the consciousness of social actors. Once consciousness is changed, then the prediction is modified or the law is invalidated. The role of discovery in the natural sciences, in which the establishment of lawful generalizations does not alter the phenomena under investigation (like the laws of planetary motion for example), does

not apply in the social sciences. Men can talk themselves into and out of crises – they can also reverse the predictions of the most sophisticated statistical techniques about their expected behaviour. Voting behaviour is a notorious example of this tendency. Seeley in a seminal article writes:[27]

> Description of a vital human activity in and by itself constitutes in my opinion, an attack upon that activity, both from the viewpoint of the participants and from the viewpoint of the disinterested (neither participant, nor social scientist) observer. To the degree that it is a successful description ethically neutral, deadpan, it tears apart from the participants the veil of unreality that is the foundation of the activity. A scientific description of a social gathering, for instance – might well yield the participants something, even something of considerable worth, but could not leave something that was also valuable to them unaffected for the worse. Everybody purports to value light, but too much light is a pitiless glare, and what goes on in and after the glare is impossibly what went on in the welcome and familiar twilight. How could a love relationship survive, for instance, an extended equitable enumeration of the characteristics of the beloved? How does other directed behaviour survive its characterization (stigmatization) as such? What becomes of the organization man, once he is identified by self and others as such? I am almost tempted to analogize: the light of social science is ultraviolet: the bacteria cannot survive the light: life cannot live without bacteria: social science sterilizes: and sterility kills.

(15)   The fact that sociology is not a mirror-image discipline, implies that its intervention in the social world has direct and indirect moral and ethical consequences for that world. It cannot remain on the sidelines and hide behind the mask of value neutrality or objectivity. At one level, the sociologist is reminiscent of the voyeur – he often assumes the role of unmasker – he is committed to tearing aside the façade of everyday social life and thereby revealing naked and ugly reality. Whenever he does this he is being more than observer. And at another level, some sociologists see sociology as a transforming and revolutionary discipline whose main function is to provide policy-makers and professional radicals with effective blueprints for social action. Wright Mills, as we know, was convinced that sociology was not a pure academic exercise for the amusement of sociologists, but was a mode of understanding and interpretation for political and social action.

In other words, sociology cannot stand outside the social world in which it is located. It is not the servant of a static and immobile view of social processes, it is very much engaged in the dynamics of social change. The symbolic reality in which men interact is an open reality, it is not a closed system. Men carry their moral and social futures around with them in that they are able to construct alternative lines of future action. In this sense, action is never really divorced from conception or from theory. There is a real commitment to praxis which transcends the specifics of academic theorizing. Gouldner[28] is absolutely right when he argues that Western academic sociology has assumed an almost doctrinaire stance in its insistence on the autonomy of sociology. Autonomy, which originally was seen by Durkheim and others as a declaration of freedom from the pitfalls of psychologism, is elevated to the status of a catechism in which the purity of sociology is ritualized. It is salutory to realize that it is only in the last decade or so that sociologists have begun to think in terms of their own hidden assumptions and self images in spite of the fact that the sociology of knowledge has a relatively venerable history. Taken to its logical ending-point, the insistence on autonomy would imply a free-floating sociology completely insulated from the pressures of the social world. The ideal of the pure sociologist uncontaminated by the world is a hangover from the classical tradition of scholarship which believed that it was undignified to soil the purity of scholarship by the dross of everyday life.

The assumptions underpin what I believe to constitute the core of the interpretative approach in sociology. I might add that I believe that they also underpin sociological social psychology.

The balance of this book will be devoted to a consideration of the concept of interaction with particular reference to the alternatives posed by exchange theory on the one hand, and symbolic interaction on the other. In general, the emphasis is on social processes, rather than social structures. However, this is not to say that I am concerned with micro-sociological processes alone. Nothing could be further from my intention. Both the problem of individuality and the concept of interaction have critical implications for any model or theory of society. The last section will examine the fragmentation thesis and its implication for social interaction.

part one

Interaction as sociological grammar

1 The concept of interaction

It might seem to be almost tautological to say that sociology is fundamentally the study of social interaction. Not only do some sociologists make this claim but there are a great number of social psychologists who believe that social psychology can be described as being the science of interaction. For example, Newcomb *et al.* write in their well-known text: 'Any textbook in social psychology nowadays must necessarily be selective, and our basis for inclusion and exclusion has been our conviction that most of the important notions can be organized around the phenomena of human interaction.'[1] The most eloquent statement of the sociological analysis of interaction, of course, derives from Simmel:[2]

> The simplest sociological form methodologically speaking remains that which operates between two elements. It contains the scheme, germ, and material of innumerable more complex forms. Its sociological significance, however, by no means rests on its extensions and multiplications only. It itself is a sociation. Not only are many general forms of sociation realized in it in a very pure and characteristic fashion; what is more, the limitation to two members is a condition under which alone several forms of relationship exist. Their typically sociological nature is suggested by two facts. One is that the greatest variation of individualities and unifying motives does not alter the identity of these forms. The other is that occasionally these forms exist as much between two groups – families, states, and organizations of various kinds – as between two individuals.

In other words, although Simmel is speaking about the forms of sociation, he is really arguing for the ubiquity of interaction in all social contexts.

At one level interaction is conceived of as the study of interpersonal behaviour, at another level it is seen as *taking into account* the behaviour of others, whether they are present or not. The relationship between two actors is usually regarded as the paradigm for the whole interactive process. But what is exactly meant by the concept interaction?

Howard Becker[3] distinguishes between three usages of the term:

(*a*) The reciprocal influencing among persons and social forces; this implies that the behaviour or conduct of an individual is somehow always responsive to the behaviour of others. In its simplest form this view can be subsumed under a stimulus–response model. Indeed, interaction so conceived is almost automatic. We can't help responding to others. At a more sophisticated level, the stimulus–response model develops into exchange theory.

(*b*) Reciprocal influencing at the human level implies the mediation of symbols, that is, symbolic interaction. The gist of this approach is the emphasized differences between animal and human behaviour. Symbolization brings an entirely new level of experiencing the other. In other words, interaction is equated with communication, particularly linguistic communication. There is, implicit in this process, the belief that reciprocal influencing is never direct but is subject to mediational transformation. By this is meant that the stimulus is never directly apprehended by the other, it is always interpreted. This leads to the third usage.

(*c*) The notion of the self as being an interactive process. Not only is the individual engaged in continuous interaction or communication with others, but he is also engaged in similar interaction with himself. Thus, thinking is essentially an interactive process in which one is talking to oneself from the perspective of others. In this respect interaction can be described as a self–other process.

These three usages are of course not all-embracing. The concept interaction is bandied around by nearly every type of theorist. There can be no doubt, however, that it is culturally mediated interaction that interests most sociologists, whether or not they subscribe to the symbolic interactionist perspective or not. Certainly, in the work of Parsons, we find the interactive process acting as a model for the inclusive system. It becomes the paradigm case for systems analysis. The relationship between ego and alter, while apparently conceived of as a system in miniature, also serves as a way in which self–other relationships can be conceptualized, very much in the tradition of certain forms of interactionism.

Historically, the concept of interaction has had an important role in the development of social thought, although not necessarily in the narrow technical sense of modern social theory. Certainly, the idea of reciprocity has been important both to moral philosophy and to political theory, not only to the social sciences. Reciprocity initially has a strong moral connotation. Men are bound by moral conventions to return benefits they have received from others. It is argued that social life would be impossible if social actors did not return favours received, that is, they should act towards others in a way which ensures that others will continue to provide favours. There are, in other words, strong moral obligations towards others which are guaranteed by the social context in which one finds oneself. More specifically, these obligations are defined in terms of 'particular' others. Initially they are couched in terms of obligations toward those who provide one with emotional and material sustenance, namely, members of one's family or kinship group.

One owes one's parents respect and love for the services they have rendered in enabling one to cope with the demands and pit-falls of living. Thus, right at the centre of the socialization process is the concept of reciprocity which makes an absolute demand that one reciprocates in kind, or in socially approved equivalences. It can be argued that it is only when actors perceive or believe that reciprocity has broken down, that we can begin to speak of exploitation or power in social relationships. This is something I shall return to later in the book. What *is* important for our purposes is the belief that reciprocity is already implicit in the social order. It is not something which is newly discovered for each new generation, but is constitutive of the moral basis of society. Thus interaction is believed never to be free and pristine, but always constrained by the implicit and explicit obligations of the role-relationships extant in a particular society.

What this implies, therefore, is some form of encapsulating moral order, which is prior to, and determinative of, the encounters between individuals. Interaction is shaped by the larger context. The degree of freedom and choice between two people in face-to-face interaction is governed by a whole complex of rules and norms which enter into the way they mutually adapt to each other. The norm of reciprocity is not generated in interaction, but helps shape that very interaction. This indeed is the root of the sociological argument deriving from Durkheim and Mauss, and modified by later French sociologists. Simply, it states that society is *prior* to any individual; and by definition, prior to any interpersonal encounters that individuals might participate in as members of that society. In a sense, therefore, I am bound by these rules even in the privacy of my bed or in the forced isolation of a prison cell.

Now indubitably there is an element of the chicken and egg

argument here. No set of interactions between individuals is likely to take place in a vacuum. Indeed human interaction is inconceivable without some form of commitment to the rules of language and discourse. And language is usually prior to interaction. Language contains within it prior classifications, categories and conceptual distinctions which provide a framework for social understanding, and also delimits the boundaries of interaction. In other words, mutual responses to certain symbols implies reciprocal mutuality by the uses of language.

Reciprocity

In another sense, reciprocity can be conceived of as the *grammar* of social relationships. Indeed, this is the sense that Parsons seems to put on the concept when he describes social systems in terms of the reciprocal relationships between ego and alter, and the attendant rights and obligations which roles impart to these relationships. It is the 'abstraction' from reciprocal or interactive processes that enables the sociologist to construct his model of the social system. Parsons goes on to an analysis of systemic properties, yet his interest in interaction is not lost and later emerges in his discussion of economic and political activity as expressing 'generalized mechanisms that facilitate and mediate interaction among people – it is a generalized symbolic medium of communication.'[4]

More immediately, our concern is with reciprocity as a grammar of social relationships. This entails a discussion of social exchange, but is, I think, basically a moral problem in the sense that social morality is premised on the notion of rights and duties attached to roles. Reciprocity is, of course, extant in the work both of Durkheim and Mauss and through them is crucial to Lévi-Strauss. It is also endemic to British social anthropology and to the whole tradition of fieldwork which derives from Radcliffe-Brown and Malinowski.

Basically, we can ask whether reciprocity entails a generalized commitment or a commitment to particular others? Am I bound to reciprocate favours received from strangers, or am I only bound by those who have helped me in the past, that is, my immediate family and friends? Or more technically, are my obligations defined by my kinship group and neighbourhood involvements? What obligations do I have to the stranger who needs help? If I do have an obligation to a stranger, then what is the origin and nature of this obligation? Gouldner[5] argues that reciprocity is universalized in one form or another in all societies. Even the most rationalized social systems are partly governed by the reciprocity norm, although in many cases it is not officially sanctioned. While Gouldner recognizes that the problem of mutual gratification is important, he believes that it must be supplemented by some idea of a general moral norm, which, when internalized, obliges the actor to give benefits to those he has received benefits from. Consequently, reciprocity is a component of social order. At the same time, reciprocity must be distinguished from *complementarity*. There is no need to assume that one man's rights are another man's duties. This puts too much onus on the notion of value consensus. The 'complementarity of expectations' that Parsons is so much concerned about does not subsume the possibility of egoistic gratification. I will only bestow benefits because I assume that others will have to bestow benefits on me if they want to optimalize gratification: [6]

> There is nothing in complementarity as such that would seem to control such egoism. Even if it is assumed that socialization transmits a deeply internalized moral code (with its accompanying conceptions of rights and wrongs), there still remains a question as to how this is sustained during the person's full participation in the social system. How is complementarity maintained within the context of social interaction. For this we need to look to reciprocity, the process through which *gratifications* are exchanged. For reciprocity unlike complementarity actually mobilizes egoistic motivations and channels them into the maintenance of the social systems. Egoism can motivate one party to satisfy the expectations of the other, since by doing so he shall induce the latter to reciprocate and satisfy his own.

Reciprocity, then, implies egoistic mutuality. The social order is maintained by the exchange of gratifications. But, of course, there is a great question mark right at the centre of this concept, namely, the question of power. What happens if I intend to maximize my own gratifications at the expense of others? This obviously has consequences for the continuing stability of the social relationship, and by extension, for the entire social system. Power is very difficult to conceptualize as a component of reciprocity. It can be argued that 'Power' does in fact determine the actual reciprocity contexts of a society. However, this is not our interest in the present discussion but will be relevant in our analysis of social exchange. What we are concerned with *is* the assumption that reciprocity is somehow a 'starting mechanism' which has somehow become internalized in the orientations of individuals to others. The norm of reciprocity is believed to be a 'Given'. It is internalized as an aspect of the socialization process. Therefore, it is subject to some form of exchange. Hence, it is *not* necessarily implicit in the moral order itself, but must be continuously reconfirmed for each new member of a society or group. Thus, while the norm of reciprocity may be defined as a starting mechanism, it can only become a starting mechanism by being part and parcel of an interaction context, specifically an interaction context which involves the agents of primary socialization. Reciprocity is learned in inter-personal relationships. It is not picked up at random from something called the moral order. The moral order is mediated through people, not through abstractions or a free-floating set of moral prescriptions. These people might presumably teach me that I only return favours to certain people, and not to others. Thus, one might conceivably be taught that one does not reciprocate or indeed enter into relationships with one's father's enemies, or at another level, one might be instructed to deny reciprocation to strangers from other groups. It follows, therefore, that it is not necessarily the moral order which is constitutive of social interaction but that the reverse might be true, that is, social interaction could be construed as being constitutive of morality and reciprocity.

Reciprocity involves a number of supporting assumptions mostly from the anthropological literature.

(A) It is believed to be ubiquitous: thus, even when the possibility of exploitive relationships is taken into account, there is the assumption that social life would be impossible without some minimal commitment to returning benefits. However, the returning of benefits is not to be exclusively thought of in economic terms but rather in social terms, what Marcel Mauss[7] calls a 'total social fact'. It is a way of confirming one's total commitment to social experience.

(B) It provides the basis for the emergence of structured relationships. Let us take as an example the famous one offered by Lévi-Strauss.[8] Two complete strangers sit on opposite sides of a table at a restaurant. The locale is France. Initially they are completely unaware of the status, role, occupation and personality orientations of the other. The two eaters are suspended in a state of uncertainty about their respective roles vis-à-vis the other. There is mild conflict developing between the appropriate norms of privacy and the relevant norms associated with community or reciprocity. Now while social distance may be maintained without necessarily giving rise to offence, there seems to be a moment when the demands of mutuality are overwhelming. The first diner finds distance to be too anxiety producing, so he offers his partner some of his wine. The other diner has two options open to him. He can either accept or reject the offer. If he accepts, then he will have to reciprocate in kind. Once he accepts, he is bound by the rules of sociable discourse. In other words, the purely fortuitous spatial arrangement at a restaurant table becomes translated into a social relationship.[9]

> Wine offered calls for wine returned, cordiality requires cordiality. The relationship of indifference can never be restored once it has been ended by one of the table companions. From now on the relationship can only be cordial or hostile. There is no way of refusing the neighbour's offer of his glass of wine without being insulting. Further, the acceptance of this offer sanctions another offer, for conversation. In this way a whole range of trivial social ties are established by a series of alternating oscillations, in which offering gives one a right, and receiving makes one obligated, and always beyond what has been given or accepted.

This episode seems to Lévi-Strauss to contain, in encapsulated form, the very essence of society, albeit in microscopic form. It can lead to a more permanent relationship of friendship and ultimately to their common commitment to a number of values and maxims of behaviour. Or, presumably, it can also lead to indifference, or the generation of a permanent state of hostility. Lévi-Strauss believes this episode is reminiscent of the encounters that individuals in primitive societies sometimes have with participants of strange and foreign groups. These encounters can either lead to downright aggression, or to acceptance, by the mutual exchange of gifts. Reciprocity, in this sense, is constitutive of the continuous emergence and reconfirmation of social structure. If reciprocity breaks down, then presumably the social order itself breaks down. But where does reciprocity derive its binding power from? Lévi-Strauss's answer, of course, is tied up with his whole notion of exchange which is more than the exchange of gifts; it is also the exchange of a society's most treasured possession – woman. The exchange of women provides society with both the occasion of reaffirming the social bond, and also the occasion of creating new bonds with other groups. At the very centre of social relationships we are presented with a picture of man as being bound together by a system of reciprocal ties which are located in the nature of the human species itself, namely the ties between men and women which are converted into the basic ties of social organization.

(C) Reciprocity is fundamentally an interpersonal tie. It might be argued that there are traditional forms of reciprocity institutionalized in a society, but this does mean that the norm of reciprocity is mediated through secondary socialization agencies. At its most direct level reciprocity is located in the role-taking process. Simply, to engage in social interaction involves the ability to take the other's point of view. In a sense this capacity is the mechanism whereby the individual comes to know himself, as well as the selves of others in social interaction. The responses that others make with respect to one's conduct are reciprocal in that they involve the taking into account the others' definition of the situation. Thus, if I present the other with a gift, my intention is not to contribute to the cohesion of the social order, but to contribute to the other's positive evaluation of me as a human actor. Simply, this means that reciprocity is negotiable at a very uncomplicated level. The mother who tells her child that if he behaves in a certain way there will be certain consequences is merely contributing to the child's learning of reciprocity. This is not necessarily to be seen as a reward–punishment contingency, only as confirming the nature of the social bond as being binding in the future. In a sense, therefore, there is a dialectical core to the learning of reciprocity, in that the child can always envisage the counter-move to his own behaviour. Reciprocity, at the interpersonal level, always implies the ability or capacity to forecast the other's behaviour with respect to the indications that one presents. Therefore, although this can be understood to be an exchange process in which some sort of cost–benefit or obligation–duty mechanism is at work, there is the added implication that reciprocity is the mutuality of understanding between two individuals. What this implies is that between any two interactors there is not only a role-relationship implicit in their respective attachments to social positions, but also a relationship which is dependent on the actual nature of the role-taking process. Its genesis is in the primitive conversation of gestures that Mead[10] has described as being a necessary condition for the growth of human conduct.

The institutionalization of reciprocity in such complicated patterns as the Kula Ring[11] is only conceivable as being the result of initial interpersonal ties. To argue that the institutionalization of reciprocity is a prior condition for cohesive social behaviour is to misunderstand the operation of basic interactive processes. Moral obligation means nothing to me unless I have been exposed to interpersonal relationships in which I can perceive that my behaviour is positively or negatively evaluated by others. The norm of reciprocity, therefore, is not a norm until I have confirmed it in my own experience. This is not to say that interactive behaviour is determinative, but it does mean that reciprocity has to be renegotiated for each new generation. And this renegotiation is basically interpersonal. It does not have to be dyadic, but must be mediated through 'actually present others'. It is only when the individual has managed to develop a fully fledged self concept that he is in a position to categorize the notion of reciprocity as a moral requirement. Before this he must learn reciprocity from others, and because he does this by taking the role of the other, it is an almost natural process.

These three assumptions, that is, the ubiquity of reciprocity, its determination of structured relationships, and its mediation through interpersonal encounters are constitutive of what we can designate as the social bond. To a certain extent, reciprocity in this sense is the central concern of sociology, especially when social structure is conceived of as being a network of interlocking roles in which reciprocity is institutionalized. However, there is great danger that we might think of reciprocity as being equivalent to, and deriving from, a prior commitment to values and norms, as being dependent on the consensus in any given society. There are times when reciprocity is deliberately violated and ignored, when the network of obligation and duties is seen as being restrictive, or even as being completely irrelevant. Again we must emphasize that reciprocity may be completely negated by the operation of power dimensions in social relationships. This power dimension is not only to be considered as being a function of the decision-making process at the centre of society, but is also crucial in interpersonal behaviour. Some of these problems relating to power will be examined under the rubric of social exchange. We can state here that the norm of reciprocity, although found universally, does not necessitate that benefits accruing to actors in an exchange-relationship will be equal or anything near equal. In the Marxist sense, the exchange-relationship can be absolutely exploitive, even in the context of family relationships. Indeed, psychiatrists' consulting rooms are full of people who have been victims of interpersonal exploitation in the family. Although the norm of reciprocity is believed to be universalized, there is no guarantee that role-performance entails a corresponding validation from one's role-partners. Parsons[12] assumes that if this validation is not forthcoming then social order is not possible. However, this is placing an emphasis on the complementarity of expectations which, as Gouldner has argued, does violence to the possibility of egocentric advantage.

Social interaction as the grammar of social organization

While it is perhaps correct to say that reciprocity is an interactive process, or is implicit in interaction, there is an important associated problem which is crucial to social theory, although it has been badly misunderstood in the past. This problem relates to the concept of the *elements* of social behaviour, as expressed or manifested in interaction. The question to be asked here is: does interaction precede and thereby entail social order? In other words, can we talk of social order as being constituted of countless interaction episodes, which in themselves are the building bricks of social structure? Can we derive a macro-theory from an essentially inter-active perspective? The classic Durkheim answer seems to be a positive 'NO'. But what exactly is meant by building blocks of social structure? Certainly it would be ridiculous to describe the interaction of two lovers as being a paradigm for the social system. Or would it? Or at another level, is the simple dyad a model for the inclusive system? Now there is a distinction to be drawn between a model for a system and the assumption that the dyad is the essential component of a system. Parsons[13] uses the relationship between ego and alter as a model of the larger social system. This does not necessarily mean that the relationship between 'ego' and 'alter' is the unit on which social order is built. However, when dyadic relationships are treated in terms of roles and role ascriptions we find that interaction is somehow trans-muted and crystallized in a set of obligations and counter-obliga-tions. Roles are treated as units of social order; conceptually they can be described independently of any particular role-player. Also conceptually we can conceive of roles as being always bonded, or paired, or related to other roles in a complex set of obligations and counter-obligations. When we do this, as is so often done in role-analysis we tend to lose sight of the actual interactive process from which role-constructs are abstracted. The dyadic relationship is obviously a role-relationship, but it is something more than the negotiation of expectations; it is in the first instance a relationship between two individuals.

Simmel's search for a social grammar

Simmel never made the mistake of regarding interaction as being purely the mechanical commitment to role-playing postures. Indeed, sociality is essentially a joyful and pleasurable experience. Men seek out their fellows for the sheer joy of interacting with them: [14]

> A superficial rationalism always looks for this richness among
> concrete contents only. Since it does not find it there, it
> dispenses with sociability as a shallow foolishness. Yet it cannot
> be without significance that in many, perhaps in all European
> languages 'society' simply designates a sociable gathering.
> Certainly, the political, economic, the purposive society of
> whatever description is a society. But only the 'sociable society'
> is a society without qualifying adjectives. It is this, precisely
> because it represents the pure form that is raised above all
> contents such as characterize those more concrete societies. It

gives us an abstract image in which all contents are dissolved in the mere play of form.

The social bond therefore is not merely an instrumental relationship in which the participants are out to maximize their benefits, but is, in Simmel's view, to be considered as intrinsically satisfying. Sociality involves more than role-taking – it involves the delight in the actual form of relationship – in social conduct as a form of play. Of course, this highlights only those aspects of social interaction which are consciously constructed around sociality for sociality's sake, that is, play episodes, parties, games, etc.

Simmel's analysis of the dyad is located in the assumption that social interaction can be described and understood, only, if we look for those *enduring* patterns or elements of interaction which together constitute the subject-matter of sociology. These 'forms of sociation' are the grammar of social relations. In the encounter between two individuals they are bound to place the interaction into a stylistic mode. There is, in other words, a style of interpersonal behaviour that is partly constitutive of the actual content of the future relationship. At one level the entire personality of the individual is involved, at another level there are role prescriptions. At both levels Simmel seems to insist that it is the grammar, the forms, which canalize the ongoing interaction. Thus, episodic interaction among strangers is in Simmel's view controlled by intrinsic social qualities. For example, the chance meeting on a train of a man and a woman, while being circumscribed by the role requirements of the male and female roles respectively, is also an opportunity for both to exercise a style of contact which is not defined by the role-prescription. If they merely play roles in stereotyped fashions, that is, if they merely play remembered parts of old sex scripts which have been internalized in the past, then it is more than probable that the encounter will not develop into anything more. It will fade away and degenerate into sheer mannerism or a mild flirtation. It is only when the total personality is involved that the fleeting episode develops into a more enduring relationship, such as friend or lover.

However, forms of sociation are not to be considered as merely being abstractions from interaction. They are the actual processes which enable men to relate to each other. For example, in his analysis of the 'stranger', Simmel postulates that the stranger's interactions with groups to which he hopes to belong, or to which he is put into propinquity by fortuitous circumstances, always involve a constant pattern of reciprocal orientation between group members and the stranger. This pattern of reciprocal orientation can be studied in different historical and social contexts but will always be recognizable because it exhibits the 'form' of the stranger *v.* group relationship:[15]

> In spite of being *inorganically* appended to it, the stranger is yet an *organic* part of the group. Its uniform life includes the specific conditions of this element. Only we do not know how to designate the peculiar unity of this position other than by saying that it is composed of certain measures of *nearness and distance*. Although some quantities of them characterize all relationships, a special proportion and reciprocal tension produce the particular, formal relation to the stranger.

The forms of sociation are replicable in trans-cultural and different historical contexts. If one can unravel form one creates a grammar or a style of conduct between actors, no matter what the content of that interaction happens to be. The distinction between form and content is not to be seen as an arbitrary division between two categories of social organization, namely interaction and normative and symbolic content. Obviously such a distinction is only made for the purposes of analysis. There is no such thing as pure sociation, nor for that matter is there a pure cultural world of ideas and symbols. No interaction takes place outside a cultural framework in which certain categories have already been interpreted, nor does culture free-float without human actors. However, their relationship is not one which is that of a causal chain from culture to interaction, or from interaction to culture. Form and content are aspects of human relationships. When we talk about strangers we are really construing the stranger in terms of approach–avoidance, in terms of nearness and distance. All cultures treat strangers in terms of the social distance criteria which have been culturally defined over a long period of time. Whether these criteria are hostile, or whether they are fundamentally hospitable is something that can be established empirically. But, as sociologists, the notion stranger is one which can be established by concentrating on the idea of the 'stranger' which is a formal aspect of behaviour between actors in a variety of situations.

It is these formal aspects of interaction that are recurrent and are, therefore, available as data in the sociologist's comparative analysis. The danger, of course, is that we can go on to say, as Simmel has been accused of doing, that it is only the forms which are the real subject-matter of sociology. Although Simmel probably did believe this, it is quite apparent that this assertion is of minor importance. The real contribution that Simmel made to social theory was his insistence that content by itself was not sufficient to describe, let alone explain, social interaction. In general, he concentrates on the patterns of reciprocal orientations between actors in face-to-face situations, that is, in dyads, but he introduces into his analysis the complicating factor of the third party. Let us examine what is involved here.

The complicating other

In a dyadic encounter we obviously cannot assume that the reciprocal orientations that individuals make to each other are uncontaminated by the influence of others. When two lovers are involved in an intense emotional relationship their mutual behaviour is not pristine, it is governed by a subtle play of expectations and rules which often may be implicit or incommunicable, but their love play at one level may yet be highly personal. In the privacy of one's bedroom it is believed that anything and everything is allowed and tolerated. Therefore, the expectations, the rules of play etc., are presumed to evaporate under the impact of emotion or desire. This relationship may possibly be transformed from that of love-making into a more permanent relationship, namely marriage. When this happens, obviously the essentially interpersonal intensity of a sexual relationship is transformed into an institutionalized and rule-governed relationship. In other words, one openly acknowledges the apparent right of the 'other' (SOCIETY) to enter into the very fabric of highly personal relationships. There is, therefore, in the relationship between two individuals, however personal, a third party always present. In a sense this presence is guaranteed by the fact that the two individuals are themselves partly the product of countless dyadic relationships with others. A dyadic relationship does not exist in a pure form. However, having said this, there can be no doubt that Simmel believed that there is a qualitative difference between the behaviour of two interactors in persistent relationship, and their relationship to a third interactor. Reverting to the family again, the birth of a first child is likely to have consequences for the relationship between husband and wife which are qualitatively different from the initial form of relationship. The baby's advent conceivably might bolster up an ailing marriage, or it might create a whole new set of alliances or coalitions which were not possible in the dyadic relationship. It is quite conceivable that the third party's arrival completely transforms the quality of relationship between the two original interactors, and that one interactor now finds himself at a distinct disadvantage. In Simmel's view, the difference between dyadic relationships and triadic relationships are far more crucial than the difference between dyads and larger groups. It is the entry of the third party which has the transforming quality – added increments do not make all that much difference.

45

Whether the entry of the third party is envisaged as that of (1) mediator or (2) tertius gaudens – the enjoying other, or (3) that of oppressor, the triadic relationship involves patterns of interaction not possible in the intensity of the dyadic encounter. In a sense, Simmel does not believe that dyadic relationships are self-sustaining over the long run. They cannot last the course. The intimacy of a love affair which develops into marriage ends up in the need for the novelty of further contact with others. In marriage this need presumably is met by the birth of a child, or the development of a triangular sex relationship, or possibly, the commitment of a friend of the family in the role of mediator etc. The essence of Simmel's position is that in both dyadic and triadic situations, there are forms of interactive orientation that will appear time and time again, although in the triadic situation these formal elements are not necessarily duplicated in the dyadic relationship. It is the sociologists' job to tease out these forms in whatever context they appear.

There is the implication in Simmel's position that even though dyadic relationships are emotionally absorbing, eventually social interaction is basically triadic in nature because the third party is always present, no matter the intimacy of the interpersonal relationship. This is certainly in keeping with contemporary emphasis in the social sciences which construes interaction as always being *audience orientated*. The third party, in this sense, is the reference group, or imaginary other, who is monitoring one's conduct even when one is apparently committed to the most absorbing interpersonal encounter. There is, therefore, present in dyadic relationship a visitation of the other inclusive context, that is, the collective. But this visitation is not determinative.

Both the dyadic and collective are dual processes, twin-born in the same way as the individual and society are twin-born. The question of what comes first then, the interaction between individuals at the interpersonal level, or the larger social context, is resolved by Simmel, and I think symbolic interactionism, by the demonstration of the presence of others in almost all highly intimate interpersonal encounters. *The differences between one level and another are the forms of sociation which are regarded as appropriate to that level.* The actual grammar of social interaction then can be studied in the relationships between two or three actors. This grammar is also operant at the collective level. Just as language is universalized in a given population, so is there a language and grammar of interaction, which takes on different protective colouring in different social settings, which is always discoverable by paying attention to the *elements* of social behaviour. Simmel thus foreshadows theorists like Homans and others who also are very much concerned with the discovery of grammar and elements of social behaviour. However, grammar without semantics gives us a very one-sided picture of language. Similarly, the study of the forms of interaction without the meaning contexts in which these elements are enmeshed is also one-sided. Language is not sheer utterance, nor is it composed of signs attached to objects. Sociologically, it is both an element of, and a product of society. It is in this sense that I think that Simmel's insistence on the ubiquity of social forms should be taken.

Social structure and social grammar

However, to delimit sociological grammar is not to specify the causal antecedents of social structure. This is a fallacy. Interaction does not create social structure. As I have implied, social structure and individuality are both processes or aspects of the way in which men relate to each other and through each other, to collectivities. But in the very act of relating, they are allowing language, evaluation, rules of procedure to permeate their interaction. And these social and cultural facts are not sucked out of the air. They are already present in the social climate. Thus interaction is never devoid of links with the past, it is never phenomenologically immediate – even love-making is subject to the pull of cultural prescriptions – and not only cultural prescriptions, but also the burden of the individual's unique experiences and endowment. It is wrong to assert that Simmel was completely sold on the idea of a formal sociology without reference to history and culture. The fact that he saw sociology's unique subject-matter as being the study of the forms of sociation was probably a reaction to the tendency of other theorists to emphasize and proclaim content and culture as constituting the only subject-matter of the social sciences. This emphasis on content was construed as being an argument against sociology's claim to an independent existence, particularly as it was believed that the other social sciences already subsumed the entire field. In discussing this vexed question of form and content we can do no better than quote Theodore Abel, who writes: [16]

> To this distinction Simmel gives a unique meaning that cannot be inferred from the common connotations of these terms. The distinction does not refer to a difference between the abstract and the concrete, the mold and its substance, the structure and its material, or the formal and the substantive. Such connotations are misleading when applied to Simmel's distinction.
> By distinguishing forms and content in society Simmel wants to draw attention to two aspects of interaction. One aspect is a mode of reciprocity between persons manifest in their actions

47

toward each other, their attitudes, and their mutual evaluations. The other aspect is the total situation in which a particular mode of reciprocity is realized. This includes all the facts obtainable needed to answer the questions Who interacts? Why? When? and under what circumstances?

Both aspects of interaction are equally substantive and concrete, and can be justifiably considered content according to the common meaning of the term. Simmel, however, reserves the term content for the second aspect of interaction in order to emphasize its variable character, which changes from an instance of interaction to another in terms of the combination of people, their interests, and the cultural and historical circumstances. For the first aspect represented by the modes of reciprocity, Simmel reserves the term form in order to emphasize their persistent and recurrent character.

Thus interaction, while being formally constituted in the typical modes of relating between persons is always enmeshed in contexts which have already been interpreted. However, this is not equivalent to saying that these contexts determine the interaction. In a sense, all contexts can be regarded as crystallized interaction. For example, the norm of reciprocity is only meaningful when it is mediated in interaction. Presumably in the past the norm has become institution- alized in interaction. Thus Homans, for example, believes that it is possible and indeed essential that we bridge the gap between elementary social processes and the institutional level. He for one goes further than Simmel in stating quite categorically that there is no real or qualitative difference between the micro-level and the macro-level. You do not need one set of explanatory principles for patterns of reciprocal orientations, and another for the larger institutional framework. The difference between the institutional and interactive level is not qualitative, but historical. The institution presents itself to initiates as a force that usually has a long history behind it. Consequently, it is impossible to pinpoint the actual generative processes which were present at the birth of the institu- tion. If one could imaginatively reconstruct the birth pangs of an institution, then one would find interactors engaged in mutual reward–punishment activities which only become institutionalized, if, in the long run, it is more rewarding to behave in a certain way than not behave in that way. Thus in the long run, a particular mode of behaving will be maintained because it pays off.[17]

No doubt the origin of many institutions is of this sort. The behaviour once reinforced for some people in one way, what I call primary, is maintained by a large number of people by other sorts of reinforcement; in particular such general reinforcers as social approval. Since the behaviour does not come naturally to these others, they must be told how to behave – hence the verbal description of behaviour the norm.

Hence the norm of reciprocity is presumably adhered to because it is found to pay off. Similarly, the institutionalization of sexual behaviour is found in all societies because marriage must be more rewarding than sexual licence? This would seem to argue that the maximization of sexual pleasure is only possible at some social cost, that in the final analysis, this cost is worth it, because it also involves the maximization of social approval from others.

Presumably, in terms of this analysis, the norm of reciprocity is continuously acting as a social reinforcer. Therefore, if institutional or normative decline is observed in a society or group, then one would expect the norm of reciprocity to wither away as well, because it is no longer rewarding to return benefits to those whom one has received benefits from. According to Gouldner, the norm of reciprocity subverts an assumed egoism in human affairs. In this connection, it could be argued that the incest taboo is reward-ing, that it is maintained in all societies by the threat of negative reinforcements. It is rewarding because without it (it is claimed) the entire social order would collapse. Men can see its apparent advantages – they can envisage the plunge into normative and sexual confusion – they can empathize with the pain and jealousy that this would involve. Accordingly, they are prepared to submit to the costs of the taboo as expressed in the moral assumptions of society, and which becomes embodied in custom and law.

Breach of the taboo, it is believed, would somehow plunge us all into the Freudian 'Primordial Horde' situation. In Homans's view, the incest taboo can only be understood in terms of reward–cost contingencies, yet, if one accepts Gouldner's viewpoint, then the incest taboo is not only a contrived reward, but also must be understood in the same way as the norm of reciprocity, that is, as being obligatory. But it is this whole question of the obligatory nature of norms that we are discussing. The argument comes full circle. If *both* the norm of reciprocity and the incest taboo are 'given', that is, they belong to the 'of-course world' of everyday assumptions about the nature of this world, then we are saying that the 'of-course world' is somehow out there *sui generis*. This, as we have continued to argue, is untenable, and so is its opposite, namely, that there is nothing more to human behaviour than reciprocal negotiation.

The search for primary elements of social behaviour can lead to reductionism. In Homans's case it leads to a form of behaviourism. But it has been argued that what is true of Homans is also true of Simmel, that his forms of sociation are ultimately psychological phenomena which have their true location in the minds of men. Duncan, for example, has claimed that Simmel stops short of a truly dramatic theory of interaction by his tendency to treat forms as emanations of psychological needs. In other words, forms of sociation express underlying dispositions and interests. There is in Duncan's view a commitment on Simmel's part to a mechanical image of man which interferes with the development of a genuine theory of social interaction. He writes: [18]

> When we try to apply Simmel's forms to an observable content of sociation such as games, play, or art, we find that his prime image of sociation – the being with one another, for one another, in-one-another, against-one-another, and through-one-another, is really a spatial and mechanical image. And, despite all his talk about the individual and the extraordinary subtlety of his analysis of the forms of interaction, he reduces the social process to a natural process. Individuals are the 'bearers of the processes of association', and 'are united by these processes into the higher unity called society'. To illustrate how individuals are united he turns to physics. 'The energy effects of atoms upon each other brings matter into the innumerable forms which we see as things. Just so the impulses and interests, which a man experiences in himself and which push him out toward other men, bring about all the forms of association by which a mere sum of separate individuals are made into a society.'

Now while this does seem to be an expression of psychologism, it is I think not quite fair to Simmel to argue as Duncan does that Simmel reverts back to a primitive reductionism. Simmel was certainly very much concerned with psychological processes but he does not regard these as primary. The forms of sociation are to be studied *sui generis* in spite of the fact that they may have a psychological grounding. However, there is some force in Duncan's view that the study of forms as process, without taking into account the symbolic matrix in which they are expressed, leaves us in a position in which form is divorced from style. The pure forms of sociation that Simmel describes are only understandable when they are symbolically mediated. There is in other words a need to conceptualize interaction in symbolic terms.

2 Non-symbolic interaction

If Simmel's search for a social grammar is seen as an attempt to construct a subject-matter for sociology whereby the forms of sociation are seen as constituting the very stuff of society, then it follows that taken to its logical extreme the forms of sociation can be described independently of the content which they carry. Simmel, as we have seen, regarded interaction between persons as being enmeshed in contexts which already have been formalized. Therefore, in what sense is it possible to speak of interaction without reference to content and symbolization? Mead[1] makes the distinction between human and non-human interaction. Interaction at the animal level does not, in Mead's view, conform to the mutual interpretation of each other's conduct which is so typical of human interaction. Animal interaction is tied to the immediacy of the stimulus field without reference to meaning. The response that one animal makes to another's stimulus or gesture is not interrupted by the interpretative processes which typify human interaction. Each animal responds on the basis of its biological endowment and its programmed range of linked ties to appropriate stimuli. At the animal level we cannot speak of intention, or of consciousness, but only of innate patterns of behaviour which are brought into play when the organism is exposed to the correct stimulus. There is therefore, in Mead's view, a qualitative difference between human response modes and animal response modes. These differences can be conceptualized along a four-dimensional evolutionary scale which Ernst Becker has derived from Leslie Whyte.

(1) *Simple reactivity* At this level a simple stimulus–response reactivity obtains. The organism is located in its environment and in its biological structure. This is presumably typical of instinctual behaviour at the insect level. At the human level, it is conceivable

that men react to objects in their environment at a very primitive level – but it seems improbable that their reaction to other humans can ever be so primitive. At present, there is no supporting evidence to suggest that human reactivity is programmed at such a primitive level, except perhaps for simple reflex arcs.

(2) *Conditioned reactivity* Here we are dealing with a simple learning paradigm. Animals, as we know, since Pavlov's time, can be conditioned to respond to stimuli other than the primary stimulus. In Becker's words: 'The liberation here is fundamental: the animal reacts to a stimulus whose intrinsic property is of no immediate interest to him.'[2] It is liberating in the sense that the animal is in a position to employ the conditioned stimulus as a trigger for action, even when the primary stimulus is not present. However, as Becker points out, most animals are not really capable of making this association, although the word 'walk' for example will usually prepare the dog for walking activity. But, as Becker continues:[3]

> an animal who can associate the sound of the gun with the death
> of one of the herd can flee immediately at the sound of the
> gun, knowing what is inevitably to follow. (But this example is
> not the best: animals don't usually make this correlation; the
> intelligent elephant remains unconcerned as members of his
> herd are shot down around him.)

At the human level simple conditioning enables the individual to engage in complicated avoidance behaviour in order to move away from the field of danger.

(3) *Relational reactivity* Here the organism is believed to *perceive* a relationship between two stimuli. This relationship is problem oriented, being partly dependent on the nature of the organism itself. The classic descriptions of this sort of behaviour derive from 'Gestalt' psychology and are supposed to illustrate 'insight' in non-human behaviour. What it implies is that the organism itself is capable of processing information without being completely dependent on environmental controls. At the human level, this is taken for granted. It is believed to be an evolutionary emergent whose elementary forms are located lower down the phylogenetic continuum. At a purely non-symbolic level, inter-personal behaviour can be construed as the mutual experience of the other in terms of the *structured organization of perception*. The other is perceived not as a pristine stimulus object, but as part of a system of cognitive organization which is endemic to the per-ceptual process itself. Even without the mediation of symbols it is difficult to imagine human interaction on a purely stimulus–response

basis. Hence, this boils down to a discussion on the relative merits of cognitive and stimulus–response models of mediational processes which is outside the competence and scope of this book.

(4) *Symbolic reactivity* In this instance, we are speaking of the typical mode of conduct of human beings. Symbolic interaction is the great liberator from simple stimulus–response chains. Symbols are not tied to the world as such, but are constructed by men in order to give meaning to their 'worlds'. Symbolic behaviour thus creates its own objects which may or may not have any referential context. In interpersonal perception, we thus never see the other as a straight object but as an interpreted object who has meaning for us. Social objects are not perceived as if they were 'there', so to speak, but are always perceived in terms of qualities, intentions, motives that we impute to them. As against this, it has been argued by learning theorists that symbolization is itself a form of behaviour which can be analysed and broken down into its constituent elements – that ultimately, there is nothing different in principle in symbolic processes which cannot be found in the simple stimulus–response model.

These four modes of reactivity can be considered as different aspects of an evolutionary continuum. Only man is believed to be capable of all four modes. The lower one goes down the scale, the greater the likelihood that only very elementary forms of reactivity obtain. It is only man who is able to create his own symbolic objects. However, these symbolic objects are dependent on the other modes of reactivity. Symbolization is not a capacity which is sucked out of the air. Typically, men respond to each other on the basis of meanings which they attach to the *identities* that the other projects, yet these meanings can only be imputed if there is another there in the first place. By this I mean that one does not respond to un-attached symbols. Human responses, although symbolically media-ted, are stimulus bound. Nevertheless, one can choose not to respond, but this choice is made in terms of the initial stimulus condition. It is therefore very important *to distinguish between the mechanisms of interpersonal conduct and the expression of that conduct in meaningful symbols*. Although symbolization is qualita-tively different from other forms of reactivity, it is intimately related to them.

Communication

Human interaction is therefore symbolic interaction. Non-symbolic interaction is only relevant at the non-human level. But is it completely true to assert that reciprocal patterns of orientation are *only* human modes of interaction? Can we conceive of reciprocal orientation among higher primates for example? Certainly we must be absolutely clear that most organic forms have communication systems which are eminently suitable for specific adaptive purposes. Communication is not confined to symbolic discourse, and is indeed a far broader concept. In this context symbolic interaction is only an aspect of communication in general. Inter-animal communication is not random but is meant to convey as much information as possible in order to maximize behaviour. The mating calls of some animals and birds are energizing stimuli which are employed to call out appropriate responses. They do not entail imputing the intention, motive and image of the other animal because, by definition, such imputation of motives is beyond the animal's programmed capacity.

Communication therefore entails a broader spectrum of behaviour than symbolic interaction, albeit there can be no doubt that among humans at least, the majority of communicative processes are subsumed under symbolic interaction. All human interaction seems to be covered by what technically has been called the transmission of messages from one actor to another actor. They convey information or make assertions about certain states etc. They are intended to convey some aspect of the sender's inner state by means of symbols which are then decoded by the receiver. The key term here is *intended*, since the sender is in a position to imaginatively construct the other's response. This is not true of animal interaction in which the response is directly related to the stimulus presented. However, there is a possibility that there might be a transfer of energy between two human interactors which is not symbolically mediated, but this state of affairs is very difficult to envisage. Presumably, if you knock somebody out and then proceed to feed him intravenously with some kind of drug etc., then this might be construed as being a transfer of energy – it is certainly not the transfer of information. Transfer of information implies the ability of the receiving organism to psychologically make use of that information – it involves a degree of consciousness: [4]

The reasons why human interaction so rarely excludes message sending lie in the facts of individual learning. That is, individuals learn that certain events serve as cues, or signs, revealing or portending some state of affairs of interest to them. Just as thunder and lightning are signs pointing to the possibility of a storm, so words, gestures and acts on the part of other persons are signposts conveying information about their attitudes and probable behaviour. In particular – we learn to attribute intentionality to other people on the basis of the cues they provide; that is, their behaviour as well as their words, contains messages, inferred from cues, about their motives and attitudes as referents, whether or not they intend to send such messages. In sum, almost any instance of human behaviour that is observable to another person carries information to him provided only that he has learned to look for it in the other's behaviour, and has learned how to find it.

Even if we suppose that two human beings from two entirely different cultures and different language systems come into contact with each other for the first time in a neutral environment, we would find it difficult to conceptualize their resulting behaviour in any other terms than symbolic. Conceivably, there are a number of ways open for two cultural strangers to meet. They could exhibit downright hostility which could lead to physical violence, they could try to signal friendship or hospitality, they might both withdraw from the scene, they could stand and look at each other etc. If there is not much perceptual difference between the two strangers, then possibly they might signal to each other that their intentions are friendly. On the other hand, if there is a marked divergence in appearance and general self-presentation, then it is likely that the appropriate response might be withdrawal or the adoption of a threatening posture.

Whatever the response, both interactors will be desperately searching for cues and signs of the other's intentions, and also for cues as to his general nature. However, if they have no common language cues, no common expressive symbols and no common value system, then it is more than probable that the interaction will be bedevilled by ambiguity, by misunderstanding, and by the breakdown of contact. Nevertheless, if both interactors persist in trying to surmount the difficulties of communication, then it is conceivable that they will be able to surmount the information barrier. Because, right from the very beginning, they have an advantage which animals do not have, namely, that they can symbolize to themselves that the other is also human, and therefore, capable of communication. In each individual's set of cognitive maps is the expectation that all human beings can communicate and that they have a roughly similar set of categories to map the world. For example, if I am hungry when I meet my stranger, it is not beyond the realm of possibility that I can manage to convey my needs to him by the use of sign language and gestures. If I convince him that my intentions are friendly and not dangerous, he might well offer me some food. Yet, this offer will only be forthcoming if he can imaginatively reconstitute in his own mind the plight that I am in. Obviously the

55

proverbial man from Mars would be unable to do this because he has not got the relevant symbolic equipment, but our cultural stranger should be able to do so. What I am saying is that, even though different cultures have different criteria governing the laws of hospitality and attitudes towards strangers – they all know what strangers are, strangers are defined culturally; in other words, the social form 'stranger' is given substance by the symbols attached to *patterns of nearness and farness*. These patterns cannot be meaningful unless they are symbolically mediated. Given that the societies of origin of both interactors tend to view strangers in a relatively favourable light, then it follows that, in spite of linguistic difficulties, some form of communication will be established between the two parties to the encounter. This form of communication could be symbolic without necessarily being linguistic. Two animals in the same situation could not even attempt to establish a symbolic relationship system because symbolization is outside their typical mode of response.

What constitutes the essential core of non-symbolic communication among animals is their location in the immediacy of the stimulus-world – in the world of the here and now. There is no symbolic future, no remembered past. Granted that the higher one gets up the evolutionary scale the greater the likelihood that animals will respond to signs and stimuli not immediately present as primary reinforcers. Even though these secondary reinforcers often serve as mechanisms reminiscent of memory, there is no reason to argue that they are in themselves equivalent to the capabilities of men who symbolize their pasts to themselves. Hence this means that communication between animals is never likely to lead to the construction of social objects which can only exist at a symbolic level.

The grammar of stimulus and response

Although we have rejected any assumption that social interaction is simply a matter of the tying together of stimulus–response chains, we cannot dismiss the whole problem of interpersonal behaviour as being divorced from some form of behavioural mechanisms. I remarked earlier that it is crucial that we distinguish between the mechanisms of interpersonal conduct and the expression of that conduct in meaningful symbols. We have partially assented to Simmel's proposition that sociology is, in one of its aspects, a search for the forms of sociation, but have argued that these forms are not to be considered as expressing the psychological dispositions of the individual as manifested in interactions with others. But before rejecting this psychological sub-stratum out of hand, we must be very clear as to what it is that we are rejecting. To adapt an anti-reductionist stance is all very well, yet we must be sure that we are not throwing the baby out with the bath-water. Homans, for example, has been attacked time and time again for his reduction-ism, which is premised on a mixture of simple reinforcement theory and axioms of elementary economics. The gist of the criticism levelled against him has been focused on the initial vagueness of his basic propositions. In Sorokin's[5] eyes they are all tautologies. He can find no real legitimation for Homans's[6] division of the elements of social behaviour into activities, interaction and sentiments. For example, Sorokin questions Homans's use of the term sentiment. This term seems to undergo a number of sea-changes. It is some-times used as a synonym for 'drive', emotion, feeling, attitudes etc. In *The Human Group* these terms are used interchangeably but always refer to the state of the organism. In *Social Behaviour* his three key terms are translated into behaviour, that is, they are no longer inferred from behaviour but are considered to be 'behaviour' – the overt response is all there is – the *unobservable* is removed out of the social scientist's frame of reference and is replaced by overt and measurable responses. This means that the concept sentiment is, in reality, equivalent to the concept activity – all other terms are redundant – sentiment is merely a convenient label to apply to a behavioural category. In Sorokin's eyes Homans is guilty of circu-larity of definition, thus placing in doubt the strength of his case for a deductive system deriving from the general propositions of behavioural psychology. In defence of Homans, it must never be forgotten that Sorokin[7] is the author of the most imposing work in 'Macro-sociology' of this century. His impatience with the small-scale and the micro-level is understandable. Nevertheless, there seems to be an element of deliberate distortion in his critique of Homans and although very perspicacious, this criticism reflects his own ego-involvement in his own brand of sociology.

More relevant from our point of view is Homans's attempt to come to terms with the grammar of interaction. In *The Human Group* he repeatedly argues that it is the so-called simple experi-ences of everyday social living which are so difficult to grasp sociologically. His tripartite division of social behaviour into activities, sentiments and interactions does not, on the face of it, seem to be all that earth-shattering. Perhaps this is because Homans does not believe that massive theoretical systems constitute the basis for the building of a science of society. It is possibly true that initially Homans started off as a functionalist, but a functionalist with a difference. His dissection of the five groups in *The Human Group* is analytical. He is interested in the actual components or elements of a system, not only in its holistic properties. Thus, he is not concerned with equilibrium as such, but rather in establishing the criteria whereby social processes can be systematically described in any group situation. His concept of a system is defined in terms of the mutuality of reciprocal relationships of all its parts, regardless of the contextual and historical aspects of the system. These patterns of behaviour are relationships which manifest themselves in any group, whether it is a family, a play group, a factory or even an entire society (although Homans never spends time on applying his analysis to large-scale societies). Certainly, they are more than appropriate when describing the reciprocal relationships between two face-to-face interactors. Every social system can therefore be described and analysed by the use of these basic constituents of social relationships. Now while Homans gets involved in a complicated analysis of social equilibrium and the reciprocal interaction between the external and internal system, this is not really of interest to us. Indeed, at a later date he rejects the holistic implications of his earlier insistence on functional interdependence.

What is of greater interest is his construction of a social grammar along the lines attempted by Simmel, although the elements that he traces in social relationships are not equivalent to Simmel's forms of sociation. Paradoxically, while in *The Human Group* he seems to be committed to a mechanical model of equilibrium, he also assumes that equilibrium in social systems depends on the '*actual behaviour of actual social actors*' who differentially approve, or disapprove, of each other's actions. In this sense, he is certainly a 'methodological individualist'. Social processes are not abstractions, they are located right at the heart of the apparently trivial minutiae of everyday living. They are grounded in the way in which individuals actually respond to others. Thus, the sentiments of individual actors are not located outside the interaction, but are generated in the interaction itself, eventually becoming elements in the interaction. Similarly, interaction generates the verbal statement of how men *ought* to act in relation to each other. Homans argues that interaction generates the norms governing the future development of relationships between group members.

Sometimes, from the point of view of the outside observer (social scientist), these patterns of interaction seem to assume the semblance of an equilibrium situation. Since this equilibrium is only a construct in the observer's head, it is not the system which establishes equilibrium, it is individuals who engage in problems of adjusting to each other's behaviour who do so, so that some degree of tolerable balance is obtained between their sentiments and the norms which are supposed to sanction those sentiments. Social systems, therefore, are nothing more than abstractions employed by sociologists for the purposes of analysis. They have no other existence. Ultimately, the stuff of social behaviour can be described only at the level of actual behaviour between men. This behaviour can be observed, not the behaviour of systems. Systems must be studied analytically.

If these elements are described as activities, sentiments, and interactions with their derivatives–norms, then this is only the first step in understanding the operation of men in social relationships. Here Homans seems to come very close to Simmel, albeit from a different starting-point. Both are interested in very simple patterns of interaction. Both argue that forms or elements of social behaviour tend to be buried under a mass of unnecessary conceptual garbage which hides the actual behaviour of men in social relationships.

Anti-Durkheim?

In *Social Behaviour* Homans moves away from a concern with equilibrium analysis in the sense that seemed to concern him in *The Human Group*. He is still interested in the elements of social behaviour, but now this interest is bolstered up by the use of mechanisms derived from other disciplines. Sociology loses its autonomy and the elements of behaviour are firmly located in behavioural propositions. To reach such a reductionist position is not a matter of arbitrariness for Homans. He has before him the example of the sociological tradition deriving from Durkheim and he finds it sadly wanting, not in theoretical sophistication, but in its claim that general propositions can be derived from fundamental sociological properties: [8]

I have been bothered by Durkheim ever since I had been told by Elton Mayo to read him, and as time went on I became more assured that his statement [that sociology is not a corollary of psychology] was absurd. Not only absurd but obviously absurd. Not only absurd now, but absurd when Durkheim wrote it, even though what he meant by psychology was not what we mean by it now: he thought in terms of psychological traits and not of psychological propositions. I even doubt whether Durkheim believed it himself. Certainly there were social facts but from these facts his conclusions did not follow. Why had we over the years surrendered our critical judgements to Durkheim and his successors the functionalists? Many of their empirical pieces of work were excellent, but whenever they got up – and they often did – on their theoretical high horses, they maundered. I have no answer to the question except that Durkheim provided sociology with an identity, which as an insecure newcomer to the sciences it badly needed: he provided sociology with a theory it could feel was really its own.

If I am right sociology must give up this kind of identity. But it need not feel too badly; it will have companions in misery, if misery it be. All the other social sciences will have to give up their identities at the same time: the general propositions of all the social sciences are the same, and all are psychological. This does not mean that each science will not retain its own special tasks. Much of sociology has rightly concentrated on social structures. Its most interesting theoretical task will remain that of showing how *structures, relatively enduring relationships between men, are created and maintained by individual human choices, choices constrained by the choices of others, but still choices.*

Now Homans's methodological individualism is not exceptionable. After all, to a certain extent, this notion of human choice is implicit both in Weber and Parsons. Yet he strikes a unique flavour in sociology with his insistence that the general propositions be derived from contemporary reinforcement theory. Note that he does not employ the social learning model of say Bandura and Walters,[9] but the strictly empirical model of B. F. Skinner.[10] There have been other reductionists, but none of them have consistently stuck to the propositions of experimental psychology. In the past psychological explanations in sociology have premised on dispositions and inner tendency systems, or alternatively, have been flavoured by some form of Freudian formulation. His interest in behaviour is thus different in kind from the classic tradition in sociology where psychological explanations took on a far more essentialist cast – Pareto,[11] for example, conceives of 'residues' as endemic to social behaviour; these residues being almost intrinsic in nature. Homans, on the other hand, is not concerned with inner states, only in the strict empirical documentation of the empirical relationships of concepts. Concepts are grounded in nature – and the only way they can be studied is by studying what is observable. In effect, we are left with the study of stimulus–response relationships. These in turn are supported by economic axioms relating to the maximization of personal advantage in an exchange matrix.

Simply conceived, all interaction involves stimulus–response chains. Indeed it is difficult to conceive of any other way of describing the mechanisms at work. Homans himself is not bothered by the simplicity of these relationships. Skinner's psychology seemed to him to be eminently suitable for the job at hand, since it was markedly devoid of theoretical pitfalls and was securely located at the level of measurement and observation. In principle, all social behaviour can be described in these terms. If stimulus–response relationships are translated into *reward–punishment contingencies* then we have an account of social motivation without necessarily postulating such unobservables as drives, motives, feelings, attitudes etc. Men behave toward each other because they need to maximize their positive and minimize their negative reinforcements. Consequently, in any encounter there is no necessity to believe that it will be continued unless it is somehow rewarding to both parties. Of course, this excludes the complication of power. Indeed, Homan himself is rather worried that phenomena such as power and status are not readily subsumed by reward–punishment contingencies – yet he manages to place power into an exchange framework by assuming that unequal distribution of esteem and resources secures unequal advantages in the interactive situation.

In spite of the contrived simplicity of Homans's position, it must be admitted that his analysis of interaction is far more subtle than is generally admitted. When employing behavioural categories his main aim is not to act as a spokesman for Skinner and others, but rather, to begin the task of genuine explanation in the social sciences. To call him a psychological reductionist is, I believe, beside the point. What we have to decide is how possible is a behavioural description of interaction?

Take, for example, our stranger paradigm. In Simmel's terms the stranger concept is focused on the forms of nearness and distance that certain social groups employ in their relations with strangers or outsiders. To establish this relationship we need to observe the behaviour of individuals who meet for the first time. There is a wide range of empirical possibilities.

First, there is the meeting of two people in the *same culture and belonging to the same social strata*. Here the behaviour is likely to be governed by a number of conventions relating to the standards of polite behaviour. Thus, standard linguistic and rhetorical devices are employed in a rather ritualized manner. For example, 'middle-class' conventions in the British Isles demand that strangers being introduced for the first time engage in the 'How do you do?' game. Nobody is interested in the answer to this question, but it is demanded by the rules of the game. However, if one should refuse to play, then this could either mean the abrupt breaking off of the encounter, or the reciprocation in kind from the injured party, who might conceivably react by making remarks that are calculated to redress the balance. More likely is the relapse into an embarrassed silence in which the injured party engages in an eloquent 'non-active presentation' as the aggrieved and yet 'so correct' party. In terms of the reward–punishment contingencies apparent in the encounter one could claim that the encounter was broken off because there was no further profit in pursuing it any further. On the other hand, if there had been no breakdown of normal social intercourse, the encounter would probably develop along lines which were mutually satisfying to both parties without the generation of too much emotion. It is, of course, conceivable that the very act of meeting strangers from one's own social class is a pleasing form of interaction, so that it is intrinsically rewarding. Certainly, the perception of the other as a member of one's own social group goes a long way to removing the initial tension of the encounter.

If the encounter is terminated abruptly, it is more than likely that the 'deviant' interactor will have to pay quite a high price in terms of future interaction with the same individual and others of equivalent social rank. The price he pays will be measured in terms of reputation smeared and the loss of esteem. If the individual values this reputation, then it is more than likely that he will make every effort to restore the situation. Superficially, this encounter can be described in the language of reward–punishment. It assumes there is nothing beyond the surface behaviour of the participants in the encounter. The prior definitions of stranger, and the implicit norms involved in interacting with strangers are marginal to this analysis.

Second, there is the first meeting of two people from two different classes. Here again there is a set of norms and rules of the game. The criteria of nearness and farness are institutionalized in established patterns of social distance which are believed to be accepted by the various social classes. Thus, for example, the meeting of a 'boiler-maker' and a 'company director' (who perhaps has been educated at Eton) is governed by ploys which are intended to cover both embarrassment and legitimation of their respective locations. If, for argument's sake, this encounter takes place in a pub, the demands and expectations of the situation are obviously partly determinative, the context creates its own ethos. Nevertheless, in terms of reward–cost contingencies, the two participants will tend to conduct their mutual drinking as a relationship in identity confirmation. In spite of the conviviality of the moment, it is these relations that are of prime importance. Presumably, the identity projected by the company director will be to emphasize his democratic nature, whereas the boiler-maker will project his commitment to his working-class origins. If both are successful, then the encounter has been successful, each taking out of it what each invested, plus psychic profits.

In a different context the meeting of company director and boiler-maker may be accompanied by rigid application of rules of procedure in which the interaction is controlled by the prior conceptions that each has of each other's role. Here, we could say past learning has shaped the execution of the role behaviour. Learning involves expectations regarding reinforcement for particular types of behaviour, and it follows that individuals will avoid all behaviour that is calculated to involve them in costs. Past learning enables both strangers to calculate the risks involved in breaching the expectations built into occupational and class roles. One is not deliberately rude to one's employer's friends – to do so is to court redundancy. Similarly, the friend does not make derogatory remarks about the working class if he does not want to instigate militant strike action. From the point of view of the observing behavioural scientist trying to explain this type of behaviour, it is easy to see that it could easily be understood in terms of the actual stimulus–response linkages expressed in the situation and also as a result of past conditioning. If social distance is violated, then certain reactions are bound to follow. Interaction will only continue if both parties believe that this course is not prejudicial to their class interests!

Third, if two strangers come into contact from different language and cultural systems, there will be an attempt to maximize their reward–cost ratios so that the acute ambiguity and embarrassment that both suffer will be overcome. However, as we have already noted, this might not be possible because of the constitutive norms covering interaction with strangers. If, for example, the norms relating to the treatment of strangers demand that they be immediately put to death, or that they must by definition be barbarians, then it is difficult to see that the encounter could turn into anything mutually rewarding.

Underlying this behavioural orientation is the example of the experimental animal in a laboratory situation. Here it is relatively easy to document the patterns of stimulus and response that obtain between an animal and its environment, and an animal and other animals. Similarly, given controlled conditions, human interaction may be observed and experimentally manipulated along a range of very simple behaviours. The reinforcement ratios that we manage to obtain from these procedures presumably could be said to illustrate the control factors at work in the eliciting of a response. From this premise it is very easy to conclude that the laboratory is, in effect, a social system in miniature, and that everyday human interaction is shaped by the same mechanisms as those in the laboratory. All that is really significantly different is the complexity of the stimulus field and the wide range of responses available to humans – this being a matter of degree, not a qualitative difference. Science is interested in the most parsimonious explanation, and if this is provided by Skinner's reinforcement psychology, then no matter how revolting it is to the humanist conscience, our first duty is to press on in the interests of explanation.

In Homans's view, these mechanisms are ignored by the sociological community because they have been seduced by the promises of a sociology in which the claims made for autonomy have been reified into a dogma. We can't explain social behaviour because we have been too concerned with erecting verbal scaffolds to bolster up our theoretical poverty. What is needed is an understanding of sub-institutional processes which are the real stuff of society – and for this, we do not have to look to any other discipline than the *basic* one of behavioural psychology. These processes are not culture bound – they underpin all social behaviour in all societies. They therefore are, in some respects, similar to Simmel's forms of sociation – the real difference between the two is that in Simmel's case these forms are ideal types in that they are all abstractions from behaviour, whereas for Homans, they can be experimentally researched and observed. The strange thing from Homans's perspective is that behavioural propositions have been available for a long time. They do not have to be discovered by sociologists, only applied. Indeed they are part and parcel of the traditional 'psychology of common sense'.[12]

Behavioural grammar and collective processes

The behavioural grammar that Homans is interested in establishing for the social sciences is not qualitatively different from the grammar of relationships established between other organisms and their environment. And here I use the word environment in its broadest sense. Homans writes in this respect:[13]

> Although our subject is social behaviour (that is, when a man's activity is rewarded or punished directly or indirectly by one or more men) we have stated our propositions about a man's behaviour under the influence of reward as if it made no difference where the reward came from; our fisherman was not rewarded by other men but by fish. And, in one sense, it does not make any difference, since no new propositions are needed to explain social behaviour. But it does make a difference to the complexity of explanation. When a man's activity is rewarded by the nonhuman environment, he acts in accordance with the laws of human psychology, but the environment does not. When a man's activity is rewarded by the activity of another man, both are acting in accordance with these laws. The activity of each is influencing the activity of the other, and in human ways. The two are (to use a common term of sociology) interacting, and it is *this reciprocal influence* that causes complexity.

Homans's paradigm assumes that the simplest behavioural responses between organism and its environment are not qualitatively different from the interpersonal relationships between human beings, the only difference being that humans respond and the natural environment does not. And from the reciprocal responses of individuals to each other we can understand the far more complex patterns of behaviour that inform structural processes. The mutuality of interpersonal responses is, therefore, governed by the laws of human psychology – we do not have to go any further for our general propositions. This is not the time or place to get involved in the lengthy and often futile debate about the validity of psychological propositions in the social sciences, except to say that it depends to a degree on what sort of psychology one is talking about. The rejection of reinforcement theory does not thereby invalidate 'cognitive psychology' or 'Freudianism'. More crucially, are the interpersonal orientations of actors to be considered as psychological processes and not as genuine sociological processes? Is Homans's contention valid that psychology is indivisible in that you do not need two separate psychologies – one to explain the individual's behaviour *per se*, and the other to explain the individual's behaviour in group and interpersonal situations? Is this contention useful and appropriate to the study of interpersonal and collective phenomena? It could be argued that it is appropriate, provided you can demonstrate that both the individual and collective phenomena are different aspects of the same underlying process. What is worrying is the assumption that, in principle, it is only a quantitative distinction that is important, implying that the degree of complexity collective phenomena exhibit can be explained by complication, rather than qualitative considerations. It would seem to me that there is a qualitative difference between interaction as conceived of in reward–cost terms, and interaction which uses language as its medium of exchange. Language is more than a complicating factor – it has consequences which are not found at the purely animal level.

Now it can be admitted that language itself is a form of behaviour – a higher signalling system, but a form of behaviour nevertheless – yet this admission does not detract from the fact that it constitutes something new in the evolutionary stakes. In human interaction, exchanges of rewards and punishments are not direct, they are filtered and distorted by the symbolic universe that men inhabit. What men want, what they approve of, what they give esteem to, what they value cannot be expressed, other than through the symbols that they attach to these values. If men do reward and punish each other in interaction, they do so through symbolic exchange. They relate to each other through symbols of sociation which have significance for them – this significance not necessarily depending on their intrinsic reward structure, only on their power to evoke cognitive orientation. I can't reward the other if I don't know who I am, and who the other is. Strangers are not interested in the immediate maximization of their profit account – all they want to do is to establish the identity of the other so that some form of interaction can ensue; this process of identification is made possible by the symbols that they employ, not by a process of jockeying into position in order to secure the maximum bargaining power. Consequently, when one is conceptualizing interpersonal behaviour as an exchange-relationship in which both parties are doing their best to come out ahead in the bargaining process, the mechanisms of exchange represent only *one* aspect of the complicated processes involved.

Nevertheless, in Homans's view the exchange is constitutive of society – and what passes as culture (values, norms and language) is really representative of *past interaction*. One is seldom 'in' at the birth of an institution. Before one can speak of institutional behaviour, one has to tease out the sub-institutional grammar. What Homans leaves out of his account is the whole problem of 'consciousness' and the symbolic representation of that consciousness that men make to themselves.

Although Homans would probably deny it, there seems to be no reason why his psychologism cannot be described as a variant of the hedonic calculus. He assumes that motives can be described and operationalized in terms of invariant reward–cost contingencies which particular groups of men have found to pay off. Behind the most complicated social process we can discover very elementary patterns of psychological gratification. He does not come out directly for a biologically located primary reward structure, yet it is there by implication. In his description of institutional behaviour, the secondary or derived rewards are always dependent on the primary reward system, albeit primary rewards are not visible but operate in hidden regions. Ultimately, in spite of his dislike of the term, Homans's elements of social behaviour are reductionist in nature. The search for an elementary social grammar predicated on behavioural psychology is really a search for the timeless and ahistorical aspects of human living – it is based on the notion of the psychic unity of mankind, supposedly discoverable in the mutuality of hedonic gratification.

But grammar is surely not the last word in social analysis. To take an example from linguistics, the meaning of a sentence is not derived from an understanding of the grammatical elements of that sentence – the meaning can only be arrived at by the consideration of the context of the sentence, by the way in which its constituent parts are related to each other and to other sentences. Similarly, in understanding social interaction, it is not necessary that we have at our command a dictionary of exchange elements in order to

66

unravel the meaning of that interaction. The meaning of the interaction is partially a function of the actor's definition of the situation.
This definition is not only produced by the immediate situation, it
is a function of a multi-dimensional reality located both in the past
and in the future. We bring to each interaction episode 'selves'
which have historical antecedents and which, to a certain extent,
are hypotheses about how the self is able to function *vis-à-vis*
other social actors. Being social not only involves trying to get something from other people, but also implies that we *see ourselves in
other people.* In other words, sociality should be considered in its
empathic form, not only as a war of each against each. The hedonic
calculus is not necessarily the only way in which we can conceive
of interactive processes. It is surprising how social theorists, whether
they are committed to a methodological individualism or not, seem
to premise their image of man on his innate selfishness. In this
connection such topics as sympathy are ruled out of court because
they run counter to the dominant ethos. There is no reason to
believe that interaction is only an exchange mechanism in which
men exchange psychic benefits. Certainly there is an element of
exchange in all interaction, but this exchange does not have to be
based on an economic model – indeed, it is conceivable that
men relate to each other simply because they are able to empathize
with each other, because they have the ability to understand how
others feel in certain circumstances although they might not be
able to predict the other's behaviour from this understanding.

3 Emotional identification and the grammar of sociation

One of the surprising aspects of the discussion of social interaction among recent sociologists is the paucity of their interest in and discussion of sympathy and emotional identification. There has not been a substantial analysis ever since Scheler's time. Presumably, one of the reasons for this lack of interest is the vagueness of the concept and its lack of empirical specification. In general, it is seen as belonging to intuition, and intuition is not really a respectable topic for social scientists. If it is discussed at all, it is usually subsumed under 'Verstehen' or perhaps as an aspect of the role-taking process. However there is a considerable problem here. Subjectively, all of us can bear witness to the fact that we do feel sympathy with others. The trouble is that we have been told by Freudians and behavioural scientists that these feelings are only manifestations of more primitive feelings or instincts. In addition, learning theory has argued that all such motives can be seen as secondary, as being tied to powerful drives. This has led to a belief that sympathy is not a suitable topic of investigation either for the psychologist or sociologist. It is considered to be one of those 'soft' topics which are better left to writers and humanists. On the other hand, aggression, power, egoism and achievement motivation have been given the status of prime factors in the study of motivation both at the individual and group level. This image of human motivation seems to depend on the contextual location of social scientists who have been exposed to the traumatic shocks of contemporary social experience. Consequently, they seem to suspect that the human animal is best described in terms of *those motives which best express the times we live in.* Presumably, given the approximation of Utopia and the good society, social scientists would be inclined to impute different motives to social actors amongst which sympathy, co-operation and altruism might rank higher than egoism and

68

aggression. Thus, the study of social motivation is itself a problem in the sociology of knowledge.

Those theorists who have insisted on the necessity for studying man's sociality as being premised on a set of co-operative pro-clivities tend to be viewed with the greatest suspicion. Consequently somebody like Ashley Montague,[1] who believes that essentially social science should pay more attention to such qualities as love or sympathy, is regarded as not being in the front rank, or as a professional 'do-gooder'. Now it must be admitted that in a century that has seen both Buchenwald and Hiroshima a belief in the essential goodness of man does seem to be a little old-fashioned and woolly-minded. But what is the exact empirical evidence that man is the opposite? If we accept that motivation is, in sociological terms, largely a question of giving accounts of situated action in Wright Mills's[2] sense, then how can we categorically rule out altruism and co-operation? Granted, the atypical motives do not fit in with the typical motives of so-called typical actors in a world in which men seem to systematically go out of their way to inflict the maximum discomfort and pain on others. Yet, *typical* motives are constructs in the same way as atypical motives are constructs. We impute motives on the basis of vocabularies which reflect the fundamental human themes of the day. Hence, we have a vast conceptual armoury which includes those 'motive' terms which point to the supposed human condition. In interaction it is believed men are trying to maximize their self-esteem, to gratify their need for achievement, to outdo their fellows, etc. Also, other vocabu-laries involve imputed needs for authority, needs for self-debase-ment. It could be said that contemporary vocabularies of motivation tend to see man as a victim, or as a self-seeking executioner. Alternative vocabularies relating to different images of man which situate him in a more co-operative frame of reference are ignored, except by mystics or professional do-gooders. When we talk of emotional identification in interaction, we are therefore, more likely to be speaking of identification with an authority figure than identifi-cation in terms of fellow feeling. Identification is thus identification with a power source, rather than with the 'other' as a suffering human being.

Sociological theory finds it very difficult to incorporate alternative models of man which run counter to the official hedonic calculus. Although programmed drives have lost out to socially induced motives, most sociological accounts of motivation have substituted motives which are really no different from their biological counter-parts. Aggression, for example, while no longer innate, still plays just as important a part in human behaviour, except that it is now seen as being an expression of some culturally induced frustration state. In this respect I quote from an influential text on social stratification: [3]

> Paralleling the argument from modern history [that is the concentration camp and Hiroshima syndrome] is that from contemporary psychology, where current theory and research undermine our faith in natural goodness of man no less than do political events. Recent research reveals the human infant is an extremely self-centred creature, motivated solely by his own needs and desires. If we rid ourselves of the romantic aura which surrounds babies in our society, we discover that they are totally involved in reducing the various tensions created by their biological nature and the environment. Their early actions are simply trial and error probings to discover methods of reducing or relieving these tensions.
>
> In time, of course, the normal child learns to take the wishes of others into account. But this does not mean he is any less motivated to maximize his own satisfactions. Rather, it means that he has learned that the attainment of his own goals is inextricably linked with the interest of others. For example, a boy who acquires a taste for football soon finds that he satisfies this taste only by co-operating with others who share his enthusiasm. Because he co-operates with them we should not assume that he is no longer seeking to maximize his own satisfactions. On the contrary, we can be sure he is.

Lenski repeats the traditional arguments about enlightened self-interest. All human social conduct, on examination, turns out to have an element of this self-interestedness, even those actions which appear to exhibit an element of self-sacrifice and altruism. He argues that self-sacrifice must always be seen in its appropriate context – there is no such thing as uncontaminated self-sacrifice; the most disinterested action is always oriented towards the interests of members of one's own group. One does not sacrifice oneself for strangers. So, presumably, if one sees a man drowning, the decisive influence will be his identification with one's own group. If he is black, then one will not try to save him. If he is white, then all things being equal, one will jump into the river, even though this might entail one's death. Hence for Lenski, self-sacrifice is associated with the intensity of one's involvements with groups, especially families, friendship groups, possibly ethnic and national groups – he writes: [4]

> When we view human action in this broader perspective – we soon discover that these groups which generate so much sacrificial action in their internal relations are often capable of

70

the most ruthless pursuit of their partisan group interests when dealing with outsiders, even though the latter are members of the same society.

The self-interest theorem as ubiquitous?

Lenski is prepared to admit that some human actions are not covered by the self-interest theorem, namely, those which are genuinely altruistic. Genuine altruism is a form of motive which is reserved for the relatively unimportant aspects of everyday life, where, apparently, very little is at stake. When decisions have to be taken which entail major values, then it is more than likely that they will be taken in the interests of oneself, or one's own group. Self-interest or egoism is, therefore, the major psychological, social, and biological drive of men in social interaction. In this respect Lenski's view of man is roughly similar to the position taken by Homans, although Lenski is more interested in the macro-level than Homans. From his premise of individual self-seeking he manages to deduce that societies are also self-seeking and, indeed, even more self-seeking than individuals.

This viewpoint is typical of the way in which human nature has been represented in contemporary social science. The alternatives are presented by philosophers, mystics and proponents of self-actualization. Homans and others are, therefore, well supported in their model of social interaction as being basically a market-oriented activity.

Is there any evidence for the alternative? How important are expressions of emotional identification and sympathy in social inter-action? We are not here concerned with the postulation of inner tendency systems which energize altruistic interaction. What we are interested in is in examining the case for interactive behaviour which is not purely an exchange activity. When the question is asked 'under what conditions does one feel sympathy for another?', the standard reply is usually given in terms of the individual's presumed capacity to put himself in the other's place. For instance, if I hurt my hand the expressions of sympathy which others offer are presumably based on their own experiences of pain and their imaginary reconstruction in their own heads of the pain that I am supposed to be experiencing. At this level, the mother of a small child, or the husband of a wife suffering from a severe illness feels sympathy, because she or he can reconstruct the other's pain. In this they can be said to take the 'role of the other'. Under these circumstances the person can express his sympathy by trying to comfort or alleviate the stress the other is undergoing. This supposed capacity to experience vicariously the other's pain or psychic trauma is not to be construed as constituting a complete identification with the other. One must differentiate between the other's suffering and my intuition of that suffering. As Scheler has argued, my intuited sympathy, and the other's actual suffering, are phenomenologically distinct. There is no fusion of the two states so that one is indistinguishable from the other. My experience of the other's suffering must be distinguished from his actual suffering.

Because they are phenomenologically separate, these two aspects point to psychological processes which are compounded of different mental mechanisms. In a way, it could be argued that one only gives sympathy to those *one knows and likes*. Hence, some form of exchange is involved. One's liking of the other is in return for some psychological benefit. I could, therefore, understand the other's pain, since I believe I have experienced the same pain myself. On the other hand, if the other is a stranger, this will not involve me in sympathetic interaction, merely by the understanding of certain expressive conduct which points to pain or other internal states. In other words, I can take the role of the other, by cognizing his state of pain without necessarily feeling anything for him at all.

Taking the role of the other and 'true sympathy'

Scheler makes this abundantly clear when he differentiates between empathic experiences of the other, and true fellow feeling. Before one can genuinely feel for the other one has to assume that one has some knowledge of the other. This knowledge is compounded of past experiences with others in similar circumstances – it implies a capacity to recognize the symbols and expressions which go with certain feeling states. Typically, these expressive symbols are culturally standardized for particular groups of people in particular contexts. Only family members, for example, will recognize that certain expressions and symbols which the father employs are meant to indicate pain or joy. They may be misinterpreted by outsiders. Sympathy, nevertheless, is not to be confused with the understanding of the other's state, but is an analytically distinct datum of experience. Even the reproduction of the other's pain in one's own reconstructed imaginary experience cannot be really construed as genuine fellow feeling. As Scheler writes: [5]

> The reproduction of feeling or experience must therefore be sharply distinguished from fellow feeling. It is indeed a case of feeling the other's feeling, not just not knowing of it, nor judging that the other has it, but is not the same as going through the experience itself. In reproduced feeling we sense the quality of

the other's feeling, without it being transmitted to us, or evoking a similar real emotion in us. The other's feeling is given exactly like a landscape which we see subjectively in memory, or a melody which we hear in similar fashion – a state of affairs quite different from the fact that we remember the landscape or the melody (possibly with an accompanying recollection of the fact that it was seen or heard). In the present case there is a real seeing or hearing, yet without the object seen or heard being perceived and accepted as really present; the past is simply represented. Equally little does the reproduction of feeling or experience imply any sort of participation in the other's experience. Throughout our visualizing of the experience we can remain quite indifferent to whatever has invoked it.

Scheler's typology of sympathy as expressing various forms of fellow feeling is, admittedly, impossible to conceptualize in the standard language of reinforcement psychology. Emotional interaction is so submerged under the weight of cognitive and cultural prescriptions that social scientists have almost legislated it out of existence because it does not meet the criteria of strict empirical documentation. Similarly, altruistic interaction is never examined with the same rapt attention as other more spectacular examples of human egoism. Yet it is surely one of the most typical of everyday episodes that sympathy is expressed by individuals for others for whom they have fellow feeling. Vocabularies of motivation are not established in emotional voids, human interaction is not only a question of the mutual negotiation of neutral symbols. Symbols are suffused with affectivity, this affectivity not necessarily being related to the maximization of a profit and loss account. It seems to me to be a mistake to see emotion as subordinate to sentiment in the attribution of motives in interaction. Sentiment, as defined by theorists like Mcdougall[6] and Kirkpatrick[7] is always a socially defined emotional state related to an appropriate object. Consequently it involves a *translation process* from primitive feeling states into socialized and structured emotions. Thus anger or aggression is transformed into sarcasm and indignation. In this process, the so-called primitive states are watered down and socialized. Given the appropriate circumstances, anger is necessarily transformed into its cultural equivalent, even though it is difficult to distinguish from its primitive biological origins. However, because human interaction is nearly always symbolic, there is a tendency to assume that it is the symbols themselves which contain the emotion: this is not true – symbols can draw out emotion, but they cannot do this unless the individual is basically capable of emotion.

73

In altruistic behaviour we have the example before us of the individual who ostensibly puts the interests of others before his own self-interest – sometimes leading to self-sacrifice. We are told that ultimately this sort of conduct is reducible to the individual's sense of identification with a particular set of individuals or a group. When I see projected large as life on the television screen the plight of war or famine victims, my reaction can be one of indifference, indignation, emotional identification, it can involve the concrete action of dipping into my pocket and sending some financial contribution to the victims, or I can down tools and actively participate in the relief and the experience of the people whose plight has shocked me. Whatever my reaction, we can be sure that there is a typical motive which will be attached to my conduct. Thus my intention of joining the victims in their struggle will be construed as being idealistic, altruistic or as an instance of my ideological commitments. The appropriate labels will be trotted out both by those evaluating my conduct and also by myself. The expression of sympathy for the victim and my consequent action of identification then situates me in a context – it places me, and presumably resolves any ambiguity about the status of my behaviour. What is forgotten is the direct impact that the original situation may have on me. Granted that this impact is mediated by the schemata that I have built up inside me about the whole question of victimage. Granted that my response to victimage is partially dependent on my individual biography, but this does not invalidate the fact that the emotional rooting of these experiences may be genuine and not compounded by the interpretations that others have put on them. Social interaction is, in other words, not necessarily a process in which cognition is divorced from feeling, and in which the imputed emotion is seen to be dependent on prior definitions of that emotion. But it is true that we have very little direct understanding of the emotional underpinning of interaction, although there is any amount of evidence offered in literature and the arts.

However, a theory of interaction which does not take into account the phenomenological aspects of personal encounters would seem to be inadequate. Interaction is exchange; it is reciprocal negotiation, it is tied to the perception of the other, it is normatively shaped, but it is also an encounter between two or more individuals who relate to each other as biosocial beings and not as some abstracted social essence as expressed in role theory. Of course, it is difficult to grasp the phenomenological aspects of interaction without encapsulating it in the language of normative discourse, yet if we fail to consider the undefined aspects of interaction we neglect an important aspect of social experience. Although, by implication, we have been arguing for situated accounts of human interaction, we do not mean to imply thereby that feeling states are purely symbolically mediated. Nor do we intend to imply that all feeling states are communicable and translatable into symbolic discourse. However, unlike Wittgenstein, there is no reason to believe that incommunicability demands absolute silence. One's feeling states are usually occasioned by one's involvement with others, and these involvements generate anxieties and tensions which are frequently inexpressible, yet the inexpressible is sometimes a constituent element of social interaction.

From the point of view of the social scientist trying to conceptualize such feeling states, one might well be forced to conclude that they were, in principle, beyond analysis and conceptualization, and therefore not a suitable object of study. This seems to me to be a great mistake. Incommunicability is usually associated with moments of extreme personal crisis: death of a loved one, the breaking off of a sexual relationship, the realization of one's impending death, pain, or even the so-called 'existential angst' of continental philosophy. Attempts to communicate such experiences often seem ham-fisted in the language of conventional everyday sociability, even attempts to translate these experiences into poetic metaphor tend to heighten their symbolic content without necessarily catching their immediate phenomenological impact. Certainly, in the conceptualization of sympathy, we are in danger of intellectualizing an experience which, by definition, is beyond intellectualization.

There is some psychological evidence that purports to show that most emotional states are biochemically very similar, and that consequently the only way that inner emotional states can be identified is by external cues. The well-known experiments of Schacter and Singer, for example, demonstrated that certain happenings in the social environment seemed to be the only means that individuals have for *naming* the particular emotion that they experienced.[8] Thus in a sense, emotions involve the tacit agreement of those engaged in the interaction to label certain physiological states in a certain way. However, this agreement presupposes some sort of consensus on the actual feeling states that both parties say they experience. If I say that I feel joy at the occasion of somebody's success, I presume that this label has meaning for the person I am speaking to, because in the past I assume he has experienced joy, that is, he has attached labels to similar inner states. But in certain immediate face-to-face situations, the only cues that one has are the actual expressive cues given off by the other. Although these cues are subject to misinterpretation, they are phenomenologically the only way in which I can apprehend his inner states, even though my inner experience is obviously not a carbon copy of his inner experience.

In general, even though it can be said that my motives, my feelings, my attitudes are only known through the indications of others, and even though the witnessing of my subjectivity is, in part, a reflection of the indications that others have made to me, there is nevertheless, underneath the apparent ubiquity of social and symbolic interaction, the notion of interaction *as being experienced*. This seems to be at the heart of the phenomenological account of social behaviour. The experience of the other is always phenomenologically immediate. It is symbolic when we attempt to impute motives and meaning to the other's conduct.

The notion of interaction as being experienced must presuppose an implicit commitment to the phenomenological self.

The phenomenological self

The experience of the self does not only depend on the categorizations of social scientists, but on the common-sense observations of so-called common men. It depends on the individual's experience and witnessing of his own subjectivity. Individuals observe their own inner states but they also define the external world in terms of their own immediate perception of that world. The world of the immediately given is always mediated through some form of self-process which relates subject to object. It follows that at one level the self is experienced as solitary and as an axis of experience. This view of the self is congenial to phenomenology and existentialism. It is expressed nicely by Maurice Natanson: [9]

> The biographical actualization of the self is the person.
> Accordingly, persons are selves whose identities have achieved
> expression. It would be misleading to think of the person either
> as somehow encapsulated in the self or as developed by the self
> in interaction with its surrounding social world. The person is not
> an essence precontained in the self, nor is the self a blank slate
> as far as identity and character are concerned. *If we drop the
> language of both original attribute and conditioning by
> environment we may begin to speak in phenomenological terms.*

The elimination of the language of original attributes and conditioning experiences allows the phenomenologist to make the so-called 'phenomenological reduction' in which all that is given to the self is the experience of the self. Sociologically, as Schutz has attempted to demonstrate, the self moves in a dialectic of multiple possibilities between the world as assumed in 'of course' assumptions, and the world as 'actively experienced' at the level of meaning. But there is also a level of experience which seems to lie outside the sociologically meaningful, which is fully related to the sense of self as immediate experience. I refer to the sense of the 'bodily me'. In this connection Allport's vivid description of the propriate nature of the body sense is of interest: [10]

> The bodily sense remains a lifelong anchor for our self awareness. It is true that in health the normal stream of sensations is often unnoticed while in a state of ill-health, or pain, or deprivation the bodily sense is keenly configurated. But at all times, the underlying support of the bodily me is there. How very intimate it is can be seen if you imagine the following situation. Think first of swallowing the saliva of your mouth or do so. Then imagine spitting it into a tumbler and drinking it. What seemed natural and mine suddenly becomes disgusting and alien. Or to continue this unpleasant line of thought for a moment, picture yourself sucking the blood from a prick in your finger, then imagine sucking blood from a bandage wound around your finger. What you perceive as belonging intimately to your body is warm and welcome. What you perceive as separate becomes instantly cold and foreign.

This example of Allport's highlights an aspect of the phenomenological attitude in that it points to those bodily experiences which are not necessarily reflected on, are not intellectualized, and yet are 'essentially actual experiences'. It is in this sense that the phenomenological self is to be understood. At a more sophisticated level it can be regarded as the essential requirement for the individual's definition of the situation. The self as experience is, of course, not insulated from the contents of experience, but is assumed to create its own experiences. It is the nebulous nature of this view of the self which is questioned by more experimentally minded social scientists. It cannot be demonstrated, except by an act of introspection and, as we all know, introspection was sent to purgatory a long time ago! Nevertheless, this is only a negative criticism. It does not touch on the crux of the matter, namely the everyday experiences of common men. These everyday experiences certainly are phenomenologically alive to the individual actor. He does not operate on a fully fledged operational theory of the self, only on his own immediate perceptions and feelings, no matter how constrained by social conditioning or inner compulsions. The intrusion of phenomenology into the social sciences probably has a great deal of intellectual faddism attached to it, but there is no doubt that this perspective is more than a fashionable pose. It is important to certain psychotherapies as well as to ethnomethodology. In this, it is allied to existentialism as articulated by Sartre in its emphasis on the self as the axis of meaning, and in its claims about the social and *a priori* significance of the individual.

Self as the axis of meaning

When the emphasis is on the *self as the axis of meaning* an assumption is made which sees human behaviour as being predicated on some need for authenticity. It is thus predicated on some of the apparently outworn clichés of humanism and the centrality of human personality. In one sense, it takes up arms against any idea of prediction or validation etc. As Frankl asserts, 'A real human person is not subject to rigid prediction. Existence can neither be reduced to a system nor deduced from it.'[11] No matter how woolly this might sound to certain hard-minded practitioners in the behavioural sciences, it does seem to be the view of a lot of people who have not necessarily sold out to some form of newer mysticism. In general, at the personality level this stance has been maintained by people like Carl Rogers[12] and Abraham Maslow,[13] the key concept being 'self-actualization'. It must be admitted that these approaches are not easily translated into the language of conventional personality theory, let alone the language of verification. This in itself is not a real objection. Thus, without necessarily subscribing to the philosophical underpinnings of phenomenology, it would seem to me that any definition or discussion of the self is helplessly untenable unless the self is defined in terms of its being a *point of sentience*, an axis of meaning for the relating of the individual to the objects in his world. It is the centre from which the world is defined – even when this world has already been defined culturally as a set of common understandings. This is similar to the symbolic interactionist view expressed by Mead about the individual's construction of his own meaningful reality, that is, the construction of his own social objects, 'things are converted into objects through acts.'[14] Essentially the emphasis is the same, the social construction of reality by a process of self-indication. But the social construction of reality is not an automatic process for the phenomenologically and existentially orientated theorist. It is premised on some idea of the *freedom* of the self to create its own objects. It is premised on the notion of *becoming*. It is premised on the notion of the primary condition of *openness* of the personality structure. This admittedly attractive point of view is summarized by Allport:[15]

> There is a tendency among existentialist writers to seek for one basic intentional theme in human life. A fairly wide range of proposals is the result. . . . Man is inherently restless and anxious, desiring both security and freedom. He strives to counter his

condition of alienation by seeking a meaning for existence which will cover the tragic trio of suffering, guilt and death. By making commitments he finds that life can become worth living.

It is precisely this feeling that the phenomenological self is experienced as the locus of pain and suffering that makes it so believable. Certainly it can't be located by the usual canons of empirical research, yet it is evident that human beings can testify to its presence.

Probably the greatest obstacle to the understanding of the phenomenological self is that it is very difficult to see how its essence can ever be communicated to other men. When phenomenologists claim that experience is always 'present experience', they imply that it is necessary to conduct an elaborate analysis of appearances and perceptions. Raw experience, as immediately apprehended, is therefore regarded as constituting the basis of all knowledge. But how do I communicate my immediate experiences? Does conventional language allow me to convey the actual immediacy of my involvements etc.? My experiences in a concentration camp could, conceivably, be communicated to an observer, but no act of understanding could possibly reconstruct those experiences in the observer's consciousness. It might be argued that what is needed here is some form of intuition, that it is only by an act of subjective understanding that we can ever enter into the experience of another's pain. This might be true, yet one thing is certain – it is almost impossible to communicate symbolically. This forces phenomenological descriptions of the self or other inner dimensions into some form of communicative paralysis. If one's experiences can't be communicated, how can the observer be sure that these experiences ever occurred, or if they did occur, how can we be certain that they can ever be reconstituted or remembered? Bucklew puts it this way: [16]

> The inability to find a suitable utterance provokes word frenzy.
> Language unfailingly reveals its derivation from an indissoluble
> attachment to the observed world. When transcending attempts
> to reject this world it must reject language or else do violence
> to it. The various devices are familiar. Words are undefined,
> continuously redefined, or definitions as well as logic are
> rejected. . . . In the effort to obtain sublimity, the linguistic
> turmoil continually turns on itself until the outline of all that
> is non-linguistic, the only thing that can give meaning to language
> is blotted beyond effective recognition.

An indictment of the language of phenomenology is not equivalent to its rejection. The phenomenological insistence that problems of social existence are only to be understood in terms of the intentional experiences of social actors is very near the classic formulations of both Weber and contemporary symbolic interactionism. What phenomenology and existentialism do, therefore, is to re-establish, both for sociology and psychology, an awareness of the tragic condition of man. In the past this condition has been the focus of the artistic vision of man – it has only been hinted at by various thinkers in the sociological tradition. Certainly alienation, anomie etc. are tragic themes, yet they never really seem to be located in the actual lives of actual people. The phenomenological self is at the very heart of this tragic situation, particularly in our realization that it presupposes some form of tragic confrontation of the individual with the society in which he lives.

4 The grammar of symbolic sociation (1) acts, scenes and agents

It is an article of faith of the symbolic interactionist position that language is both constitutive, and a mechanism, for the maintenance and generation of social structure. The mechanical images of structuralist–functionalist sociology are regarded as foreign to the real stuff of social interaction, namely, the reciprocal negotiation of self–other relationships. This tradition is expressed in a number of different forms but their rationale is derived from the work of two theorists – Cooley and Mead. In addition, two other theorists have been instrumental in creating a climate conducive to the acceptance of symbolic interactionism as a cogently argued intellectual position – Blumer and Burke. In terms of popularity, all these theorists have taken second place to Goffman and his elevation of the dramaturgical model of social interaction into one of the most influential of American social psychologies. The common strand that ties all these diverse people together is their insistence on the flux of social life as expressed in the flux of language. They are all committed to a view of man and social relationships which is essentially a sociology of 'becoming' and 'meaning'. In this respect, Stone and Farberman's division of the study of social interaction into the following six basic processual questions is suggestive:[1]

(1) What is meaning?
(2) How does the personal life take on meaning?
(3) How does the meaning persist?
(4) How is the meaning transformed?
(5) How is the meaning lost?
(6) How is meaning regained?

These six questions presuppose that meaning is basically a problem in communication and that an analysis of meaning in terms of standard epistemological criteria is tangential to the sociological context. As Mead argues, social objects are constituted in symbolic action:[2]

> Symbolization constitutes objects not constituted before, objects which would not exist except for the context of social relationships wherein symbolization occurs. Language does not simply symbolize a situation or object which is already there in advance, it makes possible the existence or the appearance of the situation or object, for it is a part of the mechanism whereby the situation or object is created. The social process relates the responses of one individual to the gestures of another, as the meanings of the latter, and is thus responsible for the rise and existence of new objects in the social situation, objects dependent upon and *constituted by these meanings*. Meaning is thus not to be conceived fundamentally as a state of consciousness or as a set of organized relationships existing or subsisting mentally outside the field of experience into which they enter; on the contrary, it should be conceived objectively, as having its existence entirely within this field itself. The response of one organism to the gesture of another in any given social act is the meaning of that gesture and also is in a sense responsible for the appearance or coming into being of the new object – or new content of an old object – to which that gesture refers through the outcome of the given social act in which it is an early phase.

This extended quotation seems to me to sum up the hub of the symbolic interactionist position on the duality of meaning and language as a social process. More than this, it establishes the communicative process as being more crucial for social order than its conceptualization as a mechanism of social control by Parsons and others. I want to examine this argument more thoroughly. Superficially, it might be allowed that symbolization is equivalent to cultural determinism. After all, language and symbols precede any one individual. The individual plunges into a symbolic sea of meanings which have already been defined and interpreted by others. Nevertheless, this is exactly the opposite of reflexive interaction as understood by Mead. Language acquisition may be governed by some universalizing transformation rule in Chomsky's sense, however, it is also, fundamentally, a creative process in the sense that its acquisition is not predetermined in any one way for any one particular culture, although the initial definitions are limited by conventional usage. As a language user, man is able to construct meanings out of old stereotyped situations, so that old situations become transformed into an entirely new meaning structure.

Hence, for each new member of society, there is a whole range of possible gestures which he might make, provided he is guided by certain implicit rules of language appropriate to the culture in which he finds himself. Of course these rules of syntax or grammar may never really be made explicit to the language users, they assume them as part of the 'of course world' in which they are located. It follows that, even allowing for these ground rules, the range of possibilities seem to be almost infinite. They are infinite because the generation of a language and its meanings is dependent on the construction of social objects, both real and imaginary. Thus social systems are more than the actual arrangements of demographic and ecological parts which interest certain social scientists. They also contain the symbolic universes of individual members of that society, some of which are articulated with one another, and some of which are mutually incompatible. These symbolic universes are not epiphenomenal. Their existence is just as salient as the actual 'objective' world of traditional empirical science. The answer to the six questions posed by Stone and Farberman is, therefore, only feasible if one adapts a view of social behaviour which elevates communication from an instrumental to a constitutive process. Communication is more than an exercise in information; it assumes a role which is equivalent, if not identical, to other sociological categories, such as structure and culture. More simply, we can agree with Eugene Weinstein when he writes: [3]

> If the sociologist's principal abstraction, social structure, has any concrete expression, it is to be found in myriad everyday social encounters. The operation of the larger system is dependent upon the successful functioning of the microscopic and episodic action systems generated in these encounters. And these in turn, require that participants are able to effectively pursue their personal goals. In the long run, if social structure is to be stable, individuals must be successful in achieving personal purposes.

Talk and social structure

Episodic encounters can only be structured and men's purposes laid bare by the mutuality of symbolic response. In a sense, therefore, we can argue that the grammar of sociation is really symbolic discourse; talk, conversation, dramatic confrontation, the playing of games, the attribution of motives, the definition of the situation, the reifying of social constructs, are all contained in, and manifested by, the way men relate to each other by employing rhetorical and symbolic devices. We are concerned with sociation as being more than the search for the pure form that was so crucial for Simmel. Talk can be construed as being representative and prototypical of all social behaviour. Because in talk and conversation, we construct social objects, they tend to be more than exercises in sociability; rather they are the stuff of social structure. In each episode or encounter that we engage in, we find that the situation is partially structured by past definitions; it has already been defined in terms of role scripts and normative expectations. At the same time, the episode is always open; it is subject to reinterpretation and the attendant possibility of the creation of new accounts and meanings. Even though we are always prisoners of our pasts and hostages to consensual definitions of the situation, there is no need to accept this as constituting a final court of social and cultural determinism.

If we accept Mead's thesis that social objects are constituted in the symbolic indications that men make to each other, then we can readily understand that a passive view of man and social structure is not one which recommends itself to symbolic interactionism, nor for that matter, to the whole corpus of theories which are subsumed under the label of interpretative sociology. However, as I have implicitly argued throughout the course of this book, this does not involve us in the denial of social structure or a negation of history. All it does is to make social interaction more dependent on the creative capacities of the individuals who use symbols and language to understand and recreate both structure and their history. It boils down to what we have called the reciprocal negotiation of meaning, or the mutual construction of identities, as 'constitutive means' in relating to other men. From our point of view, we can think of the interaction between individuals in terms of the five-part categorization of motivation that Duncan and Burke employ to describe motives. In general, this set of terms pays attention to what has been called 'situated action'. This involves social actors in symbolic definitions of their motives and their contextual location. But it also involves both the attribution of motives to others, as well as the perception of one's role as being an important component of the action. Burke's pentad of terms describing the elements of motivation can be adapted to a description of the ongoing patterns of interaction that interest us.

Burke's pentad:[4] the act

First, we consider the *act*. Mead placed the act at the centre of his social philosophy. In his view a social act is defined in terms of the concerted conduct of two or more individuals, directed toward some social goal or object. Conceptually, of course, the act does not have any hard and fast boundaries which can be isolated in the sense of a beginning or ending since all action is an abstraction from an ongoing process. The act refers to the observed mutual behaviour of social interactors – it can be translated into a description of what actually happened. When two strangers meet for the first time, their behaviour can be described in terms of what they actually do. The kernel of this view of action is that it is oriented towards the actions of others and not towards a neutral passive environment. Dramatically, in Burke's view, *the act involves what was done in a specific context*. It involves the utilization of a terminology deriving from the stage without the restrictive connotations that these terms have in the theatre. Action, therefore, is conceived of as a plot, but without the assumption that the plot is designed by some master-playwright. This means that the actions that men engage in, and simultaneously comment on, are always described in terms of symbolic reporting. History is not present – it can only be inferred from language used by those present, or by the historian who uses language to conceptualize his inferences. Language, conceived dramatically, is action, and as such constitutes the focus and locus of social inquiry. Hence, in interaction what we observe at the pristine level is a series of actions and counter-actions which are only describable at the symbolic level. Duncan writes in this connection: [5]

> Sociologists think of the non-symbolic realm as clear, while the symbolic realm is hazy and 'subjective'. But if we use words as data – and certainly in the human studies we use them a great deal – it matters little what our attitude toward their vagueness or subjectivity may be. We must prove that what we say about an event, described in words, can be shown to exist in words themselves. For if we do not, then we are in the realm of inference, not fact. But if we stick to the observable facts in words (or other symbols), we can argue that there is a sense in which we get our view of acts as facts from our sense of symbols as facts, rather than vice versa. But when we ground our proof in symbolic facts, we must make clear what inference or interpretation has been added to the words or symbols themselves, and we must demonstrate why what we say exists in symbols can yet be explained only by non-symbolic factors.

Not only is the dramatic account of the act symbolically located, it is also premised on the assumption that action is always between selves and others. Action takes on the mantle of reflexive indications of the self to the other, also of the self to itself. Action for both Mead and Blumer is not a resultant of external stimuli, but is a consequence of some inner impulse to action – there is, in other words, a tendency to cognize human behaviour in terms of ongoing activity within the organism, rather than what is done to the organism; in this respect, the activity is considered to be 'situated'

85

symbolically. There is a great deal of overlap here between the Weberian[6] notion of the meaningful act as the pivotal concept in sociology and the symbolic interactionist notion that all action is symbolically mediated. Action for Weber was a matter of the meaningful orientation of actors to the action orientations of others. Meaningful orientations towards others are possible only if they can be interpreted in symbolic terms, and if it is clearly understood that meaning is always dependent on the situated activity in which the interactors define their behaviour. Both in interpretative sociology and symbolic interactionism the notion of structure, system, group etc. are only relevant within the context of meaningful action. Systems do not behave or act or take decisions or have consciousness except through the minds of men who give them significance.

We can, like Goffman,[7] describe action as being an essay in self- and impression-management and, in so doing, place action in a context which is taken for granted. The system is there for the purposes of men so that they can realize these purposes. Other men, in different contexts, have constructed the system – dramatically, we can realize ourselves by playing our roles with the maximum masking effect; action becomes a process whereby one's audience is considered to be all powerful and the repository of self-esteem. Meaningful exchanges are, therefore, conducted in the belief that one's performance is subject to critical evaluation. In short, Goffman's dramatic image presupposes that action is oriented toward the other, so that the other is forced to accept the projected identity at its face- and performed-level. Goffman's image of inter-action is presented in a manner which assumes that interaction is 'stabilized' by some form of framework which is accepted by all the parties to the interaction. Dramatic realization consists of making the most out of the possibilities in the given situation, while realizing that underpinning the performance is the intricate net of implicit and tacit rules and assumptions about the limits of interpretation in the role or the encounter. Ultimately, Goffman, while mapping out the intricacies of 'face work' etc., is committed to a view of action which places the actor very much at the mercy of the script. He cannot get beyond the script because, by definition, the script is the total world – the stage on which his performance is validated.

Phenomenological precariousness

However, there is the distinct possibility that the veils of common sense and the ubiquity of the role and script, are not at all those believed by the so-called ordinary social actor, but are only the constructions of official definers. In other words, the constitutive rules of human interaction are hidden from obvious interpretation. The hidden constructs and models that social scientists attribute to men in society are possibly only motives that the social scientist employs to order his own perceptions, they do not necessarily exist for men in the so-called trivial and mundane world of everyday encounters and episodes. Hence, the assumption of motives which are hidden from the investigator is only plausible when we can demonstrate that they are not mere inventions to legitimate a research methodology or conceptual scheme. Thus, in addition to the notion of action as the imputation of dramatic motives to other actors, there is a sociological phenomenological reduction which involves the sociologist in the literal abandonment of his concepts and a voyage of discovery into the 'common-sense' world. Sociologists are encouraged to undertake this voyage by methodologists like Garfinkel,[8] in order to lose their false consciousness of their roles as official definers of the social world. Only will they be capable of teasing out the constitutive rules of interaction. Dramatic action is therefore not to be construed only as being true to the official script of official stage-managers, but is also to be considered as being trivialized at the level of everyday performance. By this I do not mean to say that action is only understood if it is studied from the point of view of the participants, that is, from the perspective of the actor; this, after all, is an axiom of inter-pretative sociology – what I am saying is that the phenomenological reduction points to the precariousness of the act as a datum of sociological inquiry, this precariousness being partially dependent on the sociological construction of motives, which may, or may not, be a constitutive element of the actor's real definition of the situation. Dramatically action is not scripted by hidden manipula-tors but is constructed by the actors themselves.

The scene

This leads me to the second term in Burke's pentad, that is, the scene.[9] Dramatically scenes are staged so that action can take place within a particular spatial and temporal framework. The dramatist selects his scene with the object of highlighting and illustrating certain elements of the action. The staging of an act in a scene implies a certain type of unity between action and context. Unless deliberately so designed, Hamlet is a renaissance prince in renais-sance context. The deliberate alteration of background and its translation into modern dress involves an imaginative leap in the minds of the audience. If the staging and the acting are convincing, then there is no great difficulty in making this jump. But if, for

eason or other, the play seems to be artificially contrived in
o illustrate some aesthetic criterion which is in the mind of
ctor and nobody else, then the play is likely to be a disaster.

In social interaction, all activity is situated activity – action
does not take place in a void. But action does not take place in a
designed scenario especially constructed for the actor's purposes.
To take an extreme example, the action that goes on in a concentration camp is certainly appropriate to certain social and cultural
contexts, however, it is not designed to release appropriate well-
constructed performances on the part of the inmates. Concentration camps are not constructed in order to legitimate the performances of martyrs. The camp is there for the purposes of putting into
effect the policies of racial genocide and not for the benefit of its
victims. Granted that if we accept the gas oven as the symbol of
a social drama in which victims are offered up for the benefit of
the body politic, then it might be appropriate to conceive of the
scenario as a prop to a social performance. Human conduct is
ritualized up to a point, but ritualization must not be pushed too
far. Men are often victims of their own symbols and their sub-
sequent reification. Nevertheless, this does not entitle us to accept
as given the notion that symbolic conduct is always 'staged' and
supported by an elaborate superstructure of deliberately constructed cultural props. When we speak of situated action, we imply
that men take the situation into account before acting, or that they
translate the situation into an aspect of the action. Situations, in
this respect, tend to be immediate, they are defined as being con-
textually present in the 'here and now'. All sorts of factors can
enter into the situation; the physical environment, the weather, but
most importantly, as far as humans are concerned, the situation is
specified by other people. The 'other' might be internalized as a
perpetual 'presence' in the form of a reference figure or, more
probably, as being the partner with whom one is engaged in the
immediate situation.

In addition, the situation can be conceived in 'field' terms, as in
the case of the group-dynamic approach of Kurt Lewin[10] and his
associates. Here there is the same emphasis on the dynamic role
of the situation as entering into the actor's definition. *Both in
field theory and in interpretative sociology, a fundamental distinction must be made between the situation as perceived and defined
by the actor, and the situation as it would seem to appear to an
observer, or if we can conceive of such a thing, the objective situation in the 'real world'.* Human actors are never neutral in a
situation, they are always interpreting and defining situations. Yet,
we must not make the mistake of asserting that situations cannot
influence conduct without being interpreted and defined. The per-

ception of a situation is not a necessary condition for its ability to influence behaviour, although in human behaviour we are usually more interested in the situation as defined. This distinction between perceived situations on the one hand, and undefined situations on the other, is similar to H. A. Murray's[11] discussion of the relationship between 'alpha and beta' press concepts. 'Press' is the term Murray uses for pressures on man's conduct. Alpha press is the set of factors in the environment which the so-called trained observer can infer as being partly determinative in shaping human behaviour. Thus, the demographer is in the position to make statements about an individual's behaviour in relation to population trends that he would not make himself, or would not even be able to comment upon. Beta press is reminiscent of the sociological 'definition of the situation'. So, to extend our example, while the demographer describes the individual in terms of his location in a large family with a large reproductive capacity, the individual's interpretation of his location will be entirely unique and subjective, thereby constituting his definition of the situation.

Reverting to our dramatic metaphor, we can see that the scene is not constructed in such a way that it can only be analysed from one point of view alone. Similarly, both the actor's and audience's view of the scene will never coincide because they will each define what they take to be the scenario in different ways. Also we must not forget that there is a scene which exists independently of our perception of its manifestations in the consciousness of men. Its influence may be 'unconscious' or subliminal or merely recorded in our neurological structures, but its presence is ubiquitous and cannot be denied. But, as Burke has argued in his persuasive manner, *scenes* have a way of entering into the action in such a fashion that they are capable of being treated in a dramatic way: [12]

> the concept of scene can be widened or narrowed (conceived of in terms of varying 'scope' or circumference). Thus an agent's behaviour (act) might be thought of as taking place against a polytheistic background; or the over-all scene may be thought of as grounded in one god; or the circumference of the situation can be narrowed to naturalistic limits, as in Darwinism; or it can be localized in such terms as Western civilization, Elizabethanism, capitalism, D day, 10 Downing Street, on this train ride, and so on endlessly.

Scenes as implicit understandings?

Obviously interaction between men in Downing Street will be qualitatively different from interaction in space capsules. The interaction between men in a Nazi concentration camp will not be the same as their interaction over a cup of tea in a Soho coffee or tea bar. The scene will enter into the action as a critical component of the interaction, not necessarily determining the interaction, merely canalizing it into certain directions rather than other directions. In addition, there is the possibility that the scene is deliberately staged by other interested parties in whose interests it is to obtain the maximum benefits from the situation. For example, the staging of a show trial of political prisoners in South Africa can be seen as an attempt to dramatize the activities of the 'communist conspiracy' so that the prisoners are not merely subject to legal processes, but are treated as the arch-villains of an international conspiracy. They are imbued with dramatic qualities against the backdrop of vast evil forces. The trial is the stage which makes manifest this hidden conspiracy.

At the level of everyday interaction, situations and scenes are usually aspects of role-encounters between individual actors. They constitute the props and supports for normal social discourse. The casual encounter between bus conductor and passenger is supported by symbols of role-status which provide both parties to the interaction with yardsticks as to the proper future conduct of the interaction. It is unlikely that interaction would proceed unless these guidelines, props etc. are present. In other words, there is a symbolic infrastructure which translates roles into conduct. The bus conductor does not ply his trade in a greengrocer's shop, only on buses. Nor does he usually wear clothes which are inappropriate, such as a soldier's uniform. Situations, in this sense, are symbolically structured; they are structured in such a way as to ensure the maximum clarity of role-performance. Role-performance is, therefore, dependent on the proper allocation of symbols to context and situation, or as Burke puts it, on the 'act–scene ratio'. The act–scene ratio tends to be structured for interactions between bus conductor and passenger – it is not structured for interactions between strangers, or between actors from different cultural systems. In these cases the situation has to be mutually defined and negotiated so that some satisfactory *modus vivendi* can emerge which will enable the interaction to continue smoothly. If such a solution is not forthcoming, the interaction might break down, or end in embarrassed silence or hostility.

Hence, what constitutes the scene in apparently unstructured situations is an interesting problem. For instance, if two strangers meet for the first time with mutually different definitions of the situation, then it is not at all clear that they are really both in the same situation or context. If one party defines the meeting place as a place of worship, and the other party defines it as a venue for the conduct of revolutionary action, there will be a basic difficulty in coming to some kind of mutual understanding about the nature of the ongoing interaction. There will also be difficulties relating to the attribution of motives and to the understanding of the symbols expressed by both parties. If not only the situations but the motives and symbols are not mutually understood, then it is difficult to envisage the two strangers emerging from their encounter with feelings of mutual respect and liking.

Sociologists tend to define situations in terms of implicit understandings which have been built up over a long period of time, thus providing new members of a society with a ready-made set of definitions which they internalize. The assumption is made that situations in any society tend to be typical, also that conduct in those situations will be typical. Certainly, from the point of view of certain kinds of structural analysis, there is an advantage in postulating structured conduct as shaped by closed role-scripts, yet in the actual context of everyday interaction, the situation as pre-defined by others is, in fact, problematic. We do tend to define the world in terms of the sex, class, locality, group, friendship groups to which we belong, or in terms of the identifications that we make with reference groups, but to claim these definitions are purely mirror-images and reflected appraisals of others seems to be a gross over-simplification.

Each new situation or context that the individual encounters is obviously like some situations in some respects; it is also different in other respects. Symbolization or interpretation of the situation in terms of past cultural prescriptions does not proceed automatically. If it did, then we could not account for novelty in human affairs. Each new situation is a compound of old and new understandings – it is never a carbon copy of the past. More important, what is defined as scene or context is not only the physical container within which action takes place, it is the symbolic locus through which men construct their meanings. Hence, meaning in this respect is not necessarily tied to things or objects, it is tied to the imaginary worlds that men have constructed for themselves. Two critics, for example, discussing the horrific world of Hieronymus Bosch could conceivably talk about the texture of his brush-work or his use of perspective; more importantly, they would also be interested in the quality of his imagination. It is this imaginary construction of symbolic meanings that is equally important in the sociological understanding of situations both as objectively constituted, and as symbolically defined.

We have been talking of acts and situations as if they were self-contained and divorced from the agent and purpose. This leads to the third aspect of Burke's pentad, the agent.

The agent

The agent or actor can be conceived of as being responsible for his actions, or as being directed by others. Obviously the agent is not some splendidly isolated monad in the sense that Leibniz gives to the term. In dramatic terms, actors interpret roles, they act out parts, they bring to their roles their unique personality characteristics, while at the same time keeping to the main outline of the role. The role of Oedipus is minutely structured in Greek classical drama but even here the tragic element is not dependent on absolute subservience to the script. The script in the hands of a second-rate actor is meaningless and lifeless. It takes a real full-blooded performance to tease out the tragic implications of the Oedipal situation. In interaction on the everyday level, we are not usually aware of the tragic implications of our behaviour, except when we are confronted with loss or pain. As actors, we try to present reasonable interpretations of our scripts, although most of us do not slavishly conform to the stage instructions of our parents, teachers and peers. As agents, we are aware of the fact that there conceivably could be alternatives to our interpretations, that consequently, the symbolic universes which we have constructed and invented are capable of further revision and reinterpretation. However, because most of us have been brought up in a society in which we have been exposed to the imperative demands of other men as witnessed in the subservient roles we play as children in our relations with our parents, as witnessed by our assumption of inferiority in the occupational stakes, by our passive acceptance of political authority, and by our belief in the operation of vast impersonal economic and social forces over which we have no control, because of all these apparently overwhelming determinants, we have come to believe that the agent is not really in command of his own interpretation or freedom of action. We have accepted, at least at the level of unstated assumption, the belief in the *tabula rasa* of traditional 'Lockean' philosophy.

Now, dramatically, the actor is always a creation in the mind of a particular dramatist. He has no existence outside the role that has been created for him by some writer in the privacy of his mind; Sir Laurence Olivier or Marlon Brando exist primarily because Shakespeare or Eugene O'Neill breathe life into the characters they imaginatively construct. Without the dramatist, there would be no actor as interpreter. At a more mundane level, the agent or social actor does not depend on the establishment of a character for him by others. Granted that socialization theory argues persuasively for the internalization of society into man, this notion of the socialization process seems to place men in the role of passive spectators to their own identity construction. Indeed, the whole role-taking process has been taken to imply the isomorphic relation of the self to the indications of others, very much in the tradition of Cooley's 'Looking-Glass Self'. We owe it to Goffman, more than anybody else, to place this assumption in its proper place. 'Role distance' implies the ability to stand aside from the identity that one has been ascribed by the defining others. As agents, therefore, we are not completely neutral in the situation in which we find ourselves, we can stand back and comment on the actual constitutive elements of that process.

We agree with Burke when he writes that there is a ratio between acts–scenes and agencies.[13]

> Insofar as men's actions are to be interpreted in terms of the circumstances in which they are acting, their behaviour will fall under the heading of a scene–act ratio. But insofar as their acts reveal their different characters, their behaviour would fall under the heading of an agent–act ratio. For instance in a time of great crisis, such as a shipwreck, the conduct of all persons involved in that crisis could be expected to manifest in some way the motivating influence of the crisis. Yet, within such a scene–act ratio there would be a range of agent–act ratios, insofar as one man was proved to be cowardly, another bold, another resourceful and so on.

The situations that men find themselves in will not be capable of being translated into the language of conventional determinism when it is realized that the actor has a whole range of possible responses that he can make in a situation. Thus, in the shipwreck, although we would expect panic and confusion from a great many of the participants, we cannot really predict this for all those concerned, simply because we have no generally accepted body of knowledge which would enable us to make such a prediction; all we have is what Weber calls 'behaviour maxims', namely, a situated vocabulary of motives which we apply to behaviour. Dramatically, we invest the shipwreck with typical instances of conduct which we believe describe the typical motives of the participants.

The critical characteristics of these accounts of behaviour are captured in the way in which they are symbolized. They are transformed into the language of typical motivation, that is, into the language of purposes, accounts, direction etc. Situated action, of necessity, implies motivation. Men act in situations because they are busily assessing, evaluating, interpreting, defining, revising and, most basically, symbolizing the situation to themselves. Agency therefore implies purpose or motive in a situation.

5 The grammar of symbolic sociation (2) purposes and agencies

Purposes

Burke sees the situation, act, as intimately connected with the purposes of man. Although they can be separated analytically, obviously they form part of a unitary account of social interaction. This is true of both sociological and social psychological descriptions of behaviour. However, from our point of view, it is symbolic accounts that are the basic elements of any description of motives. Our behaviour is always described by somebody who uses typical symbols to attribute typical motives. These symbols are not chosen randomly; they constitute a socially defined and legitimated set of accounts and reasons for action. We can do no better than quote Wright Mills. His discussion has been seminal in the current interest in the subject:[1]

> the verbalized motive is not used as an index of something in the individual but as a basis of inference for a typical vocabulary of motives of a situated action. When we ask for the 'real attitude' rather than the 'opinion', for the 'real motive' rather than the 'rationalization', all we can meaningfully be asking for is the controlling speech form which was incipiently or overtly presented in the performed act or series of acts. There is no way to plumb behind verbalization into an individual and directly check our motive mongering, but there is an empirical way in which we can guide and limit, in given historical situations, investigations of motives. That is by the construction of typal vocabularies of motives that are extant in types of situations and actions. Imputation of motives may be controlled by reference to the typical constellation of motives which are observed to be societally linked with classes of situated action. Some of the 'real' motives that have been imputed to actors were not even known

to them. As I see it, motives are circumscribed by the vocabulary of the actor. *The only source for a terminology of motives is the vocabulary of motives actually and usually verbalized by actors in specific situations.*

The vocabulary of the actor is not something he uses in order to merely describe the 'real' world outside himself, nor for that matter, is it merely an appendage to bear witness to his subjectivity. Language is both the inner and outer world.

Granted that phenomenologically we are aware of being aware, we can only conceive of this awareness if we translate it into language or symbolic category. Therefore, awareness is only possible in linguistic terms. I am aware of the possibility of slipping into symbolic reductionism; obviously this regress is possible only if we place language in some form of free-floating void. The language capacities of men are biologically rooted. They do not come to him from a cultural heaven. Having accepted Wright Mills's notion of situated motive, this does not entitle us to adapt a purely situational determinism – nothing could be further from the truth. At the same time, we must be careful not to say that behaviour and language are synonymous. If we do, we are in danger of regressing into behaviourism in which signs and symbols are merely points of reference tied to stimuli and their observable responses.

In interaction episodes, in imputation of motives, we are guided by behaviour maxims which are believed to be situationally appropriate. Those episodes which invoke inappropriate motives and which are counter to the established legal and moral procedures of a given society, are labelled as being immoral, deviant, abnormal or pathological etc. The social worker who comes face to face with a client who has committed some form of misdemeanour is likely to bring into play a complicated language which purports to pinpoint the apparent reason for the behaviour. Usually this language is couched in terms of imputed antecedent conditions, such as social class, broken homes, alcoholism, neurosis, lack of moral fibre or, at a more sophisticated level, terms like alienation and anomie are bandied around. These definitions breathe life and substance into the observed or imputed behaviour. 'This man is a neurotic' implies that he should be treated in a certain sort of way. It also implies that we attribute to him a number of internal 'pushes' which are supposed to explain his behaviour. Hence, if we meet somebody for the first time (our archetypical stranger), and if he behaves in a manner which seems to us to be completely lacking in the socially acceptable standards which we believe to constitute normal behaviour, then it is more than likely that we will come up with some form of behaviour maxim to cover his 'strangeness', or we will attribute some substantive motive to him such as an anxiety neurosis etc.

This imputation of motives enables us to handle the situation, even if it might be completely off beam. (The other's motives in the situation may be to create the maximum confusion or embarrassment to ego because he believes him to be an example of a social category which he disapproves of, such as a bloated capitalist.) Nevertheless, underpinning this interaction and its resultant breakdown, there is a symbolic process of self-indication going on which tries to make sense of a basically unstructured situation. The imputation of neurosis is basically a strategy which allows the interactor to make sense of chaos.

Motives as symbolic accounts

It is generally argued that even in the most unstructured situations it is the shared meanings which ultimately eliminate the uncertainty that arises from the mutual attribution of motives. Symbols, in this sense, are supposed to embody rules and common understandings and definitions of the situation. But this view seems to imply that these meanings are somehow embedded in the social system as a body of ready-made prescriptions for behaviour. A typical motive, in this view, would be one to which men have decided to attach significance, as being an important part of the social world in which they live. Thus, neurotic motives are attributed to men because neurosis has become a fashionable way of describing conduct, particularly when it is legitimated by the use of concepts deriving from psychiatry or clinical psychology. Similarly, men are supposed to be pushed by power drives or by the need to maximize self-esteem. These last two motives are given an aura of respectability by their appropriation by social scientists as elements in their typical vocabularies. Also, great indexes have been compiled to measure and pinpoint motives such as the need for achievement,[2] not only in Western societies, but as a measure of economic and political growth in so-called under-developed societies. We can, in effect, accept some of these vocabularies as constituting a fair approximation of what men consider important in their symbolization of behaviour, yet we do not have to accept them as being necessarily part and parcel of the system of meanings that men as *subjects* bring into an interaction episode.

In interaction, the imputation of motives is far more problematic than specified by the master vocabularies of the society or social groups. What we understand as the constitutive rules are not, on inspection, necessarily those which the official definitions have indicated as paramount. Men attribute motives to each other from the perspective of their internalized reference groups, but this attribution of motives is not the only imputation that goes on. To a certain extent, motives are constructed in the interaction process itself, they are part of the process of the negotiation of identity that is central to self–other relationships. *In this negotiation, new meanings are established and new meanings are really new motives.* There is therefore, in every interaction, a distinct possibility, that what is labelled a typical motive by the outside observer, is in fact *not* really a constitutive component of the interaction.

Take, for example, the interaction between two adolescents who are believed by the observing adult to be engaged in an argument about the advantages of conforming to the moral definitions of adult society. What the outsider construes and abstracts from this encounter is a belief that the participants are rehearsing, in some anticipatory way, their coming initiation into the adult world of moral meanings. But this is probably far from the case, their dialogue could be construed in a completely different manner by the participants themselves, especially when they are negotiating for an opportunity of smoking marijuana. Their dialogue could be deliberately misleading, so that it establishes for the adult outsider a 'generally accepted' situated activity and its attendant motives. Adolescents are attributed with high spirits and moral enthusiasm in our culture – it is highly inconceivable (or so it was argued until very recently) that they should be deliberately constructing alternative meaning and moral systems. Our outside observer, then, has attributed an official definition of the situation to the actors which may not be in accordance with the actual definitions of the actors themselves.

There is another possibility, and that is that neither the observer nor the actors are really aware of their motives, or if asked, could really verbalize or conceptualize them. If we accept Garfinkel's[3] view that the moral order is often equated with the so-called normal, taken-for-granted aspects of human interaction, then any activity which men undertake in concert could be construed as being normal and given. Our two adolescents who set out to deceive their adult observer, might do so on the unstated premise that this is the 'way the world works', that consequently there is no need to justify this attitude to anybody. Probably they would not even verbalize such a premise, simply because the 'world taken for granted' is so much a part of the normal way that the world is constructed and given meaning.

At another level, we can talk about the mutual impermeability of symbolic universes when these universes are defined by different perceptions and understandings. For example, in the confrontation between classical and contemporary pop music, we are faced with a common situation in which both sets of music lovers cannot hear the other's music without immediately conjuring up some form of motive to account for the apparent obsession that the other has. The world that each group takes for granted does not allow for the possibility that the other could conceivably be listening to music. A whole set of motives and explanations are invented in order to account for the other's tastes. The classics lover starts talking about exploitation, profit maximization, the 'new barbarianism' or, more simply, he talks about tone deafness (of course he might have a point here, particularly when one takes amplification into account) – the pop fan construes the older generation in terms of conformity to the establishment, as being square, etc. etc. These, of course, are imputed labels – they are imputed from the point of view of closed symbolic universes – where the normal world is defined in such a way so that it is almost impossible to make explicit the unstated assumptions that each group is operating on.

Identities and motives

When we talk of closed symbolic universes, we must be careful we do not construct an alternative form of social encapsulation. Certainly, our meanings are imputed within a framework which seems self-evident to us as participants – it is often almost impossible to break away from the trivialities and the assumptions of normal social intercourse. Nevertheless within these constraints, we can agree with Herbert Blumer[4] on the fundamentally creative aspect of the reflexive mode in social interaction. There is no need to assume that each social encounter entails a voyage of discovery into the unknown. Obviously this would be absurd. The meaning that we potentially can discover in new encounters is fundamentally the way in which we are able to project identity.

The problem of motives is really the problem of identity – both are taken for granted without necessarily actually positing the operation of some substantive energizing force:[5]

> In most situations our identity is so completely habitual and taken for granted that we virtually ignore its presence or relevance in our reactions, concentrating only upon the stimulating environment. Researchwise, it is strategic to focus observations upon those situations where identity itself is acutely problematic in order to observe its determining effect upon

behaviour. . . . When doubt of identity creeps in, action is paralysed. Only full commitment to one's identity permits a full picture of motivation. Faith in one's conception of one's self is the key which unlocks the physiological resources of the human organism, releases the energy (or capacity as Dewey would say) to perform the indicated act. Doubt of identity, or confusion, where it does not cause complete disorientation, certainly drains action of its meaning, and thus limits mobilization of the organic correlates of emotion, drive and energy which constitutes the introspectively sensed push of motivated action. We are reminded of James Michener's heroes in the South Pacific who were plagued by the question, What am I doing here? Also of William James' contention that only he who has played seriously with the idea of suicide has plumbed the phenomenon of self.

Because identity is often taken for granted, just as the common-sense world is taken for granted, there is a tendency to assume that all men are engaged in a constant dialogue between situated motives and the enveloping social climate in which they find themselves. We look at our classics lover and impute to him motives which are believed to derive from his social class or his university background. He loves Bach's music because, so it is argued, he has an image of himself as a certain type of person who has to refer his conduct to certain confirming others. Thus, his love of music is given a motivational flavour which may be divorced from his actual situation – from his actual reality as a choosing, feeling human being. Granted the situational aspects of motives are critical, yet there is a danger that we take away from men the possibility of their own aesthetic proclivities by claiming that all such behaviour is located in encapsulated symbolic worlds.

There is, of course, the possibility that motives will be described in the traditional psychological mode as being merely the result of inner pushes, or as being dependent on positive or negative reinforcement. Sociologists have reacted against this form of theorizing by building their own special vocabulary of motives, which they believe is more relevant to man as a social animal. Unfortunately, this vocabulary is generally oriented towards the maximization of self-esteem or the urgency of the achievement motive. All motives, in this view, are learned or secondary; they are acquired in particular learning contexts having no necessary connection with their presumed physiological base. Thus, the achievement motive is discovered by a close examination of cultural and social patterns. Some societies will be more achievement prone than others and vice versa. Even this supposedly social motive derives from the assumption that men will behave in a typical way because there

99

is a carrot and stick mechanism at work in the background. The need to achieve is implicitly conceived of as being necessary for the individual's reward–cost contingency schedule.

All such motivational schemes in sociology are premised on the empty container thesis – it is argued that men pick up typical motives and internalize them in such a way that they become part and parcel of their energy system. Indeed the whole weight of Parsons's[6] 'value located' theory and its emphasis on the internalization of norms is premised on this assumption. The Meadian view of motives and its elaboration at the hands of Herbert Blumer does not simply contend that motives are poured into men. Admittedly, there is the implication that the role-taking process, as construed by sociologists like Brim,[7] seems to attribute to role-prescriptions, the status of motivational agency. In my view this is a misreading of Mead. Again we come back to the question of reflexivity and its implication of self-indication. Men make indications to themselves in the same way that they communicate with others. This does not imply that their motives are established for all time by the learning of master patterns of behaviour which they automatically internalize.

We all learn motives, we develop images and translate them into plans so that we can prepare to meet the world in certain set ways, but this does not imply the insertion of a complete programme of future activity which is only waiting for the appropriate social stimulus in order for it to become fully operational. Plans and mental sets or cognitive structures are not the determinants of human activity but only enter into that activity as a filtering mechanism. We can agree with George Kelly[8] when he writes that all psychological activity is subject to alternative interpretations both by social scientist and subject.

The question of social motives, accounts, intentions, or purposes, is intimately tied up with the whole problem of mental sets and internal schemata. Ever since Bartlett's[9] seminal work on memory, and his suggestion that men and other organisms are capable of reflexively observing their own schemata, there has been a great deal of interest in the way men symbolize these schemata to themselves. In many cases, this interest has been focused on the unconscious aspects of motivation. Consequently our knowledge of them has been inferred by the decoding of symbolic constructions such as dreams, works of art and religious mythology etc. Freud[10] believed that they could be arrived at by the minutest analysis of the latent content of dreams. Lévi-Strauss[11] is convinced that their presence is best detected by the closest attention to structural analysis. Whether conscious or unconscious, schemata are not static entities dependent on mechanical stimulation – they are always dynamic; they can best be regarded as an orientation or set which enables the actor to reach an active interpretation of the meaning of the incoming stimulus. A schema is in one sense an expectation of what to focus on in the stimulus field. Sociologically, a schema is equivalent but not identical to the individual's definition of the situation. The definition of the situation implies a situated activity, which as Weinstein has suggested, is a 'Kind of shorthand summary of all the internal processes mediating between the impinging of situational stimuli and the selection and evocation of responsive lines of action.'[12] It is the 'individual's best guess as to the nature of the reality with which he is currently engaged.'[13] This guess as to the nature of the reality is dependent on a number of factors including the saliency of the role-identities he brings into play in the situation. The definition of the situation is then not merely a passive recording process which registers events as they occur, but is intimately tied up with the state of the organism (however this state is construed). And the state of the organism is not a biological readiness but is a compound of symbolic and effective sets which together combine to give man his intentions, motives, attitudes, etc.

The whole question of the motivational elements in interpersonal behaviour is also nicely summarized by Weinstein.[14]

> The effects of ego's acts on Alter's definition of the situation are not necessarily those ego predicts. Alter's definition of the situation is not only a function of the cues available to him but also the nature of Alter's mediating processes. A variety of concepts have been used to denote the organization of such processes including apperceptive mass, frame of reference, adaptation level, plans etc. All involve the interpretation of current and past experience, namely the process of *investing stimuli with meaning*. The internalized network of categories that serve the central mediating function shall be referred to as the actor's system of meanings. Here meaning is used in its broadest sense to include not only physical perceptual aspects but also connotative ones such as values and affective tone. Thus ego must take into account both the content of his own lines of action, and Alter's system of meanings.

In this connection it is interesting to note that a number of computer and simulation techniques have been responsible for the broadening of the meaning of schemata to include both cognitive maps (images in Kenneth Boulding's sense[15]) and *plans*. Plans involve the translation of the image into projected future actions. Miller, Galanter and Pribram,[16] for example, conceive of plans as being analogous to computer programmes in which the individual is hierarchically organized to behave in certain ways in certain situations. Translated into sociological language, we can say that plans imply what Blumer calls self-indication: 'We must recognize that the activity of human-beings consists of meeting a flow of situations in which they have to act and that their action is built on the basis of what they note, how they assess and interpret what they note.'[17] The interpretation of the situation is always dynamic in that images and plans are not determinants of behaviour, but are reflexively related to the interpretations of others. The flow of situations that individuals meet are always cognized in terms of a basic assumption that individuals are basically active seekers of experience. What interests the sociologist in this respect is the direction of behaviour, rather than the tendencies which are supposed to casually push individuals into action. It is in this sense that we can understand social motivation as the search for structured meaning – meaning being conterminous with symbolization. The direction of human motives is, therefore, a function of the way in which language is used both as a mechanism and as a constitutive process. This leads me to the notion of language as agency, the last element in the Burkean pentad.

Agency

In considering a social theory of motives, one is obviously trying to understand the way in which men mutually construct social worlds in their everyday encounters. We have implied that although the governing rules of interaction are logically prior to the encounter, each new encounter has within it the possibility of further growth and emergence. Language is therefore both a means and an end in regulating the way in which men regard and act towards each other. In their interactions they use language to impress, coerce, deceive, arbitrate, and construct new meanings. It is both the means of co-operation and the mechanism of conflict. Even though it is debatable, we assume that structures only exist in communication and particularly symbolic communication:[18]

> By communication is here meant the mechanism through which human relations exist and develop – all the symbols of the mind, together with the means of conveying them through space and preserving them in time.
>
> There is no sharp line between the means of communication and the rest of the external world. In a sense all objects and actions are symbols of the mind.

As we have already argued, interaction in symbolic terms is more than a means or instrumentality – it provides the very stuff of sociation. We can follow this argument up with an appreciation of the position that Burke, Duncan, Mead and others have taken in respect to language and rhetoric as an object of sociological study, and as providing the ground for a perspective on the inter-active process.

The analysis of rhetoric has traditionally been the happy hunting grounds of linguistics and logicians, but it is equally important to social analysis.

1. *Rhetoric in interpersonal situations*

We can consider the face-to-face situation as the interpersonal contact between an individual and his audience. Here a whole host of elements enters into the situation, particularly those relating to such factors as hostility–attraction (approach–avoidance and the general implicit rules governing the interaction, whether these rules are constitutive or merely legitimating is irrelevant). Even the immediacy of emotive and phenomenological aspects of a face-to-face encounter always breaks up into some form of rhetorical address and counter-address. Rhetoric is employed to influence and to create positions of power and equality in the relationship. The rhetoric between two lovers is, presumably, based on the assumption that it will finally lead to the act of love – in this sense it is highly individualized as well as stylized. The current hippy emphasis on the casualness of the love encounter is not merely a purely free expression of an unfettered free human sexual relationship, but is in reality a 'typical rhetoric' which is informed by a number of hidden conventions. True, there seems to be an infinite number of permutations available in the love act, but they are always focused and located in typical rhetorical devices. Even the apparently natural grunts of the contemporary ethos is a form of rhetorical device which is used both as an expression of individuality, and as a way of conforming to the hippy *Weltanschauung*.

Similarly, the expression of power between two individuals is not mediated in terms of a simple trial of brute force – it tends to be rhetorical even when pain is being experienced. Power in these terms is a subtle interplay between a number of internalized images that both interactors have of each other, especially when these images are not easily verbalized. Their verbalization involves an explicit acknowledgment on the part of both parties that they are in a certain relationship to each other. Verbalization involves a commitment to action, to a view of the other, to an established relationship. At the same time, verbalization also involves the

103

symbolization of motives, so that each party is aware of how the other is defining the situation.

We have already seen that Burke's description and analysis of motives involves a term to specify the situation – the scene; a term to specify the behaviour – the act; a term to specify the actor – the agent; a term to specify the motive – the purpose; and finally a term to specify the means – the agency. In the face-to-face situation, we are aware that we can use alternative interpretations of inter-personal behaviour such as exchange or game theory, but the emphasis on rhetoric is relevant since it places the most typical aspect of human behaviour, namely language, at the centre of social analysis. Rhetoric is always aimed at creating and defining both the past, present and future of the interactors.

In confronting the other, there is the sense of the 'immediate' as setting the limits of the interaction. Interpersonal conduct also involves the intersection of individual biographies which bring to the phenomenological present a form of history which is symbolic-ally translated into the interaction – and also, most importantly, the future enters into the interaction as a datum of the present. Thus rhetoric in interaction is more than just speech for the purposes of communication, it *is* the interaction.

There are a number of factors which enter into the rhetorical situation. Following W. E. Brockriede[19] we can specify them in the following way:

(a) *Numbers* Rhetorically, there is a difference between dyadic interactions and interactions involving more than two people, the rhetorical gambits being qualitatively different. This has been spelt out by Simmel in his analysis of dyadic and triadic relation-ships.

(b) *Multiplicity of groups and individuals as audiences* In any rhetorical situation, there is the possibility that the speaker is addressing more than one audience with different viewpoints and perspectives. In the House of Commons, every speaker has as an audience, both the members of his party, and also, those of the opposition. In a simple interpersonal encounter, we address our-selves not only to the other who is immediately present but also to his reference groups as well as to our own. Rhetoric is governed by the 'breadth of perspective' which we bring to the situation. At a more formal level, rhetoric will be aimed at a specific audience in a particular spatio-temporal context.

(c) *Organization* Rhetorical interaction will be limited by the degree of structure and organization in the situation. Thus, the casual encounter of two acquaintances might be highly organized in that they are both bound by a highly rigid code of etiquette which demands an almost classical adherence to a script, very much in the mode of the Japanese 'honourable sir' tradition. On the other hand, the formal requirements of a large-scale organization, with its chain of command, will generate informal structures in which the modes of address between people are open and highly capable of new meaning and growth. In both cases rhetoric sustains and creates social order. In the case of the casual encounter, it acts as a confirmation of the larger social order and places one in a context; in the formal organization, it acts as the means of creating new social relationships.

(d) *Homogeneity* Rhetoric involves an assumption that those one addresses are, to a certain extent, similar to oneself – whether one *perceives* the other as being like oneself is an important aspect of the interaction. The perception that the other is completely unlike familiar others is likely to lead to forms of interaction which are atypical and to the employment of rhetorical devices which are not in the typical experiences of either party. The anthropologist who approaches the tribal witch-doctor for the first time is not likely to have at his finger tips all the necessary modes of address which are appropriate – it will involve him in a prolonged negotiation to establish common criteria of meaning. On the other hand, amongst familiars, the rhetorical devices employed are, in general, mutually understood and acted upon. Common definitions imply a minimum degree of consensus about the meaning of situations.

(e) *Role awareness* Here we are concerned with the actual awareness, both of identity and role, in any rhetorical situation. Obviously one does not address a policeman as one's long-lost brother. In most simple encounters, the *external symbols, the appearance*, are clues as to the identity of the other. There is, in other words, a non-discursive language which enables most people to recognize who the other is, or who he claims to be. Beyond this, where symbols are ambiguous and appearances misleading, it is only rhetoric which can establish identity, even where the identity is not previously available.

(f) *Situational range* Most rhetorical situations are not uni-dimensional – they involve a whole range of relationships which criss-cross and intersect. People in situations may be treated in any number of ways – as objects, as intending and deceptive manipulators, etc. Or they can be treated as being representative of larger groups or whatever. Every situation is bounded and related to other situations, albeit it is useful to treat each as a unit with a self-contained structure of meaning.

Given these factors, we can conceive of rhetoric in inter-personal relationships as being reality-binding. If two people meet for the first time and after they establish their social and personal locations, that is, they reciprocally become aware of each other's claim to identity, they can usually build a social relationship which is symbolically structured in terms of standard rhetorical routines. This relationship will interact with other relationships impinging on the past and future of both individuals. Over a period of time, in addition to these routine conventions, some rhetorical devices will assume characteristics which are not necessarily contained in their common language systems. Two lovers, for example, will develop a terminology which is not meaningful outside the con-fines of the bedroom. Similarly, families will generate meaning-structures which are situationally specific and not translatable into the common universe of discourse. Rhetoric binds people to each other by encapsulating extant social relationships, thereby possibly creating new meaning. This is at the level where some form of mutual adaptation and co-operative behaviour is appropriate. At another level, rhetoric might divide and push people into conflict. This is due, not only to a failure in communication, but to a clash between two symbolic realities defined from two different per-spectives. As Duncan has put it:[20]

> When people cannot communicate they cannot relate. Dis-relationships are not reflected in communication; they originate in communication. If we cannot create forms for communication over new problems, or adjust traditional forms to new conditions of community life, there can be no consensus, and thus no common action. When differences become so great that symbols no longer possess a common meaning people turn to leaders who do create new symbols of community. It is not differences of station, rank, sex, age, class, or condition that create pathological states in society (as well as in individuals), but a lack of symbols we might use to express differences yet subordinate them to some great social principle of order. The study of the breakdown of symbolic integration (when by integration we mean a resolution, not an obliteration of differences) constitutes, therefore, the sociopathology of everyday life.

When men cannot communicate they not only cannot relate, they live in different symbolic universes. They use the same language, they have the same syntax, the same literature, yet they find it impossible to understand each other. They impute motives to the other which are constructs which they have abstracted out of their own mental universes without taking into account the lived symbolic field of the other. The breakdown of communication is, therefore, more than a disease of language, it is also a mechanism and a cause of social disorientation. Language binds, but, simultaneously, it pushes actors apart.

2. *Rhetoric and the social order*

At the more general level sociologists have seen language as being a functional imperative in the same way as they have identified the moral–ethical system as a functional imperative. Language has an integrative function – it binds men together (so it is argued) by creating common symbols, common values, common understandings. It follows that the problem of social order is one in which common rules are discovered which enable men to relate to each other. These common rules are expressed in the symbols of religious authority (God), or they are expressed in the symbols of the political authority (the state, the law, etc.), or more commonly they are expressed in the everyday rules of social intercourse (habits, customs, *mores*, etc.). In whatever way they are manifested they are supposed to represent the common set of understandings and rules which together are considered to be necessary for the continued operation and survival of a society. Social interaction can only take place in a climate of mutually understood rules and their symbolic manifestations.

The problem of social order, as conceived of by Parsons following Hobbes, is to explain the fact that men find these symbols binding and agree to accept their authority. It has been argued that these common understandings have been interpreted for men before they are socialized, the moral order is '*there*' as some form of ubiquitous set of meanings which newly-born children will be forced to accept as given and, indeed, will be expected to internalize in order to become members of their society. This view of society is very often a feature of the structuralist–functionalist model and its associated absolutist view of man. I agree with Jack Douglas[21] when he argues that, until recently, sociologists have been committed to this absolutist view of man and society. Certainly, this viewpoint is explicit in Durkheim; it is the cornerstone of the positivist influence in social science. Rhetorical devices are, in this respect, supposed to be at the disposal of the larger social order. Hence, in addressing each other, men are merely reflecting the forms of address which they find in their culture, where culture is defined as a system of common understandings.

Within limits, this argument has certain force, although it does not enable us to really understand how men in interaction really go about constructing moral and social meanings. There is, in the concept of mutual and reciprocal conduct, a far larger area of indeterminacy than is allowed in the official doctrine. The construction of new meanings and the confirmation of old meanings is problematic, not certain or given. Granted that politicians, priests, lovers, capitalists, trade-union leaders, deviants, official definers, all use their own typical rhetorics which seem to be standardized for some typical routines. This does not imply that they are always rigidly adhered to, or that they are continuously utilized to reaffirm old meanings.

We have already spoken about the essential openness of language and what Mead and other symbolic interactionists call 'breadth of perspective'. In interaction, the assumption of overriding normative blue-prints just does not bear up to critical inspection. For example, even in the discussion of common moral principles which both parties to the interaction are supposed to share by virtue of their common membership of an organization, church, social class etc., we find that there is no real consensus as to how these moral principles are to be interpreted. There is an official doctrine which is supposed to legitimate and guide moral conduct. Nevertheless, at the level of everyday life, the interactors find it very difficult or even impossible to interpret the official version: [22]

As we have already noted, when we actually observe everyday social activities we find that members of our society do not in fact find it easy to agree on what is right or wrong, moral and immoral, in concrete situations. In accord with the assumption that morals are nonproblematic, they do tend (or have traditionally tended) to assume that morals are obvious, but only in the abstract, independently of any concrete situation in which the individual is actually involved. This assumption of an absolute morality has some real advantages to the individual in many everyday situations, especially insofar as it provides a nonproblematic legitimacy, as he sees it, for his own ideas and actions. This presumably, is a major reason why it has been so resistant to change (until recently) in spite of the fact that in concrete situations individuals normally become embroiled in many arguments over what is right and wrong for the situation at hand. In fact, in many, perhaps most, forms of everyday activity there would appear to be more instances of disagreement than agreement over what is right or wrong for the situation at hand, though most of these disagreements are not readily observable because the individuals involved do not choose to argue openly about them. (This should be especially apparent in any situations involving authority relations.) Subordinates generally disagree with superordinates about many concrete questions of morality, but generally in silence.

It might be added that all interaction situations have this underpinning of disagreement about interpretations of what actually is going on in the situation. *There is a dialectic between the certainty of the structured expectation as given in the normative requirements of social interaction and the self-indications that men make to themselves.* Certainly, in approaching the 'other', one is aware of typical motives and typical categorizations of the probable interaction. In some respects it will be like other encounters, in other respects, it will be completely different. What really happens is that we work towards some practical compromise between what the imputed definition demands, and our actual perception of the situation. In so doing, we construct new meanings, we also impute new motives. Meanings are constructed in interaction, they are put to the test in rhetorical situations which are basically social in intention.

3. *Rhetoric as the objectification of the self*

There is, implicit in our discussion, the Meadian notion of interior audiences. Language is always employed by the user not only as a means to reach a desired state, but as a means of objectifying his inner world. What is subjective assumes some form of reality when it becomes a rhetorical action. However, it can only obtain this status if it is situated in a definite context in which both the speaker and listener are able to make comments. The speaker and listener, in Mead's view, do not have to be two people, but the 'individual' as a parliament of selves.[23] It is not only simply a question of monitoring one's language as one uses it – it is also a question of using language in such a way that it gives substance to the situated activity. Because of this, the spoken discourse of men in interaction is not merely an exercise in the maximization of self-regard – it is also an exercise in world-building in the broadest sense of the term. Undoubtedly, there is the danger that one could attribute to symbolic construction all that has been attributed to 'The Social System' or mental structures, that is, to the absolutist conception of social and moral processes, but this is not what we are intending here. All we are saying is that interaction is problematic – it is problematic by the very nature of man's symbol-making capacity. Symbols do not constitute reality – they merely indicate that reality is not only to be found in the so-called 'hard' world outside man. Reality in this sense is a construction that man makes – we can agree with Piaget when he points to the fact that it is not complete knowledge structures that men are born with; rather they *mutually construct* structures out of the material provided by the environment and the resources provided by men. The impulses to language are given to men as part of their evolutionary location in the biological spectrum, but ultimately, language is only realizable in social interaction.[24]

We all presume to know the 'of-course' world posited by official social science and derived from the common-sense interpretations of that world. The system of meanings that we believe sustains our conduct is, on inspection, found to be very tenuous. Dramatically, we realize our purposes in situated contexts by means of rhetoric aimed at sustaining or recreating the social order, but this process is not one which can be described as being epiphenomenal to the social order. Furthermore, by definition, dramatic realization in everyday life is problematic. Similarly, the social order is problematic. It is problematic because men themselves construct that social order – it is not constructed for them by agencies outside man, nor is it constructed for them by the economic system or the biological substrata.

Ultimately we must come back to the whole question of meaning and its relevance to the objectification of the inner world of man. Berger and Lachman,[25] for all their vague metaphysics, have stated this view of social reality most forcefully. In so doing they have married the phenomenological and symbolic interactionist perspectives. Their argument that all social reality is precarious is equivalent to the statement that language itself is precarious. There is always the possibility that alternative symbols or alternative meanings can be attached to conventional typifications.

In general, most men try to integrate the new, the unexpected, into a consistent framework which derives from the generally established categories of the 'world taken for granted'. But there are moments when, if we are to believe the phenomenologists, this 'taken-for-granted world' is seen for what is is – an artificially constructed and precarious meaning-structure which is always threatening to break down or move away from its everyday typification.

Goffman[26] gives vivid examples of this problematic undercurrent to interaction when he discusses some of the social silences and embarrassments caused by the breakdown of communication between actors and the misunderstandings which develop when they have constructed definitions of the situation which are completely at variance with each other. In this connection, the awareness that the other has not understood one's projected definition of the situation cannot be attributed simply to faulty socialization experiences, or to different language categories; rather it might be a complete misreading of the situated activity. If, for example, my definition of your behaviour leads me to expect you to offer me a job on the board of directors of a large corporation, whereas in actuality all that you are doing is to make casual conversation, then this is not only a misconstruction or wrong definition of the situation. If friendliness is misconstrued for antagonism and vice versa, we are not necessarily dealing with examples of potentially disordered behaviour, but with fundamental discrepancies in the interpretations of the 'of-course world'.

If I claim that there is a conspiracy directed against me, then there might be three possible reasons for this claim. First, there might be a conspiracy – and this reflects the world as it is; second, the conspiracy could exist in my head alone, and consequently, I might be a suitable case for treatment; and, third, the conspiracy may be dependent on the interpretations I place on certain symbols, on the meaning I attribute to the taken-for-granted 'of-course world' which is supposed to be my guide to social action. In the third case, we are not talking about my delusions, but the social construction of a social meaning out of the materials available to me as an actor in the 'of-course world'. The reality of my symbolic world is just as critical as that of the officially defined symbolic world.

What this all amounts to is a commitment to a view of social relationships which places behaviour fully in the symbolic context. If both structure, in terms of a learned set of cultural understandings, and interaction, as the negotiation of new meanings in that context, are endemic, or believed to be endemic to social processes, this would seem to imply that society can be conceived of as *men in communication*. There is, in other words, no distinction to be found between form and content. Because in the act of creating new meanings in interaction, we are at the same time simultaneously constructing and interpreting what has already been given to us in the past. The normative expectations which are supposed to govern interaction, in the Parsonian sense of the concept, are certainly an important aspect of the interaction. The identification of roles and their complementary counterparts can be described in the language of conventional role-analysis, but if we leave it there, we are in danger of completely ignoring those aspects of behaviour which are not bound by the role-script. And as we have continuously argued, these aspects of behaviour are creative because symbolic behaviour is creative.

We don't say that language is creative in some vague metaphysical sense, only in the sense that symbolic activity is firmly located in the biological nature of man. Particular symbols have

111

no specific location in cerebral structures, but the process of symbolization is fundamentally a biosocial activity. It is rooted in both the physical and social nature of man, and is the means and substance of human sociation. Mead recognized this long ago, yet it remains very difficult to convince sociologists who believe in the ultimate determinacy of structural constraints. It is precisely the fact that social reality never stands still that remains the most difficult aspect of studying social processes. This fluidity is understandable at the level of symbolic indications and counter-indications which are located in man as a biosocial being. Both the problematic and non-problematic are elements of social order and change. In this respect, symbolic interaction is not tied to over-socialized conceptions of human behaviour.

part two

Models of interaction

6 Interaction as drama

In our discussion of the grammar or elements of interaction we have implicitly been using a number of images of man and society which now can be made more explicit.

To a certain extent role theory is premised on the notion that all conduct can be conceived of as being, quintessentially, a matter of performance and counter-performance in front of audiences. In conventional terms, the script has to be learned and interpreted in order to make conduct meaningful. Typically, the classic drama which insists on a unity of place, time and action has provided the model for social theorists but today the emphasis has changed:[1]

> To theorists like Parsons, Merton and Gross, a role is a set of expectations held toward the occupant of a particular social status or position in a social system. Role-performance then consists of conforming behaviourally to those expectations, with the goal of attaining positive sanctions from those holding the expectations or of avoiding their negative sanctions. In our opinion, this sort of mechanistic conformity to role script is observed only in unusual circumstances, as in fairly tightly structured organizations in which roles in this sense are formally defined. Even then the utility of the model is highly limited. Although the professor and the groundkeeper both occupy roles in the same formal organization, the professor would be at a loss to specify the role relationship between them in terms of specific expectations, rights, and duties. We submit that no script exists for this role relationship, as indeed for the great majority of relationships, and therefore that the individuals involved must somehow improvise their roles within very broad limits. To the role theorist, the archetypical role is that seen in ritual or classic drama, in which every line and every gesture of

every actor is rigidly specified in the sacred script. In our view, the archetypical role is more nearly that seen in improvized theatre, such as is provided by the Second City Troupe, which performs extemporaneously within only the broad outlines of the sketches and of the characters assumed.

If interaction has qualities reminiscent of the extemporaneous theatre, there is still the problem of accounting for the nature of interaction as being dramatic. The terminology we employ in social theory, in which we never talk of individuals but only of social actors, is indicative of how the language of the theatre has permeated our thinking. Since the advent of Goffman and the dramaturgical school, all behaviour is conceptualized in terms of audiences and actors who mutually construct a performance. Traditionally, these performances were considered to be a part of the way in which men learned to adapt to the demands of the social system and the master patterns of the script writer. But there is another problem – and this is the actual empirical establishment of the dramatic model in interaction. Burke, Mead, Duncan and others have contributed to our understanding of the mechanisms which we employ in everyday life to present ourselves dramatically to others. Together with Goffman and countless others (including dramatists from Sophocles to Pinter), they have pointed to the manner in which self-observation enters into any interaction as an essential part of that interaction. To act socially is to act dramatically, in the sense that one's behaviour is underpinned by the 'self', monitoring its performances. As we have already argued, reflexivity involves self-oriented indications – the self is the central axis of meaning from which we are able to define others. There is, in other words, an element of consciousness in all behaviour directed toward others. The commitment to speech is self-conscious in that it is framed in such a way that the other's point of view is taken into account.

Now, this does not mean that social behaviour is to be seen as theatre. The theatre is an artificial construction in which dramatic performances are put on which highlight the intrinsic nature of everyday dramatic situations. As we have already indicated, in Burke's pentad of dramatic terms, men are busily engaged in situating themselves in scenes which enable them to serve their purposes through the agency of some means–end ratio. In the theatre, this is arrived at by deliberate intention. In everyday life, the roles we assume, the performances we interpret are often unconscious or automatic. We do not choose to perform the role of son or daughter, but are socialized into these roles. In interpersonal relationships we assume roles without necessarily being aware that

116

we are doing so. The coquette, for example, plays her role without studious attention to the dramatic performances of reference group, although she has probably unconsciously assimilated these roles from the television screen or Hollywood. All that is given in these circumstances is the fact that there *is* an audience which is open to influence. It is the *other* in the person of lover, or potential lover, who creates the performance. But the performance is not perceived as being a performance by the actor – it is regarded as being normal, in the nature of things. The other enters into the performance as a component of dramatic action.

At a more conscious level, socialization implies the learning of appropriate performances which can be stored up for future realization (anticipatory socialization). Furthermore, role-taking is essentially a dramatic rehearsal – roles are rehearsed in anticipation of the evaluations and appraisals implicit in ongoing lines of activity. Infants respond to their parents' indications by performing the appropriate line. However, at this stage we cannot realistically speak of back regions in which routine performances are planned. We cannot speak of deliberately staged acts in which children employ various acting strategies in order to achieve their dramatic ends. Deceit is only internalized when the child is reflexively aware of his identity as a social object. Certainly he can manipulate his parents by certain behaviours, but this is not equivalent to the full realization of dramatic roles.

Society as tragedy and comedy

The fact that behaviour is self monitored lends support to the thesis that symbolic universes and structures (mythologies, political doctrines, artistic and stylistic forms etc.) are fundamentally dramatically conceived. Art and drama are dramatic because social interaction is dramatic. Drama, of course, presupposes some tragic commitment, yet in everyday life the dramatic mode is not necessarily discoverable at the level of tragedy; it is equally relevant to the comedy of manners, or in the play activities of children and adults. Because social activity is not strait-jacketed by the rigid specifications of structured role requirements, it follows that dramatic action is subject to continuous reinterpretation. The script is merely a guideline to action – it does not determine the actual course of the interaction. In the theatre the script is given, sometimes the gestures are minutely detailed in the text so that the actors are bound to perform within definite limits. Correspondingly, there are some roles in everyday life where it is considered that the script is well known and defined. The bureaucratic role, for instance, is regarded as one in which the actors are required to

117

strictly adhere to role-prescriptions which support the legitimacy of the organization.

Role theory argues that roles can be described along a continuum – from those highly structured situations which narrowly confine action, to those situations which require the minimum of definition. In unstructured situations, even where interpretation of the role-script is given its greatest leeway, there is believed to be some constraining influence such as an internalized 'norm of reciprocity' which governs the performance. In these circumstances, what guarantees the performance, even in the most problematic situation, is the dramatic nature of self–audience relationships. Phenomenologically, the audience exerts both a constraining and liberating influence – constraining in the sense that, in order to establish some form of social rapport, the actor has to canalize his conduct so that he is understandable to the other – he must be convincing, he must perform at a level which is meaningful to the audience, but simultaneously his performance may be liberating in that, each time he performs, there is a possibility that both actor and audience mutually construct new categories of meaning.

To say that social interaction is dramatic is also to say that the network of relations which makes up a society is dramatic. If the interpersonal encounters between individuals are considered to be ones in which there is an element of interpretation and performance, as claimed by symbolic interactionism, then it is equally permissible to conceive of the larger framework in dramatic terms. Men in political offices, or in bureaucracies, relate to other men not in some entirely extra-social manner. They represent organizations or groups, but this representative interaction is not qualitatively different to their relations to other men in more intimate situations. The trade-union leader who is trying to negotiate a better wage settlement for his constituents, is not operating at a level of abstraction and reification which is completely divorced from the actual situated context in which the negotiations are taking place. He is constrained by the defined power structure, by his interpretation of his role, by the demands of his members, by the intransigency of the employers, by the burden of his own personality, yet he is also capable of stepping outside his role, of considering alternatives, of presenting new proposals, in short, of performing in a manner which is not circumscribed by the mutual definition of the situation. Granted that in the real world his performance is likely to be strictly monitored by both his constituents and his negotiating others, there is still the possibility that he can reject his allocated role and project a viable alternative.

The real difference between the theatre and the world outside is that the world outside is real only because performances are not set or prescribed for all time. Men make history not because they are forced to do so by the march of events, or because they are the victims of historical inevitability, but because they are always in the position to act in a manner which is not laid down in advance by the operations of some internalized role requirement or cerebral circuit. They literally can *act* in the strongest sense of the term – they can choose to perform and interpret the behaviour in a context in symbolic indications which are not circumscribed by the role-script.

What we are saying therefore is that the dramatic model of interaction conceives of social conduct in role terms. By roles we don't mean to imply the traditional category of script adherence. Rather, we emphasize the interpretative aspect of interaction. More than this, we imply that not only interaction at the interpersonal level is dramatic but also the entire complex of activities that go to make up the social fabric. We can extend the metaphor even further when we consider how men perceive and define their social environment.

The proverbial common man sees the world in highly dramatic terms. The metaphors he employs, the evaluations he makes of others, the assumptions he makes, are dramatic. Men are considered to be good or evil, blameworthy or blameless. The world is seen as providing the stage for the monumental battle of political forces which are described in dramatic terms. Currently, as Duncan has observed, this struggle is conceived of in terms of the confrontation between communism and capitalism or between the young and old. Yet, this is only an aspect of the dramatization of social life. In more prosaic circumstances, the sporting heroes of mass society are not described in neutral terms but are painted in vivid dramatic colours. At the interpersonal level, we attribute and impute motives in terms of symbols which focus on markedly dramatic qualities. Furthermore, there is another side of the dramatic model which is neglected by most theorists, and this is the essentially tragic side of life. Drama is premised on the human constants of birth, status passage and death. It is ordinarily saturated with the pain of everyday arrivals and departures. Art and literature long ago recognized the fact that men are not only symbolic animals, but also creatures immediately aware of their mortality and the possibility of pain and suffering. The everyday concerns of men reflect or generate these meanings. Religion in one sense is a dramatic realization of man *in extremis*. Social theory, until very recently, has tended to ignore and deny the existence of the tragic except in the broadest of generalizations about the development of society.

Communication between men in society is, therefore, not merely

119

symbolic interaction, it is also dramatic symbolic interaction. Men conceive of the world in terms of the symbols they create, while simultaneously these symbols are expressive of the drama of every-day and community life. The everyday activities of men at the subsistence level are centred on the search for food and shelter and the need to develop an appropriate method of coping with their predicament. Yet, this is only possible when they have managed to construct for themselves a symbolic reality which allows them to understand their predicament, while at the same time drama-tizing their own efforts in the scheme of things. Starvation can be explained by the 'will' of the gods. Pain can be assimilated if it is regarded as a necessary condition of one's life on earth – all things can be stoically borne provided they are given dramatic force. In all this one is acting in front of vast cosmic audiences who are believed to be the final arbitrators of one's fate. Hence, the intense attention to detail and ritual correctness in so many forms of religion. Performance is all, ritual exactitude becomes the way in which man can be sure of obtaining the attention of the cosmic order, or perhaps of avoiding its most destructive manifestations. The roles that one assumes in the stark confrontation with nature and God are therefore forced onto man by his realization that the meaning of existence is to be grasped as a drama which can only be made tolerable by the best possible performance. Indeed, the performance becomes all important.

At a more sophisticated level, when modern artists and writers find life meaningless, this meaninglessness is only communicable in dramatic terms because, if meaning goes out of life, this implies that one is really substituting one kind of meaning with another kind. The search for meaning and identity is most poignant in those who believe they see contemporary existence as dramatically null. Those who label themselves as alienated and victims of the mass political and bureaucratic institutions of our society, do so in the belief that they cannot find a significant role to play as social actors. Thus, there is a reversion from the large-scale conception of man as an actor on a social and religious stage to the notion of man as a small-part actor with his friends at a deeply interpersonal level. The comforts of pot, or the seductions of pop, are substituted for the traditional meanings of the politico-social universe. The audiences on whom one now depends are no longer the traditional ones covered by the labels family, class, church, country; rather they are the quick episodic ones provided by encounters. In all this, the dramatic metaphor is not lost, both in terms of reflexive en-actment and in the acting out of one's role in front of selected audiences.

The norm of cynicism

Thus, Goffman[2] has traced out the countless little enactments of bourgeois suburban life in the States. Self-presentation is conducted in a framework of social niceties and a need to maintain some form of front at all costs. In the back regions, where presumably one can let one's hair down, there is still the same commitment to dramatic life in miniature. Ultimately, these little performances are nothing more than a surrender to the ubiquitous and deadening impact of mass society. Of course, some men construct their performances with a great deal of skill, but they are constructed with the object of maintaining a routine, not with a view of man as a totally committed being. This, in essence, is an aspect of the Marxist critique of society, which sees the fragmentation of man proceeding in such a way that the theatre of the trivial is substituted for the theatre of social significance.

However, it would be a mistake to conceive of contemporary society as being especially conducive to impression-management. Impression-management is a feature of all interaction – it subsumes dramatic performance in preliterate as well as contemporary societies. What men offer before audiences is what they believe audiences expect. They try to maximize the efficacy and power of their performance so as to ensure the maximum degree of social cohesion. Although we believe that everybody has internalized the norm of cynicism, that is, it is assumed that everybody has become aware of the possibility of deceit in others, this does not entail a practical enactment of this belief. We accept that the carpenter will ply his trade with the maximum dedication because if he did not it would probably lead to the breakdown of normal interaction. Similarly, we accept the lecturer's claim to a knowledge of his subject, even though we have been exposed to a doctrine which places all such claims under suspicion. Nevertheless, as we have observed earlier, this does not prevent the carpenter or lecturer from merely going through the motions of dedication, that is, of masking his real viewpoint or his attitude toward his audience.

Politicians have been accused of this more often than others – their motives are often imputed as being self-seeking or dishonourable. There seems to be more evidence for a discrepancy between their moral and political commitments and their actual performances. The norm of cynicism tends to see all politicians in terms of artificial dramatic performances which are easily discoverable by their constituents and opponents. Moreover, this is only one example of a ubiquitous element in all social relationships. Masking is just as relevant in non-European societies as it is in

121

the West. As Gerald Berreman has written on the role of the ethnographer in the discovery of social relationships in field studies: [3]

> An ethnographer is usually evaluated by himself and his colleagues on the basis of his insights into the back region of the performance of his subjects. His subjects are evaluated by their fellows on the basis of the degree to which they protect the secrets of their team and successfully project the image of the team that is acceptable to the group for front region presentation. It is probably often thought that this presentation will also satisfy the ethnographer. The ethnographer is likely to evaluate his subjects on the amount of back region information they reveal to him, while he is evaluated by them on his tact in not intruding unnecessarily into the back region and, as rapport improves, on his trustworthiness as one who will not reveal back region secrets. These tend to be mutually contradictory bases of evaluation. Rapport establishment is largely a matter of threading among them so as to win admittance to the back region of the subject's performance without alienating them. This is sometimes sought through admission to the subject's team; it is more often gained through acceptance as a neutral confidant.
>
> The impressions that ethnographer and subject seek to project to one another are, therefore, felt to be favourable to the accomplishment of their respective goals: the ethnographer seeks access to back region information; the subjects seek to protect their secrets since these represent a threat to the public image they wish to maintain. Neither can succeed perfectly.

In everyday encounters we are not in the position of the anthropologist who consciously constructs a participant–observer ideology. Interaction involves participant interaction and, as such, involves us all in the attempt to get into the other's back region. This we do by imputing motives, often couched in the grossest cynicism. If the other's performance is convincing, we label the performance as being sincere or honest. However, in typical confrontations between individuals from different social strata, such as classes or generations, there is a tendency to categorize the other's performance in terms of convenient symbols which structure role-distance. For example, the encounter between shop steward and management official is stereotyped to the extent that each one believes that the other is trying to outwit him. Cynical motives are imputed, because these motives are believed to serve the real interests of the party concerned. The back regions to which both parties refer are assumed to contain within them entire vocabularies of motives which will not be made public. Thus, from the point of view of the shop steward, it is evidently clear that the management man is merely concealing the interests of his shareholders and board of directors. Dramatically, the manager might act in such a manner so that he tries to convince his audience that he is not representing the interests of any group other than the organization to which both parties belong.

In practice, this is an almost impossible task, given the prior conditioning and social location of both parties. Different class locations seem to necessitate the imputing of cynical motives. The search for ulterior motives in others is endemic to the contemporary social ethos. At the interpersonal level, where both actors do not represent organizational interests, the roles they project may be taken at their face value as exemplifying personal commitment. Consequently, it is conceivable that the imputation of cynical motives might be waived, although even here back regions are often considered to be the seat of hypocrisy and deceit.

More simply, the dramatic metaphor in sociology recognizes the elementary fact that social life is not a direct matter of response and stimulus. It recognizes that men often are aware of their inner and outer audiences and that they appeal to these audiences for positive evaluation. Consequently, men construct performances in order to facilitate the normal range of everyday intercourse; if a performance is judged to be badly conceived or insincere this leaves both parties to the transaction in an embarrassing situation. Embarrassment is countered by an implicit consensus to accept or ignore the apparent insincerity of the performance. Even when it is recognized that the other is, in reality, playing at his role, there is a commitment to evaluate that role in the most positive manner possible. Thus, we give respect to those enemies of ours who, while being completely committed to their own point of view, try to maximize the benefits of the social situation for the interests they represent. What we admire here is the efficiency of the performance. The performance becomes a work of art even though we have good reason to suspect that behind it all is the sheer face of naked self-seeking.

Psychologically, it is doubtful whether men could put up with too much truth in their encounters. They prefer to hide behind the masks and roles which they construct for themselves or which have been constructed for them. Self-disclosure is possible within the confines of the psychiatrist's consulting room, and not normally in the course of normal interaction, although it has been noted that the mass media somehow seem to act as a catalyst to the most intimate revelations of personal life. *To say that life is dramatic is to say that men are interested in preventing others gaining complete insight into their motives.* Performances are constructed in order to minimize the danger of self-disclosure.

Furthermore, and perhaps more crucially, the dramatic metaphor involves both the tragedy and comedy of everyday life as expressed in the symbolic systems that men employ to catch reality. Men confront each other in terms of dualities and polarities which are essentially dramatic at one level and farcical at another. Traditionally, these antinomies were supplied by religion, by ideology, by the confrontation of the individual and society. Always, as Duncan has insisted, the theme of victimage occurs again and again. The theme of victimage was expressed by such terms as alienation, anomie, power, pathology etc. All these concepts are attempts to come to grips with the essentially dramatic nature of social life. In everyday life men look for scapegoats, apportion blame, find explanations and construct elaborate ideologies and mythologies to understand their enemies. They find comfort in the fact that their temporal lot can be blamed on others – this is not only a question of false ideology but reflects the essential operation of the dramatic mode.[4]

Redemption through victimage, Burke argues, characterizes the 'great religious and theological doctrines that form the incunabula of our culture'. Thus Burke joins Durkheim, Tocqueville, and Weber in his insistence that the study of religious life is crucial to any understanding of social life. Burke believed the feudal enactment of redemption through victimage to be one of the great ritual dramas whose form still determines how we play our role in society. The dramas of guilt and redemption which characterized feudal Europe affect our science and technology, just as they have effected the function and structure of all modern literature, religion, and political life. Not only literary plots but plots or structures, of many community acts depict a struggle between good and bad elements. When this struggle is personified (and it usually is), we have the hero and the villain, or, in common speech, the good guy and the bad guy. Even in the science of psychology, or at least in Freudian psychology, we have a struggle between the father and the son for the mother. The resolution of such struggles is achieved through punishing the villain in the name of some great transcendent principle. Only then does the suffering and death of the sacrificial victim purge us of guilt – in literature, religion, and now, as we have discovered to our horror, in the actualities of political life.

While social theory concentrates on the determinative forces which push men into action, on the infrastructure of economic and political mechanisms, it has tended to ignore the fact that consciousness is not merely epiphenomenal to the men in the actual situation. To say that men act for purposes which they are not

124

really aware of, that they are falsely conscious of their real interest or of their roles in the social structure, is only part of the story. The way that men define the situation is more than a reflection of their interests. 'Definitions' derive dramatically from the very nature of social life – men are animals who can symbolize their own predicaments to themselves. These predicaments are not the sum total of what we like to call the unforeseen consequences of social action; they are a consequence of the essential tragic scaffolding on which social life is built. Hence, even though we are living in a post-religious age, we have not dispensed with our rituals or our social dramas. Today we are witnessing the most vivid example of this polarity which expresses itself in the drama of black against white, young against old. The attempt to reduce this polarity to the language of biological violence and aggression, or merely to the mechanics of starvation is only partly feasible. Certainly, the current drama takes place against a background of a renewed interest in the inexorable growth of population, the perception of the 'ecological Agamemnon' and the possibility of nuclear extinction, yet these possibilities are not outside dramatic construction, they are only meaningful if they are defined and perceived dramatically.

Dramatic symbolization has the effect of channelling men's energies into lines of activity which are not explicable purely in terms of the assumption of non-symbolic forces. For example, the current confrontation between Catholic and Protestant in Northern Ireland has a Marxist interpretation, it has a liberal-democratic interpretation, it has a demographic interpretation, it has an ethnic interpretation, etc., but from the perspective of those immediately concerned, their predicament is seen as being understandable in terms of real living symbolic and dramatic values which have their origin in a historical drama located in the past. You can enter into this situation as a social or political analyst and point to the operation of forces which are hidden behind the scenes, you can point to the interests at work, like the iniquity of the Roman Catholic Church, the greed of the capitalist system, the imperial ambitions of the English, the graft of politicians. However, in the final analysis, it is not these explanations that will be really effective in everyday understanding. Men perceive what they believe to be true in a situation, their common-sense explanations are just as valid as the most elaborate theoretical scheme erected by the outside political analyst. Dramatically, the enemy is seen as evil, his purposes as self-seeking, his behaviour calculated to bring about the destruction of the state. Simultaneously, the organs of social control and the mass media are continuously at work in supplementing the common-folk explanations. But it is only at the level of the immediately dramatic that men can begin to conceive of themselves as part of the larger social context.

Of course, the dramatic metaphor can be carried too far, just as role theory can be carried too far. It is important to realize we are not talking about a cosmic theatre in which everybody has an allocated role. Rather, all we are saying is that because men are capable of self-observation, they are naturally able to conceive of themselves in dramatic terms. The nature of meaningful discourse is, therefore, dramatic. Similarly, we can begin to grasp why man's sense of the tragic extends to the larger contexts in which he finds himself. Essentially, the dramatic mode is the human mode.

The dramatic metaphor is closely identified with the games model of interaction to which we now turn our attention in the next chapter. However, it differs from both exchanges and game theory by its insistence that interaction is essentially an encapsulation of the human condition.

7   Interaction as game and exchange

The notion that social interaction is understandable in terms of the application of a game analogy is very old. Certainly, the idea that behaviour is in some respects subject to game-type structuring enters into a great deal of current theorizing and speculation in the social sciences. Indeed, the mathematical theory of games provides the framework of a number of simulated approaches to the manipulation of international relations (usually at the academic level – although it also informs the thinking of strategists on both sides of the Iron Curtain).

First of all, we can talk about games in the sense of rule-oriented behaviour. Here, the premise is that the rules or norms of social interaction are analogous to the rules discoverable in the confines of artificially constructed games, whether related to the football field, or to the chess-board. Qualitatively, of course, it is recognized that chess and football embody different kinds of rule-oriented behaviour. Moreover, there is another component in game behaviour which is of relevance, that is, the element that can be roughly described as 'play activity'. It is presumed that games are played for a number of reasons, one of the most cogent being the need for the expression of some form of play or entertainment need. Over and above all the other elements that enter into a game of football, for example, is the assumption that the play element is intrinsically rewarding (in the same sense that Simmel makes claims for 'sociation' in its pure form as being, essentially, the apotheosis of play).

In everyday life we are conscious of countless game encounters going on around us. We create special temporal and spatial compartments for their operation – Saturday afternoons for football matches at such and such football ground, special chess-boards for play at various times. Basically, it is assumed that games are part

127

of, but separate from, the mainstream of living. Moreover, it has been argued that games are not additional to interaction, but are a constituent part of interaction, in the same way that dramatic reflexivity is part and parcel of interaction. Games enter into interaction as rules.

In games which we construct for our amusement and entertainment, we are first made aware of the rules of the game – it is assumed that there is no such thing as a game which is not somehow structured by a minimum agreement on some form of rule. Even the unstructured ephemeral games of children provide momentary rules which hold for the immediate present.[1] In social interaction, the rules of the game are presumably not invented by each new set of interactors; they are already there waiting for interaction.

What exactly do we mean by rules in interaction? Are we to assume that rules are guidelines or legal sanctions or merely suggestions for conduct? How do we know these rules and who is to judge whether or not we have adhered to them? Traditionally, the answer given is that we know the rules because we have been taught to obey them by our parents, or teachers, who in turn have been taught by their elders etc. There is implicit in this view the assumption that if one adheres to the basic ground-rules, one will be in a position to successfully negotiate the hazards of living. Rules are needed for the charting of the dangerous sea of human desire and moral pitfall. The public school slogan of 'playing the game' is an echo of this rather simple viewpoint. In other words, rules are seen as implicit moral instructions as to how individuals should act in social situations. In interpersonal encounters we are not free to freely erect new rules or moral codes; we are bound by rules. To play the game, therefore, is not an injunction for the cricket field only, but is the *raison d'être* of the social system at large.

Rules as guidelines

There is the further implication that just as one learns to play the game of chess by internalizing the proper rules, and the most appropriate states of preferred play, so there is in real life the same need to know the rules most appropriate to one's structural location in a society. Thus, it follows that, in a status-ridden society in which there is a relatively rigid hierarchical arrangement of classes and other groups, members of each class will learn the most appropriate rules for the behaviour expected of them. Not only will they learn the behaviour that is required of them, but they will also learn the behaviours appropriate to both their inferiors and superiors. For example, it is not enough for an individual to know what his immediate superiors in an organization expect of him; he must also be in a position to understand what is required of his underlings and also of his equals. Using the same model as Mead,[2] we can say that in this situation all individuals must 'take the role of the other' – they must internalize the rules of the entire organization, just as members of a football team must learn the rules and possible moves of all the other members of the team, that is, the 'generalized other'. In a football game the rules are not alterable by the players – they are subject to the authority of the controlling rule-making body. In everyday life rules are frequently altered and reinterpreted by players – in interaction, the rules are open to revision provided they do not completely violate the logical structure of the situation. But in a situation in which there is a definite delineation of status as given by the rules of the organization, there is not much room for negotiation unless both parties are in direct confrontation.

Can we extend the analogy any further? After all, in games there is the play element at work – men combine and agree to adhere to certain rules in order to maximize their enjoyment. Games are played at, they are not supposed to be matters of life and death. Of course, this is not to deny that some games are transformed into symbols of social cohesion, particularly in football and its national- and local-supporter syndrome, which often can verge on the waging of war by other means. In social interaction, how far can we go in claiming that rule-governed behaviour is really game-directed? It is, as we have noted, very fashionable to employ the games analogy in the field of political and strategic simulation. Here, men are considered to be pawns or units who can be handled and manipulated like the pieces of some gigantic chess set. Politicians are seen as being engaged in a deadly pastime of moving strategic pieces so that they place their opponents at a disadvantage. Strategic advantage is obtained by playing the game in as economical and calculated a manner as possible (rational efficiency). The players who can amass the greatest number of pieces (indoctrinated supporters, resources, offices etc.) can be considered to be in a position of relative strength *vis-à-vis* the other players. Certainly, in the field of international relations, especially in the cold war situation, there is possible merit in examining the positions that politicians take up in terms of game theory, particularly when game theory is supposed to exemplify the maximization of rationality in conflict situations. The assumption of rationality is a crucial one, for it assumes that men will do the utmost to maximize their advantages by the most appropriate means.

The use of simulation techniques has made this type of theoriz-

129

ing an exciting pastime for academics and military strategists, but whether in fact it really pays dividends in the actual study of inter-personal conduct is, of course, open to question. Game theory is primarily premised on the notion of power relationships between large organizations or nation states – conflict is defined in terms of the way in which players can establish and maintain advantages at the expense of others. Implicit in this theorizing has been the belief that it might possibly lay bare the essential fabric of conflict, thus leading to its minimization. In this it has failed, although it has helped us to understand some of the problems arising from the conceptualization of social behaviour in terms of gaming. In this respect, Michael Nicholson writes: [3]

> There is little doubt that the formal statement of conflict problems has clarified the nature of conflict. Further there is a great deal of work which has clearly been inspired by the theory of games, even though the purists refuse to acknowledge it as such because it does not fit into the framework of a deductive, axiomatic theory. Game theory has inspired much experimental work on how people actually behave in various game situations, and it has also suggested the description of conflict situations in game theory form. While an analysis of conflict according to the strict precepts of game theory leaves us little wiser on how people really behave, the formulations of the problem in broader game theory terms is of great help. Indeed, if the theory of games is considered to include the formalization of gaming problems, then this, the child of the pure theory of games, its more rigorous but less worldly father has added considerably to our under-standing of the problem of conflict. *It is only the hope of finding the solution of the problem of conflict by the simple application of a neat mathematical theory which has been disappointed.*

The uses of games theory can therefore be considered in terms of its ability to illuminate conflict at both the macro- and micro-level. However, this presupposes that all behaviour can be con-sidered to be explicable in terms of some conflict conceptualization. There is the added complication that games theory cuts across other perspectives, namely such areas covered by bargaining and exchange theory. In addition, conflict analysis as treated by Marxist thinkers is not premised on the notion of rules of the game, but is seen as the jockeying for position of economic and social groups with no holds barred. Our concerns here are more limited. In con-sidering social interaction at the direct interpersonal level we can also envisage the rules that enter into interaction as being 'game elements', provided we realize that games, like drama, are based on social behaviour and not the other way around. *Games, as*

130

played consciously, are merely a symbolic formalization of basic social processes. Similarly, drama is a statement of a basic social process.

Basic and preferred rules

We can define games in terms of the basic expectancies of the participating members. This we can do for both formally constituted games and informal interaction situations. Garfinkel[4] has called these expectancies constitutive expectancies. They are dependent on the mutuality of definitions of the social actors. The mutuality of expectation is, of course, also essential to Parsons's[5] definition of social interaction. If there are no expectancies, then it is obvious that there are no rules, nor for that matter, can there be any stable or viable interaction. However, in formally constituted games there are distinctions to be made between 'basic rules' and 'preferred rules'. Preferred rules are those rules which allow the players a minimum number of discretionary moves as against the required or expected moves of the basic rules. The preference rules operate more or less independently of the ground or basic rules. Cicourel puts it this way:[6]

> The independence stems from various kinds of traditional play, efficiency procedures, aesthetic preferences and the like, which are open to the player. Game furnished conditions help to fill out how the game tends to be played and correspond to each set of basic rules. The player's decisions are always constrained by them and they are independent of whether the player wins or loses. They describe the general characteristics of the game because they always enter into each decision. Garfinkel finds a good example of the game furnished conditions in chess where the basic rules provide a situation of perfect information at all times. A different game with different basic rules may not provide for such conditions. Thus in poker the situation is quite different and the game furnished conditions are such that every decision contains a varying amount of uncertainty.

In everyday life, it is highly unlikely that one is in a position to really completely predict, or even understand fully, the preferred rules of play that one encounters in interaction situations. Interactors may have some vague idea as to what the basic rules are, but even then they are subject to definitions of the situation which may be highly idiosyncratic. Certainly, basic rules do define the world as 'taken for granted'. They constitute the normal, expected world, they do not allow for uncertainty. All they allow for is what ethnomethodologists call trust – trust that the world, as constituted in interaction, is not going to dissolve into meaninglessness. But this does not necessarily enable individuals in the situation to counter the uncertainty posed by the preferred rules. Indeed, in normal interaction we cannot assume, as we do in the context of the playing of a game, that the world will remain still, so to speak, or that other contaminating factors will not enter into the situation to complicate the issue. The element of uncertainty which underpins rule-bound behaviour in common contexts is essentially not calculable – uncertainty as to how actors are going to interpret the situation makes it highly improbable that we can use the normal instruments of social prediction when studying this type of conduct.

Cicourel argues that the game model has advantages for six good reasons.[7]

(1) It points to the specification of rules – in any interaction it is of advantage to be able to pinpoint the actual adherence to basic rules and the departure from such adherence.

(2) Typification of what are considered to be the normal, or expected rules, allows the researcher to make statements about the atypical or the unusual. In other words, there is an allowance made for the atypical which can then be properly specified in one's procedures. For example, the knowledge of typical patterns of approach–avoidance in the encounters of strangers, (which to a certain extent are typified by general formal properties) can be of use in enabling us to understand novel and qualitatively different emergencies which arise in the interaction. In a poker game this is limited by a relative number of possible ploys – in real life the number of ploys tends to be relatively open.

(3) Knowledge of the constituent elements and rules of behaviour would allow social scientists to point to the stable and consistent aspects of social interaction. This implies a belief in the possibility of stable frameworks for social action – these stable frameworks are not provided by the stability of social relationships, but in the consistency of meaning structures as given by symbolic interaction. In a game, although we can speak of novelty, we are always within the boundaries of the master rules of the initial formulation, whereas in real life we find that the master rules are themselves problematic.

(4) A knowledge of both the constitutive components and preferred rules of play would enable the investigator to spell out the implications of any type of social interaction, in the sense that rule-governed behaviour is both subject to limiting frameworks and new definitions. Thus, for example, if we could really accurately describe the formal structure of interaction between strangers, we would also be in the position to specify some of the unexpected and preferred rules of play open to the interactors, although it

must be recognized that these preferred rules of play are not subject to predictive extrapolation, since they tend to be highly volatile. Nevertheless, if we accept that a sociology of action, or interpretative understanding, is premised on the necessity to tease out these rules, then it is imperative that we look behind constituent rules of the game.

(5) In addition, there is the notion of the saliency of definition that must be taken into account, that is, the 'constitutive accent' in Garfinkel's terms.[8] Constitutive expectancies change over time, definitions of the situation change over time. Thus, the constitutive accent on certain features of the stranger relationship in a social group may conceivably change when events are given different meanings and symbolization.

(6) Lastly, the game model is intimately tied up with the way in which identity is established, both at the official and unofficial levels. Role-taking at the official level involves actors in the expression of appropriate general symbols of recognition, such as appearance (dress) in the case of the relationship between passenger and bus-conductor, whereas at the unofficial level, alternative identities are negotiated. In a game we can observe the official rules, yet simultaneously we are in a position to observe the preferred rules at work. Thus, the official meanings are always supplemented by unofficial definitions which are negotiated in interaction. In everyday life it is far more difficult to untangle the official and unofficial rules, for the simple reason that they are subject to constant reinterpretation at both levels. They are also contaminated by a host of extraneous influences which impinge on the interaction situation.

Games as strategic calculation

It is not so much a question of employing the game analogy which is of use in social research, but its specification of boundary conditions for the understanding of social action. We are continuously bombarded by claims from some sociologists that social behaviour is rule-oriented, and that the prime task of social research and theory is to establish criteria whereby normative patterns can be measured and defined. But these claims are made from the viewpoint of some notion of social determination of individual action. They are subsumed under the aegis of normative determinism, and the internalization of the social definitions of the desirable, the good and the appropriate. In other words, they are usually described in terms of what Wallace has called the 'microcosmic metaphor'.[9] Game theory, when it is not tied to a doctrinaire mathematical vocabulary allows us to investigate both structural and interactionist concepts. It does so by introducing calculability into social behaviour. As Goffman writes: [10]

> Whenever students of the human scene have considered the dealings individuals have with one another, the issue of calculation has arisen: When a respectable motive is given for action, are we to suspect an inferior one? When an individual supports a promise or a threat with a convincing display of emotional expression, are we to believe him? When an individual seems carried away by feeling, is he intentionally acting this way in order to create an effect? When someone responds to us in a particular way, are we to see this as a spontaneous reaction to the situation or a result of his having canvassed all other possible responses before deciding this one was the most advantageous? And whether or not we have such concerns, ought we to be worried about the individual believing that we ought to have them?

Goffman's concern with calculable behaviour, which he conceives of as strategic interaction, is related to similar approaches in 'bargaining' and 'exchange' theory. The jockeying for position which seems to be typical of a great deal of human interaction is dependent on the way in which all parties to the interaction have *full information* about the other's intentions, that is, the way in which they successfully take the role of the other. However, there is the further implication that calculability is only specifiable in terms of some form of pay-off matrix. Taking the role of the other entails calculating what the other intends to do, so that one can obtain the maximum strategic advantage.

Game theory assumes that actors are highly conscious of their intentions – *that they are aware of the fact that they are in a game-like situation.* Thus, they ask themselves about the nature of the game they are playing and the most efficacious way of winning or maximizing their game-performance. In this connection, it is a mistake to assume that game-like behaviour can only be perceived in situations where economic criteria apply – it is not necessarily premised on the notion of the maximization of psychic profit, but also on the perception by actors that certain goals need to be secured, either for oneself, or for others. Hence, it is possible that in a game-like situation one of the actors acts in such a way as to maximize the other's self-esteem, without necessarily obtaining advantage for himself. Behaviour in this sense is calculable, yet not subject to the law of profit maximization. It is, of course, quite conceivable that some actors will not be aware of the game-like aspects of their behaviour. Thus, the old man who has always lifted his hat to the ladies is not aware of his behaviour as part of an elaborate social device to maintain his social identity, although he would soon alter his conduct if the ladies decided to respond to his gesture by giving the Women's Lib response.

Probablistic interaction

The rhetoric that goes with games theory often smacks of the pseudo-artificial world of scientism; perhaps this is a misconception. Certainly we can become seduced by a language which incorporates the prestigious symbols of mathematics. However, game theory provides us with an additional tool to add to the armoury of symbolic analysis. Games are played within the confines of language systems which have been 'situated' by certain types of rules and relationships. Nevertheless, language does not create the game – it merely gives it content. Like the dramatic metaphor, the game analogue faces up to the probablistic nature of social reality. To say that social reality is probablistic is an insight which Weber brought to his theorizing about meaningful social action – it is also central to the interactionist perspective.

Probablistic interaction may conveniently be illustrated at the analogical level by card and board games. The inventive criteria used by the creation of these games is considered to be not accidental but rooted in the game-like nature of certain aspects of interaction.

Thus in interaction situations we can speak of:

(*a*) The reciprocal nature of the pay-off or outcome. In interaction one's behaviour is always dependent on the behaviour of others.

(*b*) We can also speak of the self–other paradigm as reflexively involved in any interaction. In interaction we are continuously objectifying our own behaviour from the perspective of others. This objectification is partly premised on the calculation of how the other is going to evaluate one's performance. In a game of chess this involves the simple guess as to the other's most probable move so that one can plan one's own move.

(*c*) Both in games and interaction we are bound by a contextual pattern of rules and expectations, whether of the constitutive or preferred sort. The deviation from such rules is instrumental in bringing into play the means of social control, which, at the same time, involves the formulation of alternative modes of action (social change). In interaction, we are constantly being reminded that we are in areas of meaning which are bounded by the vocabularies of motives which actors employ to categorize their experience. It is these vocabularies which really are the *deus ex machina* of both dramaturgical and game theory.

(*d*) In addition, all games are subject to the laws of probability – interaction too is probablistic – there is no certainty that any inter-active gesture will bring out the required response, only the hope that it will reiterate past experiences. In chess, these probabilities can be covered by mathematical theory – in real life situations this is not on, particularly when actors are defining the situation from any one of an infinite number of possibilities open to them. How-ever, some outcomes are more probable than others and it is this on which so much of social theory has been based in the past. Certainly, in everyday interaction, the fact that outcomes are probablistic involves us in the construction of strategies and plans to minimize risks of undesirable or unwanted outcomes. In games, these outcomes are premised on information criteria ranging from absolute certainty to the highly improbable everyday decisions are made on the basis of information inferred from the situated context which might or might not be completely reliable or accurate. Thus, prediction of the other's intentions is always subject to some form of distortion or misinterpretation.

In general, in games these probabilities are calculable, but in interaction we face the realm of the unforeseen and uncertain. Pre-dictive certainty is perhaps obtained in highly structured situations in which variables like force, power and coercive persuasion are rigidly adhered to, perhaps within the framework of institutions such as jails and hospitals. Even here, there is no certainty that we can compute probabilities with the degree of certainty obtain-able in rule-structured games.

Strategy and concealment

It is in the sphere of strategy and concealment of motives and intentions that the game analogy is very strong. In games like poker, for example, we are supposed to hide our intentions from the other players by adapting strategies which both outwit and conceal the real moves we have in mind. In everyday life the hiding of intentions and real motives in situations is believed to be critical to normal social discourse. Goffman has had most to do with this revival of interest in concealment and deception. Taken to its logical conclusion, the prototype of this is the type of behaviour found in the art of spying (espionage). In current spy fiction this is often seen as glamorized sabotage, but in some of the more realistic novels deriving from writers such as Le Carré, we focus on the spy as an exemplar of the human condition, as typifying apparently normal behaviour.

The spy is supposed to behave in such a manner that his conduct can be construed as belonging to the particular milieu in which he is operating. In other words, he is not allowed to indulge in the luxury of his intrinsic or salient identity. Spying is both a technique and a way of life – it is a technique in so far as it enables the spy to get away with his underground activities, it is a way of life in so far as it gives the spy a legitimation for his activities, other than the obvious financial inducements. One spies because one believes that spying has consequences for some political or social ideology. Or, one spies simply because it suits one temperamentally, and is seen as one activity among many possible activities. Whatever the reason, concealment is all important. The role of a spy is one in which one cannot afford to give off cues which can be construed by others as being indicative of ulterior motives. The claims that one makes for oneself are more likely to be put to the test than under normal conditions. Thus, one hopes to present to the world an image which is in no manner inconsistent with the generally accepted images that similar others present in similar sorts of situations.

Furthermore, there is the careful scrutiny and monitoring of all one's own actions. The masks that one assumes must never be dropped. Every action that one engages in is subject to the most rigorous reflexive rehearsal and reconstruction. If one suspects one has not convinced the audience of the validity of one's performance, then the most strenuous efforts must be expended in order to correct the other's faulty impression. Moreover, as is sometimes possible, if the other knows you as a spy, and you know that he knows etc., we are left with a spiralling of perspectives,[11] in which every move is interpreted in a manner involving a set of moves like a game of chess. What is at stake here is the maintenance of an advantage which each player tries to maximize – the spies maximize each other's discomfiture by the implicit threat of revelation etc. Thus, during World War II, when espionage was rife in a neutral city like Lisbon, where agents tended to know each other, the object of the exercise was not so much to conceal the spying identity, but to pull the wool over the eyes of your opponent, by engaging in games of elaborate double-bluff, by employing strategies of concealment in which the object was to maintain certain options open to yourself and deny them to your opponent.

In everyday life, the spying metaphor is not inappropriate, especially in the context of the selling of services and self to the highest bidder on a commercial market. Hence interaction can be seen as an essay in concealment and strategic calculation. Where the dominant ethos of the age is believed to be one in which everybody is ranged against everybody else in the social approval and status stakes, it becomes easy to see why game theory (especially its emphasis on competitive advantages) comes to be viewed as explicating and legitimating this activity. In this, it allies itself to exchange theory, particularly that aspect of exchange theory which sees behaviour as a function of its pay-off.

Moreover this ignores another aspect of the notion of games in social behaviour which we have not yet discussed: the often noted phenomenon of the need for self-disclosure as documented by theorists like Jourard.[12] Here, the emphasis is not on concealment of motives, but on the absolute necessity of truth in social relationships. Evidence of this is readily obtainable in the fantastic self-castigation and truth games in which certain people indulge whenever they are pushed into a confrontation with the mass media. What normally is hidden from view is pushed into the open and the self laid bare for all to see.

Games as self-disclosure

Similarly, in normal social interaction, we are often placed in situations in which all the masks are dropped, and the interactors are involved in a game of truth and consequences. This is the opposite side of the coin to the one to which Goffman attaches so much importance. Of course, truth games may be cynically regarded as a smoke screen behind which other more cardinal and ulterior motives are operating, except that self-disclosure often seems to be cathartic in effect. Possibly, *it might be better to conceive of the game aspect of conduct in terms of a dialectic between concealment and disclosure, between lying and the truth.* Interaction involves role-enactment, it involves the striking of appropriate bargaining poses, it involves the negotiation of identity, it involves the adherence to certain rules etc., but it also involves the direct confrontation between persons as emotional beings. It is this aspect of interaction which is ignored by social theory. We do not have to adhere to the theoretical underpinning of Jourard's system, yet I think we can agree with him when he writes of some role-relationships as being fundamentally opposed to emotional functioning. Certainly the truth can be a terrible means of encountering the other. This is not a plea for a certain type of personality theory, rather it is an intuition of what actually goes on in social encounters. To assume that all social encounters are describable in terms of role-enactment, or rule-adherence, is to negate a critical component of human experience, which we can roughly equate to the phenomenological. This is not an argument for phenomenology as a philosophical system, only a redressing of the balance in social theory, where so much is taken for granted as being the result of the internalization of normative expectations. The neglect of self-

138

disclosure by sociologists is understandable, particularly in the context of their commitment to cultural and social determinism. However, having said all this, there is no reason to believe that the need for disclosure is the only critical dimension of interaction – it certainly is not. Nevertheless, behind role-performance there is the saliency of a valued 'role-identity' in which the individual has vested a great deal of emotional energy – the disclosure of such an identity is the reserved privilege of only a selected few close acquaintances, and even then we are led to believe that the identity projected will be closely monitored by the internalized expectations of others.

Certainly as interactors we are victims of an ideology which places enormous emphasis on the motives of others as being deceitful. At the same time we are subject to a dual and ambiguous attitude towards the truth as an ethical imperative. Our childhood is often governed by the categorical imperative implicit in so much of Western religious and ethical thought which enjoins us to tell the truth, no matter the consequences, but as has often been pointed out, this imperative is accompanied by its opposite, namely the injunction to keep one's eye on the main chance.

Concealment is socially given but so is the unmasking and disclosure of truth. But the premium put on truth is high, especially in the context of 'mass society' in which we are forced to accept a view of modern man as an 'other directed' role-performer. It is assumed that most men define the situation from the viewpoint of egoistic advantage. The premium put on self-disclosure has traumatic consequences as indicated in the psychic costs involved in revealing the self in psychotherapeutical sessions: [13]

Self-disclosure, letting another person know what you think, feel, or want is the most direct (though not the only means) by which an individual can make himself known to another person. Personality hygienists place great emphasis on the importance for mental health of what they call 'real self being', self-realization, discovering oneself and so on. An operational analysis of what goes on in counselling and therapy shows that the patients and clients discover themselves through self-disclosure to the counsellor. They talk and, to their shock and amazement, the counsellor listens. I venture to say that there is probably no experience more horrifying and terrifying than that of self-disclosure to significant others whose probable reactions are assumed, but not known. Hence the phenomenon of resistance. This is what makes psychotherapy so difficult to take, and so difficult to administer. If there is any skill to be learned in the art of counselling and psychotherapy, it is the

art of coping with the terrors which attend self-disclosure and
the art of decoding the language, verbal and non-verbal, in which
a person speaks about his inner experience.

The notion that self-disclosure is almost impossible in social
relationships is discounted by the phenomenon of friendship.
Friendship is seldom studied empirically by social scientists, except
in terms of liking patterns based on studies of sociometric choice.
Indeed, outside the sexual relationship, it is probably the most
obvious example of a direct phenomenological relationship between
people. It is difficult to conceive of friendship purely in terms of
role-performances – it is, of course, possible to talk about the role
of a friend as if it involved a set of expectations which are
prescribed normatively, but friendship is more than this, particularly in the context of self-disclosure. However, self-disclosure is
not confined to friendship, it is often encountered in situations
where the participants are strangers. The stranger who tells you
his life story on a train is an example of this, like the paradigm case
of the 'Ancient Mariner' in Coleridge's poem.

It is not self-disclosure which has been of interest to sociologists
unfortunately. Many sociologists are still under the spell of exchange and bargaining theory.

Interaction as exchange

We have by implication been looking at various aspects of exchange theory throughout this section. An examination of its
manifestations at the hands of such diverse theorists as Homans,[14]
Blau,[15] and Thibault and Kelley[16] is beyond the scope of this
essay. We have already considered Homans's view that interaction
can be considered partly in terms of reciprocal behaviour which is
shaped by its pay-off function. We have already admitted to the
proposition that exchange is partly present in all interaction
episodes. However, we have not accepted that it is necessary to
conceive of all exchange purely in terms of an economic transaction
mediated through the exigencies of reinforcement psychology,
although we may admit that some form of stimulus–response tie-up
may be the mechanism for interaction. What we have done is to
distinguish (in the manner of Rickman and his mentors Dilthey and
Rickert[17]) between 'mechanisms' and 'expressions'. Expressions
can be described as those culturally defined and socially validated
symbols which have meaning for social actors and through which
humans obtain selfhood. Mechanisms are the actual given biological
and physical means whereby meaning is conveyed – in other words,
in the language of communication theory, we can speak of them

140

as channels or media. In exchange theory, as considered by Homans, we can readily assent to the idea that exchange is a matter of reward–cost contingencies without violating our further requirement that all human interaction is basically expressive and, therefore, symbolic.

What passes between two human beings in indirect and direct encounters can be seen to be a matter of one party giving something (value, object etc.) in return for psychologically equivalent benefits from others. We can also admit to the possibility that such exchange generates mutual obligations, or if preferred a norm of reciprocity, but we cannot assent to the proposition that there is nothing beyond the exchange process itself, because if we do so, all we are doing is to submit a new deterministic thesis in which exchanges between mechanisms are seen as all there is to human social interaction. We also assent to the proposition that what is exchanged is, in fact, the meanings that social actors have constructed for themselves. Simmel long ago conceived of interaction in exchange terms, but he did not see it as an economic transaction. I can do no better than quote Nisbet on this and his discussion on Simmel's notion of gratitude: [18]

> Gratitude originates . . . from interaction and in interaction, specifically the interaction we call exchange. But in gratitude we have subjectified exchange, or rather the subjectified product of exchange, instead of the objectified kind to be found in the more tangible forms of goods. Simmel defines gratitude as the sentiment which, for inner reasons, effects the return of a benefit where there is no external necessity for it. For example, I may find myself in a dangerous or ticklish situation; another person stops long enough to help me out of it. In an objectified form of exchange I should pay him with goods or money. In the more likely subjectified mode however, my end of the exchange consists of the gratitude I experience, convey to my good samaritan, and, in a very real sense, store up in my own consciousness. Did the good samaritan come to my rescue because of his desire for gratitude? Such an ascription would be too simple. But were I to reward his assistance to me with chilly indifference or hostility a vital exchange relationship would have been ruptured. My ingratitude would be exchange, no doubt, but of a sort not likely to aid the social bond.

There is, in other words, an element of exchange in every social relationship, but this does not mean to imply that exchange is a calculative relationship. I give gratitude to those who have helped me, not because I believe it will stand me in good stead in the future, but because I have no other way of responding to the others' actions – in this sense the exchange is almost automatic. Subjectively, gratitude does not have to be objectified – all that is needed is some sort of symbolic acknowledgment that the helped one is aware that the other has acted in a helpful way. Moreover, as Nisbet notes, gratitude does not have to be expressed to an individual in the interpersonal situation – as long as an individual exists for whom we express admiration, like a musician or an artist, we are in some form of exchange-relationship, even though it cannot be conceived of as a bargaining-relationship. It is the introduction of the notion of bargaining into exchange that highlights the Homans model. Yet bargaining does not have to be considered as being essential to a theory of exchange, particularly at the subjective and phenomenological level.

The assumption that exchange is purely an interpersonal process is, of course, not tenable. At its broadest, exchange in economic terms is a network of transactions which have international ramifications. At the structural level, it is appropriate to see the relationships between role players as exchange-relationships which they negotiate as representatives of interests or groups. Exchanges are, therefore, governed by normative requirements. Societal interaction is seen as being negotiated by organizational representatives who exchange values and goods with other such representatives so that cost–benefits are psychologically equivalent. In an ideal equilibrium state, it would seem that a social system would approximate to its optimum state when it ensures that exchanges minimize social costs. Thus, if a social system could be devised in which all exchanges are aimed at the maximization of benefits for all participants, then we could talk about psychological and social equilibrium. If exchanges were perceived and felt to be unequal, then it follows that the system would not be satisfactory.

These equilibrium assumptions are appropriate to systems theory. When applied to exchange-relationships, it is likely that we are on very dangerous ground. We can say, descriptively, that men at both the interpersonal and organizational level are busily engaged in exchanging subjective and objective values. We are on slippery ground when we go on to extend the metaphor to such processes as power, and the unequal distribution of resources and facilities. We are also on dangerous ground when we assume that economic exchange is a paradigm for social exchange. Men exchange because they need other men in order to cope with the demands of an overwhelming environment; they also exchange with others in order to become men. In this respect, socialization is not simply the internalization of the social requirements of other men but is a process in which men mutually construct identities. It is in this sense that we can conceive of exchange as being a central process in social bonding and not merely the reward–cost schedule.

Power, love and trust

Blau has extended the framework offered by Homans and others to include such dimensions as power, love and trust. Again the reward–cost relationship is stressed. Exchange-relationships, in this view, are inversely related to the degree of commitment that interactors bring to the relationship. Thus, in a love affair the more committed men and women are to each other in purely emotional and feeling terms, the more likely is it that we cannot bring exchange-analysis into play. Bargaining is, in theory, at a minimum. Nevertheless, there is always the possibility that in such a relationship, one party is more committed than the other. In such a situation, the person who is not so involved can easily put himself in a position of power, in the sense that he or she is acting from a perspective in which the other is at a disadvantage. It follows that exchange between individuals at the interpersonal level will be shaped by non-calculable factors. It is only when the exchange is perceived to be uneven that questions of exploitation come into play, that is, bargaining postures are struck. However, Blau argues strongly for a prevailing rate of exchange, that is, for a generally accepted set of norms which legitimate the ongoing activity. In other words, exchange is governed by non-exchange considerations. Exchange at the social level is based on what Blau calls an intermediate relationship between pure calculative conduct and the expression of love: [19]

> However even economic transactions and love relations rarely express the polar processes in entirely pure form, since the multiple gains and costs typically involved in any economic transaction prevent unambiguous calculation of advantage, and since extrinsic benefits are exchanged in love relationships and often help to produce mutual affection. Economic institutions, such as the impersonal market and the contract that stipulates the precise terms of the exchange, are designed to separate concern with distinct objects of exchange from other considerations and to specify the exact obligations incurred in a transaction, thus maximizing the possibility of rational calculation. Social exchange, in contrast, involves unspecified obligations, the fulfillment of which depends on trust because it cannot be enforced in the absence of a binding contract. But the trust required for social exchange is generated by its own gradual expansion in a self-adjusting manner.

143

Trust, therefore, is generated in exchange, but we are at the heart of a paradox here. Presumably, before one enters into an exchange-relationship, we have to somehow take a jump into the unknown by committing ourselves to the other in the hope that he will reciprocate in kind. In other words, the conditions of trust precede the actual exchange, yet we are told that trust itself is generated in exchange. We are faced with the same difficulty as with the norm of reciprocity. We have to assume an established pattern of norms – a climate of trust which exists independently of the interaction. And yet, the main thrust of exchange theory is to pinpoint those actual processes which are believed to be at work in the construction of social relationships. However, these difficulties are overcome (in theory at least) by the assumption that exchange can be treated in two ways, namely, indirectly and directly. When it is treated in the indirect manner, it is seen as being macroscopic and organizational, it becomes institutionalized in a set of rules and norms which are historically extant in a society at any particular moment. Norms are crystallized exchanges which have been found to be rewarding in the past. At the direct level, interactors are busily engaged in conducting themselves in such a way that their current interactions are reminiscent of a gigantic spider's web, so that future generations will find themselves facing the crystallized products of present interaction.

All exchange theorists, including Blau, see exchange as being based on the self-interests of actors who are ultimately interested in the maximization of their own well-being by engaging in a process of exchange with others. Over time it is believed that these exchanges develop into secure social relationships as expressed in the rules, procedures and culture of a society. Ultimately, these norms, rules and cultural definitions become rewarding in their own right. Their origins are forgotten and blurred. A close analysis of behaviour would allow us to discover the same forces at work in indirect exchanges as are at work in more direct exchanges. We can, of course, get involved in a complicated analysis of the pay-off matrix in the manner of Thibault and Kelley,[20] but this would be beyond the scope of this book. Certainly, the whole question of bargaining involves us in the notion of strategic interaction and the assumption of game-like behaviour.

Exchange and power

There is also the added complication arising out of the question of power in an exchange-relationship. In its simplest form it can be argued that power derives from an inequality of exchange resources. Thus, if one partner in an exchange has not got access to the same facilities and resources of the other, then he is at a disadvantage since he has to offer more of his services in order to obtain less. At the psychological level, if one actor withholds approval from the other, and approval is the sole value that he desires, then the second actor can profit by withholding or rationing approval. In a sexual relationship, where the woman desires both the love and approval of her lover, she might find herself in a situation whereby she offers him sexual services and monetary and material inducements in order to maintain the semblance of a relationship. In this way, the man in question can and does achieve a position of power, the woman having become completely dependent on him for her self-regard and her emotional satisfaction.

At the organizational level, power can be conceived of as a set of exchanges between individuals and groups with differential access to scarce resources. Exchange-relationships are maintained, or believed to be maintained, by the manner in which all parties to the exchange see it is to their mutual benefit to exchange unequally. Moreover, some of these exchanges are not direct, but indirect. This means that exchanges have their origin in prior conditions. Furthermore, unequal resources are a function of past accumulation and education, and cannot be regarded as a consequence of current interaction.

In a sense, exchange theory seems to live in the eternal present, where power is analysed in the context of unequal allocations taking place in the 'here and now'. It seems to ignore the fact that most inequalities are historically located. Certainly, new power relationships are constructed in the process of interaction, but it is not easy to ignore the results of the past.

There is also the possibility that individuals in an exchange may become the victims of tactical alliances and coalitions which force the outnumbered party against the wall.[21]

In multiperson encounters, some of the participants may band together, tacitly or explicitly, as a coalition to influence the bargaining process in the encounter as a whole. They may do so in an attempt to coerce others into granting concessions in return for the particular resources controlled by that coalition; at an elementary level, this behaviour can be seen in gatherings with unequal sex ratios, which place the scarcer sex in a favourable bargaining position. Coalitions may also form to protect individuals' common investments in an identity that they legitimately share but that is now claimed by an unproven outsider: if a party includes a number of political scientists, for example, and some other person begins to hold forth very knowingly on the political crisis of the day, the political scientists are quite likely to cooperate tacitly in putting him in his place. These reasons are but two of those which coalitions may form in an encounter, but, whatever the reason, it remains true that coalitions more easily acquire power than individuals through such restrictions of free trade.

Exchange theory, like so many approaches in sociology, tends to become a full explanation of all processes in social life. Like game theory it assumes the essential rationality of social actors – it also assumes the essential ubiquity of the hedonic calculus. But, like all metaphors and analogies, it has the tendency of taking over the whole substance of social theory. This is a danger inherent in all theories which purport to give us an alternative to the official paradigm. Exchange theory was offered as an alternative to the official systems model; it stresses the importance of the construction of a set of categories which are supposed to be true to everyday interaction. The trouble is that it has led to the erection of a deductive system which sees exchange as the *deus ex machina* of social interaction. Certainly, exchange theorists have, as yet, not managed to erect a remotely satisfactory structural theory. This presumably is true of all perspectives which start off with an interaction base.

This leads me to the discussion of interaction as the negotiation of identity. This model is a compound mixture of exchange, game and dramatic metaphors. It also has great difficulty in handling structural and power relationships. Yet having said this, we must not assume that power and structure are not conceivable in an interactive framework, nor must we necessarily assume that they belong to different levels of discourse.

8 Interaction as the negotiation of identity

The interaction model derives its rationale from the Meadian position and goes beyond it. It differs from Mead in the way in which the multi-person aspect of the self is emphasized. It tends, in certain versions, to ignore the reflexive nature of the self process and to concentrate only on masking and performance. The key term is *identity*. Who am I? is the fundamental question posed and the answers given are very often couched in the language of social labels. Beyond the assumption of the reflexive self, the contemporary emphasis is on the self as exchange. Identities are bargained for, and once established are put on the market again at a higher price. This means that identity is not considered to be a fixed quality. It has to be constantly confirmed in a complex matrix of social exchange. Thus identity becomes a mask behind which the 'individual' temporarily finds some stability and satisfaction. It does not provide a permanent base for social location. On a superficial level, this trading process would seem to be just as deterministic as the more conformist sociological models. There seems to be the same obsession with the determinate nature of the socio-cultural environment, albeit a social environment which is fantastically fluid, so that the self is never at rest or perceived as a unity. This impression is buttressed by the terminology used by Goffman[1] and others. Terms such as performances, fronts, regions, appearance etc., bear all the marks of externality, that is, they are used to refer to the self as perceived in action, they do not refer to the self as reflexive. However, Goffman does not necessarily suggest that this is all there is to the self. Implicit in the notion of impression-management is the belief that the performance will allow the individual to maximize his personal satisfactions and values. Thus the self is presented for consumption in the hope that the consumers will exchange other values which the individual needs to maintain his own identity (at least that identity which is being used as a bargaining issue). In this respect impression-management entails a commitment to fragmented experiences and a fragmented 'self'.

The need to put on a performance for audience consumption is described in strangely rational and conscious terms. Pushed to its extreme, it seems to imply that a specific identity can be constructed for each particular social situation. We can, therefore, in theory conceive of a multiplicity of identities, each of which is negotiable in interaction. How these identities are related to each other is open to question. Thus, if we assume that each encounter involves a unique identity, and that the performer is aware that he is projecting this identity, then is it not fair to suppose that the actor is using a further identity, a hidden identity to manipulate the projected identity? Goffman[2] argues that we operate between *a back region* in which performances are planned, and where routines are rehearsed, and *a front region*, in which the performance takes place, where ultimately the performance stands or falls. Identities are managed from behind the scenes. Standing behind each performance, then, is a hidden manipulator. Yet we are never certain about this hidden manipulator. Is it to be construed as the 'I' in Mead's sense, or is it yet another identity behind which stands yet another identity? Without doubt this is the crux of the matter. Goffman's manipulator is being taken for a ride – it is being manipulated by an unknown self which is never really acknowledged. This hidden self is apparently a master strategist, a consummate game player, who knows in advance all the minutiae of the interaction field. It is no accident that Goffman has now turned to game theory to further his model of identity management.

Nevertheless, it must not be forgotten that there is another dimension to Goffman's analysis, namely the 'self *qua* character'. The implication here is that if the self is presented, is consistently successful, that is, it is validated by others, the actor will become convinced by his own performance. His interpretation will become or be perceived to be real. The actor achieves the character he tries to represent. Thus, the successful 'con-man' becomes such a proficient expert in the trade he plies that he becomes convinced of the respectability of his profession and justifies it to himself as being in line with the nature of things. Some people are fools and are born to be taken in by other people. Similarly, the individual who successfully sells himself as an intellectual and is accepted at face value because he has played the game so well will in time begin to be convinced of his own intellectuality. The labels that others attach to his performance are internalized as part of the way he begins to perceive himself. Thus, what starts off as a trading gambit, ends up as value capital for the actor. He now believes in himself intrinsically as an intellectual.

Role identity

McCall and Simmons have extended and elaborated the interpretative function of the performed self. Their emphasis is on reflexivity, and they do not give the impression of complete subservience to 'externality', although they seem committed to exchange theory and impression management. The central concept they use is that of role-identity. Role-identity is defined as:[3]

the character and role that an individual devises for himself as an occupant of a particular social position. More intuitively such a role identity is his imaginative view of himself as he likes to think of himself being and acting as an occupant of that position.

This role-identity is always being imaginatively rehearsed for presentation in social encounters. Every social encounter is a negotiating situation in which identities are marketed at their current market value. This current market value is dependent on what the authors call the overall 'salience' of a given role-identity. Salience is defined by the actor's 'definition of the situation' and by his unique configuration of role-identities, which enable him to organize his behaviour in any situation. Thus, the salience of an individual's identification with his role as a university academic will depend on the way in which he perceives himself as a 'character' in other roles. If the role of academic does not make much demand on him, or if his identification with the role is minimal, then it is probable that his performances as an academic will not be convincing, either to himself or to others.

Role-identities are continuously being rehearsed in preparation for performances in the hope that performances will be supported and rewarded by role partners and audiences. In addition, there is also apparently a need for role-legitimation. We need confirmation of the way we interpret our identities from other people, but experience teaches us that there is always a discrepancy between our own interpretations, and those of our role partners. The identity we project in interaction is subject to misinterpretation. As a result, the actor is motivated to bridge the gap between his projected idealized image, and the image that the audience holds. It is in this sense that interaction can be conceived of as being a transaction – a bargaining process, that is, a negotiation of identities. Interaction becomes a contest with the participants engaged in legitimation of their identities:[4]

If an important role identity has been unequivocally threatened by loss of role support from an important audience, one is likely to experience misery and anguish. He may attempt partially to alleviate this reaction by shifting his identity hierarchy by giving higher salience to his more successful role identities. He deprecates the threatened identity – chiding himself for being so obsessed with it and derogating the audience that holds it to be so important. That is, he tries to maintain a going concern psychologically by reducing his investment in the threatened role identity. In a sense, he thus sacrifices a role identity in an attempt to save the standing of the self as a whole.

What constitutes the standing of the self as a whole is, of course, the real problem. If it is assumed that the identities will be sacrificed for the maintenance of a minimal degree of self-regard, then we are assuming that the individual needs to see himself in some form of favourable light, and that identities are donned in order to maximize self-esteem. Presumably, at the centre of the layer of identities that the individual clothes himself in there is one which is crucial and important to maintain at all costs. This core-identity will be defended by all the psychological weapons in the individual's system of defence mechanisms etc. Psychological balance is achieved by maintaining a delicate relationship between the salient core-identity, and the countless 'encounter-identities' employed to sustain its integrity. McCall and Simmons are very much influenced by the work of Weinstein and Deutschberger[5] and their social bargaining model. There is implicit in their work, the constant necessity not only to negotiate one's own identity, but also, to predict and altercast the other's identity. Thus one's own identity is partially dependent on the identity of the others in a particular context. A misinterpretation of an identity leads to embarrassment and to psychic pain. Always, there is the implication that the individual is under pressure to alternate his identities to meet the other's presentation.

This is still the reflexive self making indications to itself. It is still the self as 'duration' – as 'memory' – referring back to its past experiences, as yet not completely fragmented.

Logically, it must be admitted that the claim for fragmentation can only be made by assuming that behaviour is constituted by thousands of discrete units which are not co-ordinated in any way at all. Complete fragmentation would necessitate a belief in the possibility of social existence being constituted of a multiplicity of individuals who themselves are a multiplicity of insulated identities. What fragmentation means is not the severing of any rational contact with social existence, but rather a feeling that the lives that individuals live in mass society are not genuine but hidden and masked. In order to survive, the individual must lie to himself and to others so as to maintain a modicum of self-esteem. But the strain of having to project relevant identities in different situations proves too much for most of us, so consequently, there is an element of inconsistency and dissonance between identities in various contexts (inconsistency being variously described in metaphors of alienation and anomie).

Masking, lying and deception

The image conjured up by this description of man is not very pretty but is believed to fit the facts, just as the image of economic man was supposed to fit the facts in the last century. Indeed, on closer inspection, man as a 'hypocrite' is really an updated version of 'Homo Economicus'. Goffman has unwittingly become its most eloquent spokesman in sociology. At one level, there is the belief that social existence is predicated upon a minimal amount of lying. Without lying as a safety valve, the social system would find it very difficult to maintain itself. Truth is believed to be unbearable in certain circumstances and situations, particularly those associated with death and disease. Also, in everyday interaction 'white' lies are institutionalized, so as to provide the mechanisms for smooth social transactions. There is nothing startling about this, but recently there has been a tendency to see all social behaviour in terms of performances which are basically nothing more than dramatic lies.

If I manage to perform well as a lecturer and convince my audience that what I am doing is 'intrinsically believed in', and that I believe in my subject, then I have managed to carry off a successful lie. But at the same time, my audience is set to pick up cues about my performance. They have been programmed to believe that it is conceivably only a performance and not a character which they see. In other words, they expect people to put on acts, to present selves, to project identities. Also, they have been exposed to a tradition which legitimates scepticism; science itself argues that things are not what they seem. Moreover today this attitude goes further than healthy scepticism. The mass media and the advertising syndrome have had one striking unanticipated consequence. They have convinced audiences that the goods for sale are dressed up and packaged, and that underneath the brand-names, they are still the same standardized products. Similarly, performances put on by actors are suspect and, in fact, are recognized as performances. Behind the performances are believed

151

to be scheming manipulators. Genuine identity is never presented for confirmation.

Identity or mask?

But what is one's real identity? Is it purely social confirmation from relevant others? If identities are conceived of as masks, is there nothing else but masks? If social interaction is only the negotiation of identities, then it follows that what is established in interaction is nothing else but a transitory mask which one assumes until the next encounter. In addition, we are faced with a dilemma, namely the belief that some identities are donned *at will* to meet appropriate situations, while simultaneously we also assume that some identities are *fostered onto us* against our will. Some identities like that of the introvert are labels which others employ to describe our behaviour and which we might be forced to accept. To be called a thief, for example, depends on a whole number of criteria, including the official definitions of thief. Yet is there any criterion by which I call myself a thief, other than the one employed in the current official definitions? Can I play the role of thief without some commitment to my activity? Is a point reached in which my entire self-definition is coloured by the role-identity 'thief'? If thieving is a mask for another identity, then conceivably, this other identity might be considered to be more salient and real. However, this more salient identity might again be employed as an interaction ploy which we bring into play in order to convince appropriate audiences. My identity as thief is one which I believe that I have been forced into by circumstances beyond my control. My identity as 'environmental victim' is one that I play for all its worth in front of selected audiences. In front of another audience, presumably, I will play the role of thief again, but possibly 'cynical thief'. Am I ever in a position to reveal my essential *core-identity*, my essential being so to speak? Not if we construe all social behaviour as being essentially one of performance and counter-performance. Goffman argues, in all his works, that the human scene is one of pretence and cynicism. He seems to imply that it is the sociologist's job to look behind the scene and expose the monumental fraud perpetuated by men in social encounters. The trouble is, we are never sure of exactly what is left after the dissecting process is over. Impression-management, while constituting a crucial element in social interaction, is surely not the whole story. There are moments when the presented self is intuitively cognized by the actor as being a mask, behind which, possibly, there is a suffering anxiety-prone human being. There is also the possibility that the actor manages to transcend his role-

152

identity, in the sense that he is able to perceive his involvement in social relationships, not only as performing animal, but as a historical actor, that is, his relationships with other men are perceived as being partly dependent on the pattern of dominance and subservience of the society of which he is an active participant.

The trouble with the masking thesis is that we are never sure of the exact relationship of men to other men in actual institutional contexts. Granted that the category thief is a label used by one group of men to label another group of men, we have no way of understanding the mechanisms behind the labelling process unless we look for identity in negotiation processes which not only point to the *naming* of parts, but *also* to the operation of power in social relationships. The stigmatized person is not stigmatized at the personal whim of particular individuals. He is usually stigmatized according to socially enforced rules and norms. In a society of thieves there is no stigma attached to the act of thieving. It is only those whose property has been stolen who attach stigma to the category thief. It is precisely because those who do the labelling are able to exert pressure on law-enforcement agencies that the identity thief assumes meaning. Labels are internalized, but they are not internalized in some hit-and-miss fashion. Those people who have been treated as thieves will often assume the identity of thieves.

Identities then are not worn on one's sleeve. They do tend to relate to critical life experiences. Masks, on the other hand, are forms of identities which are employed to maximize the benefits or minimize the losses accruing from social contexts. Masking employs the tactics of everyday hypocrisy and lying, whereas identity is intrinsically related to the self process itself, albeit a fragmented self. For Goffman, identity seems to have evolved into the mask. This is a reflection of the superficiality of human relationships in modern Western society and is intimately connected to the view of man implicit in the 'mass society thesis'. If all behaviour is seen as a façade, or even charade, then the substance of the human is nebulous and indeterminate. In a sense, masking is the sociological equivalent to the dream world of advertising, in which products are sold without any conviction that they really do represent anything of value at all. The loss of meaning that contemporary men are believed to experience, or the identity crisis that they are supposed to be facing, is precisely the realization that identity has been replaced by the mask.

If this is true, then perhaps identity fragmentation is not necessarily the imaginative construction of way-out social scientists, but may be the actual picture of the actual social world as it is now experienced. Individuals find relief from the pressures of society

153

by adopting poses, masks, identities which enable them to cope both with their *perceived potential psychological* fragmentation and the *fragmentation of social relationships*. The thief finds meaning in his thieving because it indicates to him that there is a component of his person which is different from the *personas* approved by the official agencies of the society. The deviant identity then becomes perceived as being valuable in a world of make-believe. It becomes a point of sentience, an axis of meaning. Thus, what was a mask becomes a crucial focus of personality. The thief solves his identity problems by accepting his deviancy as expressing his real nature! It is not a solution which is presented to him as a completely free option. Nevertheless, there are possibilities for improvisation even within the most rigidly prescribed labels. The identity of Jim Crow, for example, is traditionally believed to depict subservience, the smiling image of black acceptance. It never occurred to whites, social scientists included, that the Jim Crow role could be played with one's tongue in one's cheek. At best it was believed that the shaping forces of the white world had created this identity, yet it is equally conceivable that this identity was used as a strategy of survival by blacks, that they were masking in order to survive.

Goffman[6] has spelt out the role-distance situation with a great deal of insight. There is no need to assume that identities are accepted automatically once they have been prescribed. Indeed, the choice of identity is often up to the individual. He does not have to 'become' the identity. Usually, he presents the identity for approval to confirming others. If they confirm the identity, then the identity is appropriate for future negotiation. This is the case in stable social contexts in which the rate of social change is within manageable limits. The problem of identity-management in periods of rapid social change is another thing altogether. The rate of change, it is argued, has the result of forcing people into a constant process of revamping. The old cues disappear, the old roles and identities are no longer valid. Faced with the impossible task of keeping up with the technological and occupational revolution, men are faced with identity crises. They find it difficult to negotiate their identities at the old market value. For example, the identity of 'classical music lover' is not only regarded as being 'square' but is considered to imply some rigid political attitude. The question Who am I? becomes more than a parlour game, but an obsession. If there is no fixed point of location, no firm ground on which to stand, the individual finds himself in a constant search for a reference point from which to sail the seas of social change. Sociologists point to the superficiality of human relationships, to the mobility of place and status, to the flux of friendships and to the frequency of mass media fads etc., as indexes of identity frenzy.

Yet this does seem to be an over-statement. Role-distance does not necessarily imply complete detachment from reality. To say that nobody knows who he is, is tantamount to saying that the social world is completely formless and meaningless. It is true that men project different identities in different situations, but surely this is not the same as saying that they are not aware of some type of structure in their self–other systems. Probably it is appropriate to speak of the *alternation of identity*[7] rather than the full assumption of a new identity. Men are exposed to different symbolic and behavioural situations at an increasingly accelerated rate and this involves the individual in committing himself to alternative identity projections. Yet these projections are not necessarily permanent, nor do they imply a complete reinterpretation of the social world, except in extreme cases.

Alternation?

What they do involve is a feeling of anxiety, a lack of structure, a lack of belief in the 'givenness' of the social world. If today I have to assume the identity of *cynical* sociologist to meet the ploys of colleagues in the senior common room, and later on the identity of *committed* sociologist to students, this might be regarded as being part of the normal condition of the category academic. What is certain is that one does not *become* a cynical sociologist in one situation and a dedicated sociologist in another. The contexts and situations are different. There should be no difficulty in recognizing the same individual masquerading behind both identities. At another level, the consequences might be a bit more profound. The alternation between Jewish identity at home and student identity at university could have results which entail not only anxiety, but also a degree of dissociation. It is precisely in these cases that we begin to talk about fragmentation. Yet, there is no need to talk about complete commitment. There is no reason to suppose that a Jewish student can't assume *both* identities without becoming two *different* people. Some students alternate without any trouble at all. However, when Jewish identity is challenged by the identity of a radical student, then we are faced with the situation in which one set of self-perceptions colours both identities. The Jewish identity becomes submerged; in Freudian terms, it becomes repressed. Moreover this alternation is not achieved without some psychic costs, particularly costs accruing to one's sense of location.

Alternation does not have to imply commitment. The student

L

radical identity involves a set of behaviours, meanings, symbols, expressions, which are confirmed by other student radicals. It does not involve a complete revamping of the self concept. Ironically, in other contexts, the student radical might very well be working for an organization which is a mainstay of the 'establishment'. (Respectability is yet another identity which is situationally located.) The problem, then, is to specify the actual situations to which an identity refers. The old group identities such as status, class, ethnic affiliation, region, family, are not regarded as constituting firm enough bases for affiliation. Again, this is the 'mass society' thesis intruding. Some theorists like Orrin Klapp[8] have gone so far as to argue that since these secure anchorages have disappeared, the search for new identity becomes the sole activity of Western man. Clichés like the search for meaning and identity voyages are spun out with great aplomb in the belief that all human existence can be understood in terms of the quest for symbolic significance. This may be so, but it does not demonstrate the thesis that the self is completely fragmented. All it does is to reinforce the view that different aspects of the self are mobilized in different situations; it does not demonstrate the equivalence of the self and society.

What is described as fragmentation may be the normal way in which men relate to each other. This seems to be what Gregory Stone is getting at when he argued that identity can be conceived as the result of the interplay between the processes of apposition and opposition.[9]

Identity is established as a consequence of two processes, apposition and opposition, a bringing together and setting apart. To situate the person as a social object is to bring him together with other objects so situated, and, at the same time to set him apart from still other objects. Identity is intrinsically associated with all the joinings and departures of social life. To have an identity is to join with some and depart from others, to enter and leave social relations at once.

Identity as announcement v. discursive identity

Stone goes on to distinguish four types of connotation that the term identity has in social contexts.

(a) *Terms relating to universality* Such as age, gender, group, etc. These identities conceivably are to be considered as being immutable, or at least they *were* often defined as immutable. Today, however, immutability is no longer taken for granted. Sex identity

156

for example, being subject to alternation and the juxtaposition of both male and female roles.

(*b*) *Names and nicknames* Names place one in a context, but do not provide substantive identity except, perhaps, in the case of status–passage identities. Nicknames can sometimes serve as the passport to a wholly new identity. Thus, the naming of an individual in terms of personal characteristics often has the consequence of defining those characteristics for the individual as an aspect of his identity. In the case of stigmatization this process has far more serious consequences both at the psychological and the interactive level.[10]

(*c*) *Titles* Such as typical marital and occupational role-specifications. As we have seen in our discussion of role-identities, a role can have salient identificatory dimensions for the social actor. Also, role-identifications often function as mechanisms of anticipatory socialization. More prosaically, titles are indexes of social placement. They indicate the socially defined expectations of both the actor and the other in future and present interaction. Hence, the title carpenter, while having reflexive meaning for the individual carpenter, is also a means whereby he announces his identity to all and sundry.

(*d*) *Relational categories* By this, Stone means transitive interactions which are institutionalized without necessarily becoming a substantive aspect of identity. Thus, the relationship between bus conductor and passenger is not necessarily one which looms largely in the passenger's consciousness.

What Stone is doing here is to place much neglected emphasis on the notion of identity not just as a labelling process, but also on identity as an *announcement* on the part of an individual about his interpersonal and structural location, his situation. (Stone does this in the context of a discussion of the importance of clothing as a symbolic announcement.) Thus, the individual answers the question Who am I? by declaring on the open market his own claims to an approximate identity. If others accept this announcement and cash the claim, his identity is established. This announcement must not be confused with the discursive identity that is appropriate to Mead's discussion on the self as an exercise in symbolic role-taking. Before one can take the role of the other, one must be able to identify the other. Certainly, we know ourselves through the reflected appraisals of others, but we can't know ourselves without identifying the other. Stone argues that, in the first instance, this involves an *identification of* and, in the second instance, an *identification with the other*. We can only identify the other if he is in the position to announce his claims to a specific and relevant identity. The child would find it very difficult to take the role of significant others if he was not provided with the appropriate cues which enable him to recognize the significant other. Indeed, one would find it impossible to take the role of the other unless the other has successfully announced that he is such and such a person.

The failure of sex-identifications reported from the clinical litera-ture is not only due to breakdown of discursive role-taking, it is also partly to be attributed to the inability of the child to recognize the appropriate stimuli emanating from his two parents. If the mother *gives off* impressions, or announces herself in an identity which is atypical or ambiguous, then the child is not likely to internalize his cues successfully. Therefore, in the context of asking 'Who am I?' we must be careful to distinguish between identity as announcement and identity as role-taking. They both constitute aspects of the total process of self–other relationships. Analytically they have been confused in the past, because it has been too readily assumed that appearance is subsumed in *identification with*.

In this respect, it is quite conceivable that if I announce my credentials as those of a respected or serious academic, I might fail to get my message across, my 'symbols of recognition' are not taken to mean what they were intended to mean. They are mis-interpreted, either because I have been careless in their presenta-tion, or because they are perceived as being false, or lacking in conviction. The identity that I want to establish, my need to be taken seriously is sabotaged by my inability to present appropriate cues, symbols and mannerisms. Although I am recognized as a male sociology academic, my credentials may be regarded as being bogus or superficial. It is only when the claims I make for myself are symbolically exchanged with others that we can say that we have established a mutually acceptable identity. But the snag here is that the cues and symbols that I present could be construed as being artificial and contrived. They could be attributed to faddish masking, rather than the individual *qua* character. It follows, that if both the discursive and announced aspects of self-presentation coincide, then there is no problem about the genuineness of my performance. This coincidence of 'appearance' and 'believed-in identity' is only obtainable when the mask that I am assuming is not consciously contrived, or the act I am putting on seems to be completely authentic, both to myself and to my audience.

Apposition and opposition

We are told by various authorities that the old dimensions of class, family, deprivation etc., are no longer the critical dimensions of human experience, that instead entire groups are busily engaged in searching for meaning or in looking for appropriate identities. Black Power, for instance, is conceived of as a search for Black Identity. This assumes, that without an appropriate identity, the individual, and indeed the whole group, is hopelessly floundering in a morass of meaningless social relationships. To define oneself as a Jew or a Black implies the ability to locate oneself within the confines of a larger domain. If one looks inwards at one's Jewishness, what does one find? Traditional identifications with old expectancies, a commitment to certain family patterns, a belief in the immutability of suffering etc. If one argues that one's Jewish identity is disappearing in the face of a complex bureaucratic society, this is countered by asserting that it is precisely because of these demands that this identity must be cultivated. To call oneself a Jew will often depend on who one believes is noticing one's Jewishness. Noticing can mean anything from mild disapproval to the extremes of the pathological anti-semite. One's self-definition as a Jew is only brought into play when others are pointing fingers. Typically, one's response might be to *announce* Jewish identity in as elaborate a way as possible or, alternatively, to mask by assimilating.

In either case, announcement or masking involves the individual in a modification of other levels of self-functioning. If, in addition to his announcement, he has already staked a claim to the identity of intellectual, then the original impetus of the Jewish identity will have pronounced implications for the intellectual claim. It will come to colour his entire existence, particularly at a time when Jews are under attack. Similarly, the masking or hiding response will have equally far-reaching effects. When, for example, the stigmatization of the category Jews becomes legitimated, then masking becomes an intolerable strain. Other identities are put to the severest test by the anxiety that the hostile gentile world might find one out. The technique often employed here is to join the enemy – emulate his behaviour, even become a Jewish anti-semite, or completely to control and repress Jewishness. In so doing, one's other identities are subject to constant supervision in order to ensure that the slightest hint of Jewishness does not show through.

To go back to Stone: we can conceive of Jewish identity as being dependent on the two processes of apposition and opposition. Jews are situated in a context by belonging to a specific category; they join together with other Jews mutually to construct an identity.

159

At the same time, they set themselves apart from other groups and relationships, and in setting themselves apart, they find they are helped or forced to do so by others who have defined them as a certain kind of social object. They will tend to exhibit the characteristics implicit in the original social definition. From the other's point of view, Jewish identity can be defined along the four criteria discussed by Stone. Jewish characteristics are construed as universal, their names point to their Jewishness, their titles and typical roles exemplify Jewish traits and there are relational categories which exemplify their typical behaviour. Thus, even in the most casual instrumental encounters, such as a passenger on a train or bus, the social definition of the Jew intrudes. Jewish identity, then, is maintained by a subtle interplay between announcement and social definition.

Announcement and authenticity

What we really want to know is how the announcement really is freely determined? One does not claim a Jewish or Black identity automatically. We know that parents initially define this identity. Does this identity colour one's entire existence? It might be argued that ethnic identity, especially in the context of a ghetto existence is a crucial element in the individual's self-perceptions. In the Negro child's case, he is faced with the constant reminder of the facts of life, of his poverty and his general deprivation. It is claimed that Negro self-conceptions or identity will reflect these pressures, thereby becoming a focal element in his life. In other words, Black or Jewish identity is the central fact of existence. It is much like the discovery that the thief or other deviants make about their own essential nature. They might conceivably argue that their thieving is purely instrumental, yet at another level, might it not be claimed that the thief is the essential person? Obviously it is not an identity to display to legal enforcement officers, but it demonstrates a claim to some form of authenticity. As Matza puts it in a marvellous passage:[11]

> Without building and conceiving the meaning of his own deviant
> identity the subject would be unprepared for the constructive use
> to which he is to be put. Just as earlier, building the meaning
> of being devious prepared him for meaningful apprehension by
> compounding his deviation, in the same manner conceiving
> himself as an essential deviant prepares him for meaningfully
> representing the deviant enterprise. Apprehended by himself in
> the full philosophical sense, no longer simply one who has been
> bureaucratically apprehended, the subject has become suited

for collective representation. The thief will stand for theft. Though he may resent the part he has come to play, the social use to which he will be put, though he may regard it as unjust, simultaneously he will concur in the common sense that, after all, there is a certain justice in employing an admitted thief whenever an account of theft is sought. Having been cast in a part, he should be put to work. The essential thief is employed as a regular suspect; so too is the one who has not colluded the building of deviant identity, but being unprepared for such socially valuable work, to him the job will have different meaning. Only the ordained thief – one who has witnessed his own deviant identity – can see the limited justice of so strange an employment, only he can build and conceive its full meaning. Those who have not collaborated with Leviathan or have not suffered the misfortune of turning witness against themselves may easily and properly discount the unquestionable attempts by Leviathan to employ them too as regular suspects. With unmitigated indignation or carefree toleration, they – but not the essential thief – may regard such attempts as casual and meaningless employment, or as a temporary mistake, as laughable or as irritating injustice. Their response may be likened to mine when as a doctor (but of the wrong sort) I am asked to prescribe a cure for delinquency. It is simply a case of mistaken identity, or so it may be conceived.

The indignation of the essential thief is marred by his concrete realization of a deviant identity; his toleration is ruined by the care he must take to keep his realization to himself. Innocent of the theft for which he is employed as a suspect, he has philosophically witnessed himself in another and thus he will occur in the poetic justice of being cast a thief by Leviathan. His sense of poetic justice will exist side by side with a more fully displayed sense of injustice. Thus complicated, he becomes even more devious.

The essential thief, or the essential Black, or the essential Jew is thus brought face to face with his identity when that identity is signified by others, but this signification is not to be regarded as merely being the operation of the 'generalized other'. It is not only a question of the internalization of role-expectations, or the attaching of labels to types of behaviour. There is behind the labelling process a far stronger sense of outrage, a cry for authenticity which is not readily available in the official political world around one. Everywhere there are the representatives of authority who are busily concerned with the naming and typification of deviance. The Jew, while constructing his own identity out of a mosaic of his-

161

torical materials which emphasizes his own role as a suffering victim, as the sacrifice to some inevitable historical process, also willingly seems to invite others to the sacrifice. The concentration camps legitimate his need for confirmation as being different and unique. At least this is what the metaphysical identity that he adheres to prescribes for him. In actuality, when the concentration camp functionary presses the correct buttons, the cry of pain is not one of metaphysical *angst*, it is the final surrender to the ultimate significant other – the 'state'. More simply, the identity 'Jew' implies a counter-identity – a Jew hater. The Jew begins to see himself in the same terms as those who have stigmatized him, he becomes the thing that his persecutors believe him to be. Ultimately the gas chambers confirm the Jew's need for martyrdom. But the tragic confrontation in the concentration camps has another result. Jews begin to search for new identities. They go to Israel and revert to a rampant and nationalistic militarism. Becoming Jewish no longer involves the mantle of suffering but the active participation in political and nationalistic activism. Similarly, the old Jim Crow identity which was a well-established stereotype for decades has now been replaced by a more aggressive statement of Black identity, which is constructed out of the Black's own conception of what his identity should be.

The loss of meaning

There is an aspect of identity-negotiation which I have looked at in a peripheral way. This is the often stated postulation of the loss of meaning and location, brought about by revolutionary advances in technology and science. Usually this viewpoint describes the Copernican revolution and the Darwinian apothesis as being blows to man's self-esteem, constituting damaging attacks on his sense of social and metaphysical location, depriving him of his privileged status as the axis of a world view and the centre of meaning. Hence, these erosions of man's self-confidence are partly attributable to the growth of the biological and physical sciences. In addition, it is further argued that it is the social sciences which deal the final death blow. The ugly spectre of social and psychological determination is seen as providing the final step towards 'insignificance' in an indifferent universe. In this respect, the Freudian demonstration that men were not really masters of their own mental worlds, and the sociological claim made by Marx, Durkheim and others, that social behaviour is not random, but subject to the operation of forces outside the control of any one individual, reinforced the belief that men no longer control their futures.

The contemporary experience of war, economic boom and re-cession added fuel to the notion of man's insignificance. In this context, we are left with an identity which, to say the least, is rather tenuous. The old verities of church, family, country, neighbour-hood have evaporated. Thus the question Who am I? is no longer answered by reference to location in a system of meanings deriving from traditional sources. Instead, they have to be answered from the perspective of the individual's own idiosyncratic experiences. The identity that he finds satisfactory will probably be a hit-and-miss affair, since there are no longer any reliable guidelines to chart his course. If both 'God' and 'metaphysics' are dead, then the only substitutes are to be found in personal relationships or 'identity voyages'.

Conceivably, this is only true when we are considering those strata in society who define themselves as intellectuals, or have been placed in a position in which they have been exposed to systematic doubt or scepticism. Strangely enough, this doubt is not *felt* by those whose occupational roles are premised on systematic doubt, namely professional scientists and technologists. It is the new philosophers and social scientists who seem to articulate this loss of meaning. Existentialism finds a ready home among those who believe that there is no appropriate identity for modern man, except the identity implicit in the recognition of the absurdity of the human situation, in the recognition that the human social scene is a façade, in the recognition that this façade is maintained by the use of the most inappropriate means. Thus the cry for authenticity is really a cry for man's true identity, which is be-lieved to be discoverable in his essential solitariness in a world of dead matter.

It is all very well to luxuriate in identity-search when one has the symbolic apparatus to do so – it is easy to discover insignifi-cance on a full stomach. Can we truthfully say that the quest for meaning is part and parcel of the everyday experiences of those countless millions who man the structures of society? There is a sense in which the description of identity-voyage may be seen as the preoccupation of middle-class academics and intellectuals. What importance can one put to the concept when one is talking about cholera in India or genocide in Vietnam?

Selves, identities, roles and fragmentation

All these terms that I have been bandying around seem to have the ability to undergo a 'sea-change' in exposition. What, for ex-ample, is the exact specification of identity *vis-à-vis* 'self concept' or role? As we have noted, McCall and Simmons[12] employ the

163

notion of role-identity which seems to indicate that roles are crucial for the examination of the identity thesis. Both identity and role are relatively new concepts in the social sciences, although they have had histories in other disciplines. Similarly, the self concept has been pivoted to both philosophy and psychology for a long time. Now sociology in particular, has taken over all these terms, especially in the context of trying to get to grips with the problem of social motivation and interaction. Mead,[13] for example, while subscribing to the idea of the self as a social product, was not committed to an over-socialized concept of human conduct. The very fact that the 'I' is not completely under the control of the 'generalized other' assumes that the incipient acts that he talks about, are capable of introducing novelty into otherwise structured situations. The 'already interpreted world' cannot be construed as embodying a mosaic of role-scripts from which the individual faithfully mirrors his own identity. The identities that he constructs are typically his *own* identities, and not those of other men.

Pessimistic sociology argues that these identities are fragmented, and the self concept lost under the weight of role prescriptions and the resulting tension arising from conflicting roles. In this connection, Parsons puts it rather optimistically:[14]

> The fact of increasingly prominent role pluralism, means that individuals are subject to centrifugal pressures in that each context of role involvement has its own distinctive expectations, rewards and obligations. It becomes an imperative of personality functioning to achieve a sufficient level of integration of these components. *The internal conception of what the individual is, is the natural reference point for this integration. . . .*
>
> It seems to be useful and correct to use the term identity in a technical sense to designate the core system of meanings of an individual personality in the mode of object in the interaction systems of which he is part.

It is precisely the expectation that personality will be subject to centrifugal forces around each role-involvement that makes the sociological case so disturbing, because, if the personality is not integrated, if its elements are all pulling in opposite directions, then there can be no core-system of meanings in the Parsonian sense. Whether this is in fact the case is an empirical matter. It can only be resolved clinically in the clinical psychologist's consulting room. If we are to take notice of the evidence from the admission rates into psychiatric institutions in the Western world, then it is a fair assumption that fragmentation is a major problem, at least it is a problem as defined by psychiatry. The construction of identity under these circumstances could be considered to be almost impossible. At a more analytical level, is it possible to speak of a stable self-conception or a sentient identity when the participants in identity-construction are always changing? Or putting it another way, doesn't the interaction process itself vitiate against the stability of the self-conception? As Parsons and others have noted, the criss-crossing of role-relationships in industrial societies makes it very difficult for the individual to establish a core-system of meanings which are in any way related to each other. It is a commonplace of interaction theory that individuals in an interaction episode each define the situation from different, or slightly different, perspectives. It is also a commonplace that the way each actor defines the situation varies from situation to situation, and from time to time. How then can we speak of stability when interaction is subject to continuous reassessment of the other, and his continuous reassessment of me? If my identity is only known from situation to situation, then it must need continuous reaffirmation, and it can obtain confirmation from others who are always there to maintain that identity. In the past, these others were my parents, or my siblings, or the friends that I made in the neighbourhood, or community. Today, the rate of geographic and social mobility is so great that I never have the opportunity to establish social relationships of any great duration or meaning. They are always transitory and highly instrumental.

There is, therefore, a very real commitment to fragmentation in the 'negotiation of identity' model of interaction. In this aspect, both the 'unitary self' and 'social structure' seem to have disappeared. Yet, in a sense, there is a great deal of ambiguity involved here, because of the rather dubious way in which the role concept has been used and abused, especially as a substitute for the self concept.

This theme will concern us in the penultimate chapter.

part three

Conclusion

9 Interaction, selves and social fragmentation

The burial of man under the weight of role specifications is one of the unfortunate consequences of the almost obsessive interest that some sociologists have shown in the role concept (the uses and abuses of role theory demands a library to itself). Although the dramatic metaphor provides the rationale for most of the classic formulations in role-analysis, it does not of itself explain why the role concept has come to be the cardinal conceptual tool for relating the individual to society.

Initially at least, the role concept was used as a unit of analysis, which was, in principle, independent of the individual actors who occupied roles. They were supposed to provide scripts and guidelines for performance, they were not concerned with problems of personality or interpretation. Thus, a role-map of an organization does not make any statements about the unique characteristics of the role-players in the organization. However, the associated notion of role-taking is explicitly concerned with the way in which men learn to play roles, so that they incorporate into themselves the demands and expectations of others. As Gerth and Mills have put it:[1]

Man as a person is a historical creation and can be most readily understood in terms of the roles which he enacts and incorporates. These roles are limited by the kind of social institution in which he happens to be born and in which he matures into adult. His memory, his sense of time, and space, his perception, his motives, his conception of his self – his psychological functions are shaped and steered by the specific configuration of roles which he incorporates from his society.

Now, although role theory is often cast in an interpersonal framework, there is always the implication that roles are dependent on

169

a larger more inclusive system. If the family is considered as a system of interaction between role-partners, then the form of this interaction is seen as being responsive to the inclusive system. And since the family is treated as the primary agent of society, it follows that the individual's personality is produced by the society, albeit differently manifested, depending on the sub-group to which the family belongs. Even though role theory places the locus of determinancy in structured interpersonal encounters, there is no doubt that personality is the dependent variable. Gerth and Mills employ the role concept as the link between the individual and society. The biography of a person is, to a large extent, a reflection of his relationship to the network of institutional orders extant in a society at a particular period of its history. Personality is, therefore, a historical and social creation. Each historical epoch produces its own typical personality. At the same time, the self conceptions of men in society will reflect (it is claimed) the general need of individual men to obtain the approval of significant others. These others, or reference groups, are not only in the immediate family circle or primary group, but are also located at strategic positions in associated institutional orders. In a society in which the military order is emphasized, the individual biography will be exposed to symbolic pressures which endeavour to legitimate a military career and prowess on the battlefield. The soldier's role is incorporated into the self-image by mechanisms attributed to the need to obtain the approval of other members of the institutional order. But since the entire socialization process is directed towards the inculcation of the soldier's role into the personality structures of the members of society, it is not surprising that the individual finds it difficult to develop a self-image which is at variance with the dominant institutional order. In this sense, the individual's 'vocabulary of motives' is not determined by his own unique personality needs, but by the social definition of these needs. The institutional order provides a ready-made set of motives which the individual adapts as his own.

Admittedly, Gerth and Mills[2] are very much aware that there are certain pitfalls associated with a thoroughgoing determinism that the individual is not a mere cipher, yet this does not prevent them emphasizing the fact that role-requirements condition the manner in which the individual construes and reacts to his world.

There is, in other words, a commitment to a view of social interaction which stresses the isomorphic relationship between the individual and society. The concept of individuality is meaningless without the concept of society. Similarly, phenomenological accounts are congruent with, and dependent on, structural determinants. Ever since Durkheim, the emphasis has been on society as the prime mover in the genesis of individuality. Now while one can readily admit that individuality is dependent on the development of certain institutional forms, it seems to be a rather dubious proposition to see individuality as being merely the product of specific socio-cultural forces at a particular historical juncture. There seems to be no reason to doubt that men have always *felt* that there was a fundamental divergence between their own interests and the interests of society. Indeed, this divergence has been intolerable for a great number of people at different points of time.

Hence, there is the implication that interaction is contained within the container of society. Not only is individuality expressible in terms of some notion of the *tabula rasa*, but interaction between individuals is tied to the notion of structured expectation as manifested in the behaviour of two or more social actors. Social exchange, games, self-presentation, the negotiation of identity, etc., are reflections of the larger more inclusive system. Alternatively, the institutionalized relationship between 'ego' and 'alter' becomes a paradigm for the social system. Whatever alternative is chosen, there is the belief that both the micro- and macro-worlds stand in a causal relationship to each other. The opposition of man to society is thereby pushed aside, because it is a cardinal assumption of the sociological credo that there is no such opposition.

Indeed, some sociologists have become so obsessed with what they regard as the false dichotomy between the individual and society that they have completely buried motivation under a vast weight of role-specifications. What image of man does this project?

(1) In the first place the individual is pictured as being infinitely plastic. There is a biological substratum which can be moulded by social forces. This viewpoint is very much in the tradition of John Locke and the notion of the *tabula rasa*. It also fits in with contemporary academic psychology and the ubiquity of the learning process.

(2) Man is primarily motivated by the maximization of self-esteem. Self-esteem is the mechanism whereby individuals are supposed to do the work required for system-maintenance. Self-esteem is intimately tied up with the need for the approval of 'significant others' who tend to push the individual into a position in which his self-esteem coincides with his perception of group norms. Thus, failure to achieve a picture of oneself consonant with the standards of the group forces the individual into even greater efforts to bridge the discrepancy.

(3) The typical mode of adaptation is that of conformity, where conformity is defined as the integration between individual and society. Man conforms because he wants to conform, and he wants to conform because he has no alternative but to conform. In

M

171

other words, society is ubiquitous and the individual merely a manifestation of that society. There is the further implication that men are not responsible for their individual choices, since they are merely the playthings of impersonal social forces.

(4) The deepest core of the subjective testimony of the individual's own sense of self is seen as being dependent on the social sphere. Thus when I ask 'Who am I?' the answer will always be given in terms of the appropriate social labels which I have internalized. There is no escaping the overwhelming presence of society, even in the privacy of paranoia. The dialogue between the 'I' and the 'Me' is contained in the larger dialogue which constitutes society. The answer to 'Who am I?' depends, therefore, on the way *others* have treated and acted towards me.

(5) The individual is thus an embodiment of his group anchorages, either real or imaginary. He becomes the roles he plays, even when he plays some roles with his tongue in his cheek. Nevertheless, some roles will be more salient and rewarding than others and these will tend to generate role-commitment.

(6) Among 'culture and personality' theorists, the commitment to the microcosmic metaphor means that the individual is regarded as a mirror image of the culture in which he is encapsulated. But culture is also an image of personality. They entail each other. Human actors cannot, by definition, act other than in terms of the desired ends which their culture has prescribed for them. They cannot act outside cultural limits, because their motives are themselves cultural products. Thus, internalization implies the embodiment of society in man. Because this metaphor is often saturated with psychiatric notions, it follows that both personality and culture are seen as belonging to the realm of mental illness. The image of the individual that this extreme position implies is one which leaves him dependent on the machinations of a sick society. It also involves the assumption that social and cultural processes themselves are somehow abnormal. We then have the possibility of a neurotic society continuously reproducing itself. In this context, the individual is anxiety-prone, neurotic and open to the whims of any social engineering ideology.

(7) Although there are Freudian overtones in both the anthropological and sociological approaches to personality, there is no doubt that the 'body' and psychological characteristics of individual men are pushed aside. If social structure or culture are conceived of as the main determinants of personality processes, then it is difficult to see how we can usefully talk of individuality except as some form of afterthought. Milton Yinger,[3] in a much neglected work, has pointed to the inherent danger of ignoring one set of behavioural variables at the expense of others. If we are trying to

understand human conduct, then obviously there can be no exclusive approach which includes everything under its conceptual umbrella. To reify the social and demote the psychological is, to my mind, an excessive over-reaction which has bedevilled sociology ever since Durkheim. (It is one of Parsons's[4] merits that he has recognized the importance of variables other than the socio-cultural.) *It seems what is really needed is a biosocial view of man which does justice both to the symbolic aspects of man's nature while not neglecting the biological substratum on which all such symbolic modes are based.* This is not to say that we must immediately embrace some Freudian metaphysic, or jump into bed with ethologists; it does mean that sociology cannot proceed in a theoretical limbo which reifies the autonomy of the social. Yinger writes:[5]

> The effect of the Freudian tradition has been in my judgement, to define these limits too narrowly; but the opposite assumption by some behaviourist psychologists and some anthropologists that the biological influence is almost infinitely malleable seems equally wide of the mark. If the character types developed by Freud in terms of psychosexual development seem at once too biological and too universal (that is, too little affected by cultural variation) the remedy is not to forget that man has an inheritance.

The sociological man which contemporary social theory pre-supposes is then a product of forces outside his control. The individual is compounded of a number of intersecting lines of influence which ultimately are presumed to constitute both the 'form' and 'contents' of his personality. Thus, his typical way of interacting in typical situations is informed by typical definitions of those situations. All this implies a belief in the mechanism which ensures conformity to social and cultural prescriptions, namely internalization.

The problem of internalization

How individuals become social beings occupies a great many social scientists. To say simply that they internalize role-expectations or normative patterns is one thing, but to demonstrate the mechanisms whereby this becomes possible is another. Certainly, at the naïve level, it might be useful to suppose that there is a 'stamping-in' process whereby parents, or other agents, shape behaviour of young children by the application of some reward–punishment schedule. Children become social beings because they learn to be human through precept or example. They learn typical role-requirements, they learn to control impulsive behaviour, they

173

learn how to cope with unexpected situations, and they learn how to adapt to their structurally located positions in the allocative system. They even learn to project appropriate self-images in appropriate situations. What is assumed here is that some form of stimulus–response paradigm is, in principle, all that is needed to give us an account of the way in which individuals learn to conform to social expectations. Social control is replaced by *social self-control*, that is, individuals do not need carrots and sticks to guide their behaviour; it is assumed that they have internalized their own individual carrot and stick systems. Self-control replaces external control, yet it is presumed that conformity is obtained just as effectively as if there were actual carrots and sticks in the external world. This is a caricature of some of the sophisticated models used by social scientists, especially those who employ a social-learning framework; nevertheless, it does highlight the essential features of the learning model of internalization.

The difficulty arises when we ask exactly what is being internalized. Is it the reflected image of the social, or is it the 'shoulds' and 'don'ts' of the normative system, or is it only language and symbols which are internalized? How exactly does one take the role of the other? How does the superego become effective in controlling impulse-behaviour? More generally, in what way can it be said that internalization involves the translation of one conceptual system, namely society, into another conceptual system, namely personality?

The abuse of transitive metaphors

Is it really true to say that internalization means the actual translation of one system into another system so as to generate the complete modification of the second system? The fact that the concept personality seems to contain some of the same dimensions as the socio-cultural system does not entitle us to claim that the one system determines or contains the other. In this respect I quote Wallace: [6]

> the concept of culture is a set of propositions about some of the same propositions which are included within the concept of one or more of the personalities within the society. Thus to use transitive metaphors like internalize, impact, mold, and so on, to describe the relation between culture and personality, is precisely comparable to claiming that a circle has an impact on, or molds, the points which constitute it, or that the points are internalizations (or expressions, or phrasings, or transforms) of the equation describing the circle.

The use of transitive metaphors tends to obscure the real relationship between personality and society. There is no need to conclude that because we can observe the apparent similar behaviour of a large number of individuals in a social context that this similarity means that they are products of the same socialization process, or that they have internalized the same role-prescriptions. If we were in a position to observe the conduct of the inmates of a concentration camp in the last war and found that all of them exhibited the same behaviour patterns, this would not entitle us to draw the conclusion that they are behaving in the same way because they were socialized in the same way. Similarly, when the anthropologist observes uniformities of behaviour in the community he is studying, there is no need to assume that these uniformities are necessarily expressive of personality dimensions which have been shaped by the inclusive culture. The sharing of a culture does not mean that personality is shared, or that everybody interprets the world in the same way. Uniformity of behaviour might be a consequence of social control, as expressed in the naked exercise of force. Certainly, in the concentration camp environment it is primarily the fact that the SS guard had the means of enforcing life or death decisions that ensured uniformity of behaviour. There was only one possible role that the prisoner could play. Any small departure from the script meant the gas chamber. Its sanctions were so explicitly defined that there could be no question of an individual interpreting his role. Conformity to role-expectations, that is, absolute obedience, made all the difference between life and death. The concentration camp was a closed system – there were no alternatives to the prescribed role, the only way to survive was to rigidly conform to the rules and regulations of the camp. It might be argued, that the pressures of the camp were such, that the individual was completely *resocialized* by the internalization of a new set of role-prescriptions.

To a certain extent this is true, but this 'atypical internalization' is not to be considered to be on par with the way in which most of us are socialized in the context of everyday life. Because so much behaviour is repetitive and stereotyped, this does not mean that society is necessarily a super-concentration camp which is constantly imposing its will on its inmates by monitoring their innermost subjective life. *To assent to this proposition is to assent to the microcosmic metaphor and the hypostation of an underlying social current or force.* Internalization does not mean the *subservience* of man to society, nor does it mean the *equivalence* of the individual and society. The mechanisms underlying internalization relate to the process whereby men learn how to cope with other social beings. It does not refer to the encapsulation of one set of variables by another more inclusive set of variables.

Agreed that there is a false dichotomy between social processes and individual processes, yet this false dichotomy can be mis-construed. It can boil down to seeing individuality as expressing the values and ethos of the social system in which it is contained. We do not have to accept the notion of an abstract set of concepts from which both the individual and society are simply to be con-sidered as phases or aspects. While it is appropriate to talk about interpenetration between various levels in the functioning of the individual personality, it is *not appropriate* to talk about inter-penetration as constituting the aggregated properties of these levels. There is no reason to suppose that the individual cannot conceive of himself as being separate from, and also partly responsible for, the social environment of which he is a participant. Although the individuation process involves us in a commitment to a belief in some form of interiorized dialogue between the 'I' and the 'Me', this does not mean that the indications that men make to them-selves are traceable to the historical past, or the immediacy of the situation.

We have noted that there seems to be a tendency to subsume the sociological account of individuality in terms of role theory. Not only does role theory provide the motivational system for person-ality functioning, but it also provides the framework for the develop-ment of the self. The self, as the 'learned repertoire of roles', replaces the self as the self-regulating agent of traditional person-ality theory and philosophy. Both consistency and personality differences can be accounted for by demonstrating the unique exposure of the human organism to different aspects of the social structure. Individuality, from this point of view, is the learning of appropriate norms, values and prescriptions attached to social positions. It assumes that individual behaviour is a pay-off from a location in the social structure. What is completely ignored in this view is the phenomenologically located anchoring of the self process, that is, the self as an axis of meaning. Granted that one can only become aware of the self as a result of social interaction, this does not mean that the individual is incapable of experiencing reality except through the eyes of the other. Although difficult to pinpoint, the experiential self is the focus of the way we define the world and ourselves. It depends to a certain extent on our capacity to announce our experiences no matter how vaguely articulated : [7]

One of the marks which differentiates what is intrinsic to the identity of a person from what is not – often the principal and pragmatically sufficient mark – is that the person has the capacity for spelling out that identity. To spell out, as has long been noticed, is to exercise a peculiar authority, an authority intimately associated with one's existence as a particular person. The point has been both familiar and central in the western philosophical tradition ever since Descartes. This special authority and this intimate relationship to personal identity have traditionally been attributed to the supposed privileged access to the contents of one's own consciousness afforded by introspection. Essentially the same issues have been raised in more recent times by referring to the peculiar force of certain typical uses of the first person present tense of mental verbs. With an authority that no one else has, I can speak regarding what I desire, feel, intend, experience, think and do.

To say that all my desires, feelings, motives etc., can be subsumed entirely by role-playing is to argue that individuality is nothing but role-playing. In other words, sociological theory contributes to the fragmentation of the self. It correctly argues that social life demonstrates fragmentation with the increasing division of labour. From this, it assumes that the self has become split into a multiplicity of identities which tend to become insulated and isolated from each other. Empirically this may well be true, but there can be no doubt that sociology contributes to the very process it is analysing. The sociological definition of alienation, anomie, mass society masking, identity, management, and the positing of inauthenticity in human relationships, in itself constitutes a mechanism of fragmentation. The fragmentation of sociology is both a reflection of, and a factor in, the fragmentation of the individual's experience of daily life.

Fragmentation and role differentiation

Sociologically, the fragmentation thesis has been tied in with the realization that the social division of labour generates a division in the social personality and a corresponding fragmentation of the individual consciousness. In this connection, the role concept has tended to lend support for the view that human conduct can be understood in terms of 'performances in situations'. Now while the idea of a performance is not startling, it has the further implication that since there is a multiplicity of performances, there is also a multiplicity of selves which are brought into play at each performance. There is, in the extreme statement of this position, a belief in the self concept as a refractory surface which mirrors each situation yet is never integrated. Statements of this

177

position are made with great panache by exponents of dramatism. Each performance reflects the requirements of a specific situation. But because society has so many situations in which performances must be given, it follows that the sheer impossibility of co-ordinating each performance leads to a fragmented consciousness, or to a multiple identity. For each situation there is an accompanying identity – each performance therefore brings into play a specific act of self-presentation.

Long ago the fragmentation thesis was put very cogently by David Hume:[8]

> I may venture to affirm of the rest of mankind, that they are nothing but a bundle or collection of different perceptions, which succeed each other with an inconceivable rapidity, and we are in a perpetual flux and movement. Our eyes cannot turn in their sockets without varying our perceptions. Our thought is still more variable than our sight, and all our other senses and faculties contribute to this change; nor is there any single power of the soul which remains unalterably the same, perhaps for one moment. *The mind is a kind of theatre*, where several perceptions successively make their appearance; pass, re-pass, glide away and mingle in an infinite variety of postures and situations. There is properly no simplicity in it at any one time, nor identity in different; whatever natural propension we may have to imagine that simplicity and identity.

What Hume said two hundred years ago has become a commonplace of contemporary social thought. In sociology, fragmentation is seen as being the end result of the industrial revolution. The multiplicity of roles that men are forced to play shatters the unity of the self. Men are divided against themselves – roles contradict each other and often are in direct confrontation. Occupational roles are divorced from family roles, friendship roles are estranged from citizen roles etc., etc. There is no 'still centre' in which men can take refuge from the demands of the world. At least this is how contemporary social pessimists see the situation.

Role-differentiation

Simply stated, fragmentation can be construed as being dependent on occupational specialization. The division of labour necessitates greater and greater role specialization. It is no longer specialization of the entire product, but specialization of process. Specialization of process leads from specialization of a 'person' to specialization of specific aspects of a person. Thus, 'organic solidarity' creates an interdependence of parts, while at the same

178

time separating and encapsulating those same parts. The demands of the job generate a specific type of response repertoire. The typical bureaucrat, for example, following Merton's analysis,[9] is compounded of compulsive rule-following, and an often observed arrogance and high-mindedness in front of clients etc. However, in different contexts, the same bureaucrat may be a hen-pecked husband, a lover of Marcel Proust, a sexual athlete, a rugby international player etc. It is not sheer enumeration of roles that an individual plays that is being discussed here, but the possibility that each one of these roles tends to remain insulated from the others. Now we know, intuitively at least, that some roles are more salient than others, that for example, the bureaucrat might conceivably play all his other roles as versions of the bureaucratic role in which he has invested so much of his energy and emotion, yet this does not necessarily demonstrate the hypothesis of role-insulation.

What exactly do we mean by role-insulation? In the *first place*, role-insulation implies the commitment of the individual's energy resources to an interaction context in which the performance takes place. By this is meant that each situation demands a *degree* of allegiance. The workman on the assembly line may be completely bored with the job he is doing, yet he must invest a minimum amount of effort to maintain an even and socially accepted flow of production. His insulation from other role-demands in this situation is crucial for the productive process as a whole. In the *second place*, role-insulation implies the surrender of a part of an individual's autonomy to the requirements of the more inclusive system. This surrender entails the substitution of external norms of behaviour for an aspect of the unitary self. Hence, specialization of function entails role-differentiation.

It might be argued that one can approach role-differentiation from a different viewpoint, that is, from the viewpoint which sees particular types of personality gravitating towards particular types of occupation or role. For instance, in a classic paper on the relationship between role-playing and personality, Edgar Borgatta examines the degree of congruence between personality characteristics and role-specifications: [10]

The common view of the relationship between personality and social structure includes two important propositions (*a*) Personality types tend to gravitate to positions with consistent normative demands; (*b*) Occupancy of positions with given normative demands tends to alter the personality towards consistency with the normative demands. Stated in mundane language, an individual tends to do things consistent with his personality and what he does tends to effect his personality. Concomitant with these propositions, is a notion that when persons of given characteristics are placed in situations that make demands of them consistent with their characteristics, they will be able to satisfy the demands well and will do so with relatively little discomfort or with relatively more enjoyment.

Of course, the assumption that there *are* personality characteristics that can be described independently of role-specifications is one which some sociologists would probably reject. However, Borgatta's study is not aimed at establishing criteria for partitioning personality – its aim is really to show that personality characteristics (no matter how they are defined) are not absolutely determinative in any given situation. In so doing, he and other small group researchers hope to erect models of social interaction which demonstrate the *relative priority* of role and situational variables. This is particularly true of the proliferation of studies emphasizing the 'situation' as a factor of leadership. Perhaps, it would not be too far off the mark to state that most studies in the leadership field treat the leader as a product of group determinants. This is not to say that small group studies always relegate leadership to the interplay of role and situational variables, but it does indicate that interactive processes themselves are regarded as having significant consequences for leadership roles, and also for the differentiation of other roles.

Similarly, 'interaction process analysis' points time and time again to the way in which certain types of role are manufactured in the course of group interaction. Role-differentiation seems to be dependent on the development of a well-defined division of labour in the group. Bales's[11] demonstration that problem-solving behaviour in small groups usually generates three types of specialist role (namely, the task specialist, the social specialist, and the over-active deviant) is a function of the necessity of finding solutions to problems relating to group productivity and group solidarity. Bales argues that the three types of role are not necessarily complementary but often in conflict. They depend on qualitatively different types of behaviour, basically implying different types of personality. Hence, it is role-differentiation which seems to be consonant with these types of behaviour or personality.

Now while it is relatively easy to hold variables constant in a small group context, this is obviously not the case when we look at the larger context. In this larger context, we are usually faced with a large role map in which each role is interlocked with other counter-roles. The division of labour is allied to a process of role-allocation. This view of the social system is basically static, and

180

as such, is not controversial. It acts as a descriptive model of structure at a given moment in time. Therefore, the role map of an organization like a university, is a point of reference for identifying the type of categories of person in the university, e.g. vice-chancellor, registrar, professor, lecturer, student, porter. It does not purport to explain the organization.

It is not the role maps of organizations which illustrate the fragmentation thesis, but the inference that role-differentiation has the consequence of divorcing and estranging the individual from himself as a self-contained unit. In other words, we are attempting to get to grips with the philosophy of role-estrangement. Intuitively we know that role-differentiation cannot mean complete insulation. My identity as a university lecturer is not completely insulated from my identity as a husband. To accept the thesis of complete isolation would be to indulge in a form of sociological schizophrenia.

The Kafkaesque view of man

To assent to the argument that each situation projects its own identity, is to accept at face value the Humean notion that each individual is a bundle of different and unconnected perceptions. But this is not being claimed by those theorists who emphasize the notion of a multiplicity of identities. Their precise point is that it is the quality of modern industrial life which pushes men into isolated relationships; it is the quality of their occupational roles which alienates them from themselves and their fellows; it is the quality of their emotional and psychological experiences in a complex and mass society which generates emotional frigidity and the stultification of social relationships.

This line of thinking, all the way back from Marx to the present day existentialist school, sees men being constantly turned into 'things' by the ravages and impersonality of political, cultural and social processes. The roles that men are forced to play are believed to be fundamentally inhuman. They demand absolute conformity even when they are perceived as being antithetical to the individual's real needs. Men are forced into situations in which the roles they play are merely performances which must be confirmed by others to be accounted successful. The performance does not have to be believed in by the performer; all he has to do is to convince others of the validity of the performance. He must be able to project an appropriate identity to meet the requirements of the situation. He must convince his audience that he 'really is who he claims to be', and this claim is usually couched in the language of impression-management – the selling of one's image at the highest

181

possible price. At the same time, this bargaining process always takes place within the framework of the larger scenario in which performances are merely fragmented interpretations. Performances, therefore, are dramatic, but they are dramatic in a completely haphazard way. There is no director or set of authoritative dramatic conventions which give the actors a feeling of participation in a cathartic experience – contemporary life is not Greek tragedy, nor is it Shakespearean drama. Rather, it approximates to the Kafka-esque view of man and society – the roles that are performed are never understood by the actors; they are always performed in some sort of nightmare situation; men are isolated, and their lives are enmeshed in a constant interplay of performances and counter-performances which are often deceitful yet have no *qualitative* exchange value. This image, so pertinent to Goffman's description of identity-management, is related to the mass society thesis. It is also related to alienation, and is implicit, in Marx's view, of the personality as a saleable commodity.

Identity and the rape of the self

Fragmentation of consciousness is, therefore, apparently dependent on the fragmentation of social processes. It is a by-product of industrialization and, for Marx at least, it is implicit in capitalist development. The unitary self begins to break down when the feudal order is disrupted by the growth of capitalism and the elaboration of the social division of labour.

Traditionally, the self concept has been the focus of philosophical speculation, but it has also entered into the social scientist's conceptual world. It took a long time for psychologists in particular to rid themselves of the 'essentialist' cast of thought which attributed to the self some kind of inner force and substantive reality. However, with the advent of behaviourism, the self disappeared together with 'subjectivity'. There was no place for the incommensurable in academic psychology. Paradoxically, the self concept reappeared as the 'ego' in certain versions of Freudian and Neo-Freudian psychology. Not only was the ego conceived of as the executor of motivational processes, but it subsumed cognition, perception and learning. What really is at stake here is a fundamental methodological and theoretical divergence about the status of subjectivity and objectivity in the social sciences. Sociologists, on the whole, have tried to escape this dilemma by treating the self as though it was entirely understandable in socialization terms.

In general, the dichotomy between the subjective and the objective is usually blamed on Descartes – as James Diggory writes: [12]

Descartes had distinguished mind as knower or subject of knowledge from what is known, or the object of knowledge. If in the Cartesian formula, 'I think therefore I am', we emphasize the personal pronoun 'I', we come near to a source of the confusion which still troubles many thinkers. If it is simply a defect of language there is no problem. We might as well say, as James did (1890) that we cannot doubt that thinking occurs. But Descartes is a little more definite than that. He concluded that since thinking occurs, 'I' exists. But does 'I' refer to the whole person or only to a part? Is it a sentient (incorporal) entity to which messages from sense organs are presented, something like a recording camera film, or the spectator at a play? Is 'I' in the Cartesian sentence the same as self?

The promotion of the 'I', unfortunately, always tends to lead to the reification of the self and in extreme cases a self is posited which proposes a psychic agent or inner manikin. In discussing this issue, Allport[13] compared the tradition of Locke with that of Leibniz. For Locke nature was passive (and the individual was a *tabula rasa* on which experience is impressed). For Leibniz, nature is active (the individual is self-determining). There is nothing in intellect, said Locke, that was not first in the senses. Nothing, replied Leibniz, except the intellect itself. (It is strange how this debate is echoed in contemporary discussions about universal grammar and deep structures.) The first tradition in its extreme form leads to behaviourism and stimulus–response psychology; the second tradition leads to personology and instinct theory.

The confrontation becomes translated into the self as agent or the self as product. (Symbolic interactionism attempts to merge both traditions – the dialogue between the 'I' and the 'Me' can be said to consist of both the learned responses ('ME') and the agent ('I').)

Contemporary formulations owe a lot to William James. Indeed, James already noted the possibility of a multiplicity of selves and perhaps should be credited with the notion of 'identity in interaction'. James postulated a social self (the self as perceived by others), a material self (the self in terms of 'mine', my possessions, my belongings) and a spiritual self (one's psychological faculties). For James, these different selves were arranged in some form of hierarchy in which the appropriate self would only come into play in the appropriate situation. However, each one of these self-images was not insulated from all the others; there was no fragmentation. Hierarchy presupposes order, whereas fragmentation is premised on the lack of fit between one self-image and another, or between one identity and another. James does not assume that consciousness is fragmented into a number of competing and un-related selves. Identity is always being modified and changed, but the individual has no great difficulty in recognizing himself by introspection, by memory of past events etc.[14]

> Yesterday's and today's state of consciousness have no substantial identity, for when one is here the other is irrevocably dead and gone. But they have a functional identity for both know the same objects and so far as the bygone me is one of these objects, they react upon it in an identical way, greeting it and calling it mine and opposing it to all other things they know. This functional identity seems really the only sort of identity in the thinker which the facts require us to suppose. Successive thinkers, numerically distinct, but all aware of the same past in the same way, form an adequate vehicle for all the experience of personal unity and sameness which we actually have. And just such a train of successive thinkers is the stream of mental states (each with its complex object cognized and emotional and selective reaction thereupon). . . . The commonest of all, the most uniform, is the possession of some common memories. However different the men may be from the youth, both look back at the same childhood and call it their own.

James, therefore, while concerning himself with the stream of consciousness still remained convinced of the functional identity of the human being. Memory serves as the locus of self-perception. There is no implication of sociological schizophrenia here.

Self versus identity

Since James's time, psychologists and other social scientists fol-lowing his example have emphasized three aspects of the self concept, namely:

(1) The self object
(2) The self as agent
(3) The self as social product

The self as object implies that man is capable of developing attitudes towards himself. He can interpret his own experience. He can make indications to himself. He can step outside himself, metaphorically at least.

As an agent, the self can be regarded as the prime mover in the execution of activities. It controls perception, memory, motivation etc. In other words, it acts as a power house for the generation of behaviour.

The self as product is usually conceived of as the result of exposure to learning experiences, particularly experiences with significant others. This does not mean that the self is not an object to itself. It only implies that before it can become an object it must be socially produced. In Mead's words: [15]

> The self as that which can be an object to itself is essentially a social structure and it arises in social experience. After a self has risen, it in a certain sense provides for itself, its social experiences, and so we can conceive of an absolutely solitary self. But it is impossible to conceive of a self arising outside the social experience.

This last emphasis is relevant to social-psychological and sociological approaches to the self.

If one categorizes these general approaches in the language of experimental social science, then the self as agent is equivalent to an independent variable directly controlling behaviour, the self as product can be regarded as a dependent variable; the self as object being viewed as an intervening variable. The obvious danger is that a reliance on the formulation of self concepts which rely exclusively on any one of these categories is likely to mislead. The idea that the self is a force energizing behaviour has long been rejected by the majority of contemporary psychologists and sociologists. Nevertheless this does not mean that they reject any motivational implication that the self concept might involve. However, today we are faced with a situation in which the self has been demoted and has been replaced by *identity*, not one identity, but a multiple identity in which insulation seems to be the rule rather than the exception.

The notion of a multiple self makes possible the construction of models of interaction which emphasize the episodic and situational aspects of conduct. If the self is fragmented, then it is difficult to conceive of structured social relationships. It is also difficult to conceive of the 'self' as an axis of meaning in social relationships. Indeed in this respect it has been argued that dramatism and ethnomethodology are expressions of a fragmented way of life, expressing a sterile, new, middle-class style of life. It is argued that there is nothing of the historicity of a Marx or Weber in these perspectives, only a constant interest in social episodes. The self is employed in some form of game for the amusement of bored middle-class sociologists who somehow have given up the job of serious structural analysis. Social scientists who give themselves up to the present preoccupation with 'episodes' are, therefore, believed to be outside the mainstream of sociological concerns.

If this were true, then it would mean that people like Simmel, for example, have not anything of importance to say as sociologists. This of course is rubbish. If Goffman and Garfinkel have sold the pass, then both Weber and Simmel have sold the pass. It seems to me that a concern for the episodic, an interest in self-presentation, and an analysis of the tacit, never stated premises of social and self processes is more than a middle-class preoccupation, although it can be seen as being highly modish. After all, Marxism, systems theory, structural functionalism can and have been faddish. The important thing, from our point of view, is the capacity which these perspectives have for helping us understand social conduct. To say that a perspective is middle-class or bourgeois does not detract from its insights or its validity. Goffman's image of man might be unattractive, it might reflect a middle-class preoccupation with superficial externalities, but it does not reflect a conscious flight from the centrality of sociological commitments.

Recently, Gouldner has argued very plausibly for the importance of a reflexive sociology which enables the sociologist to some-how transform both the image he has of himself, and through this transformation, transform his activity in the world. He writes: [16]

Conventional Positivism premises that the self is treacherous and that, so long as it remains in contact with the information system, its primary effect is to bias and distort it. . . . The assumption that the self affects the information system solely in a distorting manner is one sided: it fails to see that the self may also be a source both of valid insight that enriches study and of motivation that energizes it. A reflexive sociology looks therefore to the deepening of the self's capacity to recognize that it views certain information as hostile, to recognize the various dodges that it uses to deny, ignore, or camouflage information that is hostile to it, and to the strengthening of its capacity to accept and use hostile information. In short, what reflexive sociology seeks is not an insulation but a transformation of the sociologist's self, and hence of his praxis in the world.

Gouldner stresses the precariousness of the sociological self-image in the contemporary social thought. In this respect he takes both Goffman and Garfinkel to task for their episodic approach to the self. There is, in Gouldner's view, an implicit anti-humane and ahistorical element in both ethnomethodology and drama-turgical sociology. He argues that both approaches seem to legi-timate a licence to inflict pain by withdrawing from a commitment to the norm of reciprocity in their research procedures. Now, while there might be a grain of truth in this, there seems to be a basic misunderstanding involved here. Granted that the intrusion of ethnomethodological procedures in the observation of the constitutive procedures of one's own family are fundamentally at variance with accepted human relationships, this in itself does not detract from the claim that ethnomethodology does dramatically highlight the artificiality of the rules which we establish for ourselves as social actors. Nor does it detract from the insight that the self itself is premised on unstated assumptions about its pretensions. I agree with Gouldner when he deplores the uses to which ethnomethodology can be put, but this in itself is not really the issue. Garfinkel's methods cannot be dismissed because they do violence to human dignity. They faithfully reflect social fragmentation as experienced by middle-class man.

Fragmentation: fact or fantasy?

The problems that we have been examining under the general rubric of fragmentation are often ones which are not taken seriously by academic sociologists. Very often, they believe them to be suitable for presentation as 'pop sociology'. We are told that the problem is exaggerated, and that in the final analysis fragmentation is purely a function of the way some intellectuals define the situation. Alienation, for example, is regarded as not worthy of serious academic attention. How tenable this position is, is extremely debatable, particularly when an entire generation in the United States and Europe tends to apply these labels to themselves.

The whole question of 'identity crisis' or alienation, might be spurious, but if it is, then the individual's perception of his own role in society is also spurious. If somebody tells us that he finds life meaningless, that he finds it difficult to relate to others, then are we merely to see this as evidence of false consciousness, or a total misinterpretation of social reality? It might be argued that typically the only people who make this sort of statement are those with a certain sort of vocabulary, with a certain sort of education, with a certain form of life-style, with a typical location in society, that they are, in fact, representative of a middle-class life-style. If this is so, then does it invalidate the general thesis? If only middle-class identities are perceived as being subject to fragmentation, then is this only a pseudo-problem dreamt up by trendy popularists to legitimate their boredom? My perception of my social identity as being anxiety-prone surely is not a psuedo-problem.

Fragmentation presupposes that there are real conflicts which cannot be explained away by distorted definitions of the field of

N

action. The operation of the mass media, the impersonality of power, the remoteness of decision-making from the everyday concerns of human beings, the exploitative nature of so many social relationships are not pseudo-problems. The middle-class identity search is not remote from these problem areas, it is squarely at the centre of them. It is not only middle-class man who articulates his fragmentation. All men are fragmented by the very nature of the social processes which modern science and technology have unharnessed. The confrontation between man and society then is one which he himself has created. The divisions that men have erected between themselves are understandable, precisely because they are man-made, symbolically mediated, socially defined.

In Marx's[17] conception of alienation as a multi-dimensional process of estrangement from the product of work, from meaningful relationships with others, from the sources of the individual's own basic creativity, and from the actual control of the work process, we still have the most eloquent account of the felt estrangement of man from his society. But it is no longer fashionable to stress alienation as being directly dependent on the relationship between the mode of production and the worker's participation in production. Today the emphasis has shifted to alienation as some form of psychological malaise which is best treated at the psychiatric clinic. The confrontation between individual and society is then given a mental health connotation. Alienation loses its political and social connotation.

At another level, the fact that it is youth culture which *describes and defines* itself as alienated is indicative of the way in which a unique misinterpretation of a concept becomes an aspect of social reality. If men define themselves as alienated, then there is no power on earth that can convince them to the contrary.

10 Reservations

Over-emphasis on self-consciousness

The central argument of this book has been centred on the notion of dramatic realization. Yet I must admit to a certain uneasiness about the rational nature of this model. It assumes that performances are constructed, put together so as to realize some object or value. It therefore tends to ignore and devalue non-rational, irrational or, if you like, unconscious elements of the interactive situation. Are we to assume that all interaction proceeds as if the actor is aware of his purposes and knows what the other's purposes are? Obviously, this we cannot do. Yet at the same time, to say that men are not aware of their purposes some of the time, is not to say that they are not aware of their purposes all the time. What the dramatic model has tended to do, therefore, is to ignore the emotional underpinning of human behaviour. We too readily assume that motives can be situated. This was referred to when we discussed Scheler's analysis of sympathy.

What applies to the dramatic model applies with equal force to both the exchange and game model. Here again we discover the commitment to rational behaviour in terms of calculative advantage. In some forms of bargaining theory we are left with a highly sophisticated network of strategies which seem to place actors in a constant calculative posture.

Is it possible to conceive of interaction which does not require an element of self-consciousness? If we accept the basic premise of this book, then presumably the answer has to be no. One way to escape from self-consciousness has already been spelt out – namely, assuming that all interaction can be conceptualized as a form of stimulus–response linkage. Alternatively, self-consciousness withers away if we are prepared to follow an extreme pheno-menological position by assuming that the self is merely a hypo-thesis about the way the body acts in the world. Although, in theory, it is possible to conceive of the experiential self without social commitments, in practice, such a self is intuited, not empirically grounded. Nevertheless, we cannot afford to neglect phenomenological accounts of interaction, simply because they do not fit into traditional categories.

Indeed, the current emphasis on episodic encounters, while being highly dramatic, is also symptomatic of the intrusion of phenomenological methods and procedures in the social sciences. In these encounters, the individual faces the other, not only as a player of parts but also as a total person.

Perhaps it is more appropriate to say that it is existential pheno-menology which argues for episodes as total encounters between persons. This notion of the person is put eloquently by Natanson in his discussion of phenomenological typifications and existentialist assumptions about personal concreteness.[1]

> The argument for the uniqueness of the person, for his
> existential fervour and identity, for everything opposed to the
> anonymity of roles can be put straightforwardly: We can and
> do distinguish between the Other who confronts us as a
> distinctive fully individuated person with his own character and
> flair and, at the other extreme, someone whose greyness,
> conformity, almost built-in uniformity assures a sovereign
> mediocrity.

In everyday encounters, most sociologists are far too ready to ignore what actors really say about their experiences of others. One of the better things that comes out of the ethnomethodological[2] position, is that ethnomethodologists really take the definition of the situation seriously. Most sociologists pay lip-service to notions relating to the definition of the situation, but in practice they tend to ignore them, by seeming to act and believe that they know better what the definition of the situation is for those involved. They usually do this by talking about culture as a complex of common understandings and, consequently, they assume that men are all busily defining the world in the same way.

Ethnomethodologists actually listen to what men have to say, they allow men to typify their own behaviour as well as en-couraging them to construct their own moral meanings. They do not attempt to strait-jacket these typifications in the bounds of some prior commitment to a conceptual scheme. Hence, they are concerned with actually investigating life as it is lived by men in contemporary society, not in inferring how it is lived. Although

190

one can object to the way in which they try to tear away the typifications and assumptions which men employ for understanding their own behaviour, this does not necessarily argue against their real interest in the mundane social world.

When men say they experience others as persons, it is no good saying that this is not consonant with what we know about role-mediated interaction. In a sense, sociologists have become victims of their own propaganda. They fail to take account of the world as reported to them by men in that world. They believe that socio-logical insight gives them some form of privileged access to the world, entailing the right to legislate for that world from the point of view of the detached observer. Now while detachment may be desirable up to a point, it is also highly dangerous. It is dangerous because it entails two different types of knowledge, the social scien-tist's and everyman's. This duality has the consequence of rarifying sociology into a system of self-contained meanings which is only accessible to the initiated and committed.

To a certain extent, this explains why sociology is so unpopular amongst the general public. They see sociologists employing a highly specialized vocabulary about areas of conduct to which they themselves have direct access. Hence, what they see in this 'specialized language' seems to bear no resemblance to the every-day world they recognize all around them. Sociology seems foreign, strange and completely divorced from their concerns in everyday living.

It follows that if we see interaction in terms of self–other encounters, we do not necessarily have to subscribe to the view that encounters will always exhibit rehearsal effects. We cannot assume that interaction is always 'on stage'. Nor can we assume that calculative rationality will always inform interaction. This is not to say that we should not make such assumptions – it is evident that we cannot help doing so. Yet this does not entitle us to assert that this is all there is to social interaction.

The demotion of the psychological

While sociologists have reacted with a great deal of vehemence to the threat of reductionism, they have done so in a peculiarly negative sort of way. Homans has been attacked for his particular brand of reductionism. Yet, in part, this attack is misconceived. Granted that Skinnerian reinforcement theory is not congenial to a sociology which stresses 'meaning' and 'intention', this does not imply that we should reject psychological assumptions from our models of interaction. Indeed, this would be impossible. The fact that we have constructed elaborate vocabularies of motives to

191

account for the inferred subjective dimension of man's social behaviour is a measure of the way in which sociologists continuously make use of psychological constructs. But in constructing these typical vocabularies we have tried to get the best of both worlds. We have implied that motives are social in origin, while simultaneously we have conceded that they have energizing properties. There is nothing inherently wrong in this, provided we recognize that social behaviour is basically biosocial. Yet, most of us are not somehow prepared to take this step – we have become so obsessed with the autonomy of the social, that we tend to relegate energizing factors in motivation to predisposing tissue needs which have become so modified by cultural conditioning that they no longer have any analytical and empirical reality.

We have over-symbolized motives and intentions. Furthermore, we have unwittingly allowed ourselves to be deluded into treating human 'needs' as if they were merely expressions of culturally defined categories, such as the achievement motive, or the need for social approval. The point is, that needs like the ones just mentioned are not merely 'internalized cultural prescriptions', they are also intimately related to personality and emotional proclivities. Having said this, one is immediately aware that the terms personality, or emotion, often are defined in terms of social criteria, so that one gets involved in an incessant circularity of definition. To argue for a social account of motives must not force us into the position in which we subsume both the psychological and biological under the roof of symbolic construction. The over-socialized conception of man might be old hat, yet we cannot afford to ignore Wrong's warnings about the burying of the 'body'.

Derek Phillips, writing about the way in which American sociologists have tended to ignore human needs, puts the point we have been making very clearly.[3]

One of the most remarkable things about present-day American Sociology is the almost complete absence in the literature of any sustained discussion and consideration of human needs. There is a good deal of concern with such concepts as 'significant others', 'reference groups', 'values', and 'social norms' – all of which are utilized to help explain various types of social phenomena. But the argument in which these concepts are contained seldom tells us why people behave as they do. To say, for example, that people vote as they do because of the influence of reference groups, that they have birth rates because of religious values, or that they use alcohol because of the norms of the groups to which they belong, is to go only part way in terms of explanation of social phenomena. For the question still remains as to how reference groups, values, and norms exert an influence on people's behaviour.

In other words, in what ways do symbols become energizing? To argue that they become internalized does not help us to understand how they become aspects of typical vocabularies of motives. Obviously, the answer to such a question is not resolved by merely delineating the problem. Yet, in doing so, we acknowledge that there *is* a problem which is not resolvable in terms of simple socialization mechanisms. We can assent to the postulation of the self as a social process, without surrendering completely to the belief that the self is nothing but the 'generalized other'. Similarly, we do not have to accept without reservation the notion that needs are explained by social determinants. This is to assume that men have no needs other than those provided for him by the socio-cultural system in which he has been socialized. Although we might reject Lenski's view of man as basically a self-interested and egoistic animal, this does not mean that we reject the view that some such psychological proposition is at the foundation of most human behaviour. The difficulty here is that the empirical specification of such a need is not demonstrable at the present time. Even if such needs are not empirically demonstrable, their intuition by an increasing number of sociologists points to the dissatisfaction that many feel with the current emphasis on the self and personality as end products of the 'reflected appraisals of others'.

The separation of individual needs and 'social facts' seems to be a prerequisite of any discussion of the influence of symbols in man's interactive behaviour. In practice, social scientists seem to confuse these two levels by deriving both individual and social needs from the social environment. This social environment is compounded of many things including demographic, ecological and cultural elements. But for many sociologists in the symbolic interactionist tradition, such factors are only important in so far as they enter the actor's definition of the situation. Social structure is, in this view, perceived as an interpreted reality. It is not surprising that this subjective view of social structure is somehow forced into serving the dual purposes of society and personality. The danger is, that if society is believed to be constituted of the sum total of everybody's definition of the situation, then we are committed to the belief that psychological and social variables are in fact the same. Even if we accept that psychological needs or motives enter into any account of social behaviour, we do not have to accept that they are fundamentally the same kind of fact as those which we have called demographic, ecological or cultural.

The obsession with meaning

Earlier in the book I gave the impression that language was a constitutive element of any interaction. This is an assertion, not an empirical demonstration. It is grounded in the corpus of linguistic and philosophical theories[4] which point to the way in which linguistic categories and classifications colour both our perceptions and behaviour. When one asserts that language is constitutive, this is usually done in the context of denying the validity of a 'functionalist' position which regards the symbolic system as a means or mechanism of social integration. Usually such a position stresses the communicative process as epiphenomenal to the system of structural relations which it presupposes. Traditionally, the idea that language existed solely for purposes of communicating messages fitted in very nicely with the associated idea that social structures cohere through the medium of language.

Social theory, as has been argued by Duncan,[5] tends to see language as the medium through which certain forces express themselves. Hence, the meaning of an event is not found in the symbolic account of that event, but in the actual relationship of the event to the symbol. Meaning therefore, in this sense, refers to the way in which symbols are tied to events, even when events are broadly defined. It follows that events determine meanings, not the other way around. Duncan and other symbolic interactionists argue, that while it is true that events influence meaning, it is also true that meanings influence events. When this is being asserted they are saying that language is more than a mechanism for the expression of content or force; it becomes a shaping and constitutive element in the generation of meaning. The style of communication between people is, therefore, just as important as the contents contained in the communication.

When Mead says that 'symbolization constitutes objects not constituted before', he is implying that it is the constructions that men make as interactive beings that allow them to attribute meaning to the world. Symbolic interaction in this sense, provides men with their social objects. Now this argument is the cornerstone of the symbolic interactionist position on meaning. It is the position on which this book has been partly premised. Yet, there are objections and reservations to this view that must be kept in mind. If we completely assent to symbolic determinism, then we have merely substituted one form of social determinism for another. In addition, we would also be guilty of denying the influence of constraining factors in everyday life. Poverty, for example, can be described in terms of relative deprivation etc., yet it is too easily assumed that relative deprivation invalidates any discussion of poverty as experienced in the raw. Similarly, symbols, although permitting the construction of imaginary worlds, are not divorced from the world from which they have emerged.[6]

Mead cogently argues that symbols permit meaning, but this is not enough. 'Perspective' without an assumed reality, without some 'animal faith' in the more or less veridical relationship between the thing or the relationship between things and their meanings makes taking the 'role of the other' a hollow, meaningless, memorization of noise. Symbolic interactionism means nothing if the symbol is confused with the word or sound. The analysis of the interaction of value perspectives is only a concern with conceptual smoke and disembodied soul unless there is something real. Why do people change their minds? What makes them admit they were in error? What makes them refuse to admit they were in error? What makes them right? How can we possibly explain or predict the synthesis of values in contradiction to facile analysis of this synthesis after the fact.

Bill Harrel is disputing the symbolic interactionist assertion that meaning derives from symbolic accounts of interactive processes. Just as there are real relationships and events which are handled by physics and other natural sciences in the language of mathematics, so there are real relationships in the social world which are translated by the symbols we employ: 'The knowledge of relationships requires symbols but the fact that some relations are persistently described by man in time and space suggests that relations are not only symbolic events but real events as well.'[7]

This is undoubtedly true. There does seem to be a tendency amongst symbolic interactionists to treat the social world as if it were merely an afterthought, or an appendage to symbolic analysis. This is reflected in their cavalier treatment of social structure and social change as if they were artificial categories. However, while this is true, there still remains the problem of trying to account for the way in which men symbolize social structure. This relationship is not isomorphic. Indeed, it is often completely divergent. There are times when the symbolic accounts of the actors in situations seem to be completely opposite to the structural accounts presented by sociologists. Are we to assume that this is an example of false consciousness? If men define their situation in terms of religious categories and the sociologist employs structural concepts in order to explain why men hold the definitions of the situation that they do, then does the structural account logically entail the symbolic definition? Obviously it does not, because if it did, then the whole question of infrastructure and superstructure would have been settled a long time ago. Ultimately, the relationship between struc-

195

tural and symbolic aspects of social reality is far more complicated than simply asserting that one is the consequence of the other.

What we have to assert in one way or the other is the duality of symbolic and structural processes. We have to demonstrate the dialectic interplay between ideas and 'bodies', between culture and structure, between symbols and objects. Similarly, although we can analytically distinguish between norms and interaction, between the 'norm of reciprocity' and the actual exchange process, this distinction does not exist empirically. One can quote Simmel at this juncture.[8]

> Every relationship between persons gives rise to a picture of each in the other; and this picture, obviously, interacts with the actual relation. The relation constitutes the condition under which the conception, that each has of the other, takes this or that shape and has its truth legitimated. On the other hand, the real interaction between the individuals is based upon the pictures which they acquire of each other. Here we have one of the deep-lying circuits of intellectual life, where an element presupposes a second element which yet in turn, presupposes the first. . . . In their alternation within sociological interaction, they reveal interaction as one of the points where being and conceiving make their mysterious unity empirically felt.

In other words, the symbolic interpretations that we put on the other's behaviour are always distorted. Perhaps it is in this sense that we can conceive of the influence of symbolic construction, not as encapsulating, but reciprocally related to the actual interaction. It is this distortion which gives rise to the belief that symbolic reality is of a determinative nature. We act towards the other on the basis of partial information and cultural prescriptions which do not in themselves actually represent the empirical interaction accurately. Thus to say that symbols determine interaction is just as misconceived as to claim that interaction determines the generation of meaning. Meanings are constructed in interaction, yet simultaneously, interaction is based upon symbolic pictures that each individual has of the other. It is in this context that we sometimes speak of false consciousness, although this is usually seen as ideological distortion, not as necessarily pertinent to the entire interplay between symbol and reality.

The pejorative implications of the fragmentation thesis

It is too readily assumed that a multiple identity is a consequence of the fragmentation of social relationships. Even if this can be empirically demonstrated, there is no necessity to deduce from

196

this that the fragmentation of the self is undesirable. It is quite conceivable that fragmented self-processes are the normal condition of men in society, just as symbolic distortion is normal.

In the models of interaction that we have been evaluating in this book we are aware of the constant interplay between fragmentation assumptions and assumptions relating to the microcosmic metaphor. This interplay is expressed in terms of episodes on the one hand and internalized role scripts on the other. In addition, the self concept becomes subject to the same polarization. Episodic interaction implies a multiple identity, whereas structured, role-mediated interaction presupposes a self concept which is consonant with normative integration. Whether interaction is episodic or not depends, in the final analysis, on whether or not we have a view of social structure as being highly integrated, so that interaction follows highly predictable channels. Moreover, in dramatic inter-action, as we have noted, we are faced with the problem of self-consciousness. Indeed, symbolic interactionism is rooted in metaphors which purport to demonstrate that performances are always put on in front of audiences. Although dramatism allows for the unpredictable, by assuming that the 'I' confronts the 'Me' in some form of audience–actor relationship, this unpredictability often seems to be dependent on normative requirements.

What this means is that self-consciousness seems to be highly problematic. If we assume that performances are strictly controlled by audiences, then we are saying that the actor presents himself in such a way that he merely reflects their appraisals. Logically, we could say that he *becomes* his audience. When this occurs, his self-consciousness is at a minimum because he has no means to evaluate his conduct other than those provided by his reference group. This implies that we are also assuming a high degree of cognitive and motivational unity which may not reflect the empirical situation of men in everyday interaction. Hence fragmentation may be a prior condition of successful interaction. In this context, Wallace attacks the concept of motivational homogeneity as a supposed index of cultural uniformity or behavioural regularity. He argues, it is a mistake to identify behaviour and motivation. The uniformity of behaviour that typifies interaction in an institu-tional setting does not imply psychological uniformity among the participants. Nor does the fact that institutions are shared by members of a socio-cultural system mean that cognitions are shared. In Wallace's view, the basis of social living is to be found in *complementarity*. In any interaction it is not essential that cogni-tions or motives be shared; it is only necessary that the conduct of each actor is relatively negotiable and predictable. Thus, if one visualizes the social system as a network of roles, then this network will not depend on the way in which individuals conform to role-expectations, but on the complementarity of these roles. Similarly, in any interaction episode, it is not necessary to put one's salient identity on the line for confirmation from the other – all one has to do is obtain a minimum recognition or response from the other that he intends to act on your gesture. *You do not have to have a theory of the other before you interact with him, nor do you have to expect that the other will want identity claims to be established by you before the interaction can continue.*

Highly complex and stratified social systems are able to function, precisely because the individual is relieved of the burden of under-standing the motives of everybody with whom he interacts. In a sense, a great deal of interaction goes on in the context of a mis-perception or misinterpretation of the other's motives. Culture and symbolization imply that men have similar *cognitive capabilities* which enable them to predict the behaviours of others without necessarily sharing the same hypothetical cognitive maps. All that is necessary, is to show that certain patterns of behaviour are cognitively equivalent, that is, they can be predicted by the parties to the interaction: [9]

Indeed, we now suggest that human societies may characteristic-ally require the non-sharing of certain cognitive maps among participants in a variety of institutional arrangements. Many a social system will not work if all participants share common knowledge of the system. It would seem therefore that cognitive non-uniformity may be a functional desideratum of society (although – it is certainly not a formal prerequisite any more than is uniformity). For cognitive non-uniformity subserves two important functions; (1) it permits a more complex system to arise than most, or any of its participants can comprehend, and (2) it liberates the participants in a system from the heavy burden of knowing each other's behaviour.

In the relationships between the multiplicity of groups and individuals in modern industrial society a fragmented personality structure has decided advantages over the monolithic personality posited by certain varieties of socialization theory. A 'basic per-sonality', for example, would be a distinct hindrance, because it would be inflexible and maladaptive. All that socialization has to do, is to instil the notion of behavioural predictability into indivi-duals, so that they can interpret the other's behaviour as being related to their own. Interaction can proceed without assuming that men have to be psychologically alike before they can interact. Nor is it essential that men reveal many aspects of their personality to those with whom they interact. Thus, the identities projected in

198

interaction are not necessarily to be seen as being a measure of personality disintegration or alienation, but rather as the adaptation to complexity:[10]

> Thus, reciprocal interactions between the representatives of geographically separate groups as alien as American Indian tribes and colonial or state governments, have proceeded for centuries with only minimal sharing of motives or understanding, on a basis of carefully patterned equivalences. Similar observation might be made on the relations between castes, social classes, professional groups, kin groups, factions, parties and so forth. In no case is it necessary that a basic personality or a basic cognitive framework be shared, but it is necessary that behaviours be mutually predictable and equivalent. Thus, we may say that as any set of persons establish a system of behavioural expectancies, an organized relationship comes into existence.

There is, in other words, no need to assume the homogeneity of society, nor the functional unity of personality. Social living demands a system of behavioural equivalences without postulating some form of internalized image of the common values and cognitions of that society. The identities that one projects in interaction are correlated with the identities of the 'others' in the situation, not with the 'Identity' of the social system. Wallace believes that personality and cultural data are related only by means of correlations which, in the main, are considerably less than unity. He is influenced by those cognitive theorists who emphasize tendencies to maximize cognitive organization. In assuming that social interactors maximize cognitive organization, all that Wallace is saying is that their cognitive maps are complementary to each other.

This is tantamount to saying that men's cognitive capacities are fundamentally the same, but that the contents of cognition are volatile. Hence, fragmentation in the alienative sense only occurs when the individual is unable to make sense of the behavioural cues in his environment. If he not only misinterprets the other's motives but fails to make the appropriate cognitive connections between his behaviour and that of the other, then there is a good chance that some form of communicative and behavioural paralysis will obtain. In general, most interaction proceeds *as if* men understood each other's behaviour. They are able to predict behaviour in terms of behavioural equivalences which might not be related to each other's vocabulary of motives. It is conceivable that as long as there is this element of behavioural predictability between certain types of interactors, that interaction could proceed without the necessity of imputing the actual motives of the other. For example, in rigidly structured institutional contexts such as hospitals

199

we do not have to know the motives of nurses, doctors, administrators, patients, porters, etc. All we have to know is that certain behaviours are related to other behaviours, that is, they have meaning for those who are involved. I do not have to make any assumptions about the motives of doctors, provided they fit into patterns of behavioural equivalences.

Although I impute motives to the doctor, these imputations do not have to be accurate as long as they allow me to establish predictive criteria which satisfy me – perhaps me alone. All that is needed in this situation, is my belief that the motives I impute to the doctor are roughly equivalent to the way in which they will manifest themselves in the course of the interaction. If I define the doctor as idealistic, whereas in fact he is materialistic, this will not be a barrier to successful doctor–patient relationships, provided the behavioural expectancies are realized.

Over-emphasis on the situation

All along we have assumed that we cannot obtain a macro-theory from any consideration of micro-processes. This assumption may be untenable, particularly in the light of the current revaluation of sociological thought brought about by the focusing of interest on everyday life. In the past, interaction theory has been premised on the notion of the application of the traditional canons of naturalistic observation and empirical research to interaction. In general, this has been a reaction to the interest of macro-theorists in the development of a science of society. The assumption is made that a science of society is dependent on an understanding of both 'sub-atomic social behaviour' as well as the 'holistic molecular behaviour' at the macro-level. In addition, there was the belief that interaction could be conceived of as providing the concepts for a building-block sociology. On the other hand, macro-theorists have been in the habit of telling us that, just as it is possible to study macro-systems in the natural sciences, as evidenced by the study of the propositions of astronomy, so it was possible, and indeed imperative, that we undertake the study of macro-phenomena in the social world. In other words, it was believed that the study of 'entire societies' did not necessitate the complete, or even the partial understanding of what went on at the micro-level. Unfortunately, this happens to be an inappropriate analogy.

Although macro-sociology should perhaps be concerned with the range of problems specified by Etzioni,[11] this is not to assume that there is in fact a qualitative difference between the two areas. Indeed, social life is everywhere made up of the same stuff, it is everywhere subject to symbolic presentation, to interpretation and to revision. At the so-called higher levels of abstraction men are not passive victims of large-scale organizations. These organizations don't suddenly assume an extra-dimensional existence outside the concerns of men in everyday life. As ethnomethodologists are now insisting, when we examine the conceptual elaborations of some sociological theories, they are found to be verbal constructions, implying a level of abstraction not warranted by the material used. Theoretical elegance might be a highly desirable ideal in social theory, yet if this elegance is obtained at the expense of the actual life of men in actual situations, then we have moved away from sociology into the realm of social myth.

All theories of interaction, even of the most blatantly positivist kind are fundamentally premised on the assumption that the focus of analysis in interaction *is the meaningful behaviour of actors in situations*. Even when meaning is treated as being tied up to stimulus complex, action is seen to be important both from the point of view of the observer and the interactor. However, there is an assumption built into behavioural approaches to interaction which believes or states that the actor has no privileged status with respect to his own subjectivity. It is argued that it is only in external behaviour that we can really talk about patterns of interaction, that is, the patterns of interaction observed by the social scientist as investigator. The internal states which the actors report are not admissible, and even if they are, they are only admissible as being examples of complex behavioural linkages.

In addition, there are other approaches to interaction which, while not emphasizing stimulus–response linkages, tend to see meaningful conduct in terms of a relationship between programmed actors and a given symbolic environment, where the symbolic environment is defined as a set of common cultural understandings. In either case, behaviour is fundamentally prescribed and determined for the actors in the situation. Thus if we know the values and norms of a particular society, the dispositions of the actors, and the saliency of the situation, we are presumably in a position to specify the actual operation of all ongoing and future interaction. However, it is readily admitted by most theorists who subscribe to such a viewpoint, that such a high degree of predictive efficiency is a pipe dream. But there is another more serious objection to the notion of mechanical interaction or to norm-internalized interaction, and that is that it does violence to the interpretative nature of self–other relationships. To construct a deductive theory out of material which is basically intractable to mechanistic treatment is to deceive oneself that one has managed to construct a trans-situational set of laws.

More serious, however, is the belief in the over-determination of the contextual base of interaction. It is assumed that a simple set of observations in an interaction setting can provide the basis for a number of theoretical propositions which can be applied to other interaction settings at different times and places. But this in itself is only possible when we have fully documented and understood what the world is like to the actors in the situation. It is no good merely relying on the belief that men are busily defining the situation from a common base. More critically, one must allow these actors some capacity for constructing meanings in the ongoing interaction, and this cannot be allowed for if we attribute to actors some form of stereotyped interpretations of the world as being indexes of what actually occurs. Everyday meanings are ultimately the stuff out of which it is possible for sociologists to erect their own everyday interpretations.

Yet we must not make a fetish out of 'everyday life'. Everyday typifications can become another dead end, if we allow ourselves to be taken in by a completely relativistic account of social interaction, in which episodes are elevated to the status of the prime unit of methodological and theoretical interest.[12]

Understanding the situational nature of human existence is crucial for developing any science of man. But an over-concentration on the contextual effects to the relative exclusion of trans-situational meanings leads, however inadvertently, to a failure to consider adequately the most crucial aspect of man, the symbol maker and user: his awesome capacity to transcend himself and his immediate situation, to bring a vast realm of previous experience to bear in constructing meanings and actions, for his immediate situation, to co-ordinate (order) his immediate situations with those of many others beyond his immediate grasp, and to project himself into as yet unrealized future.

The creation of a trans-situational sociology which is not contaminated by the shifting sands of relativism and the demands of socio-cultural determinism may, in the end, prove to be the most difficult task facing sociology. We are now told:[13]

The world is essentially without meaning. In contrast to that sociology which seeks to discover the real meaning of action – a sociological reality, such as the 'functional' meaning of social behaviour – this new sociology asserts that all systems of belief, including that of the conventional sociologists, are arbitrary. The problems previously supposed to be those of the sociologist are in fact the everyday problems of the ordinary man. It is he who must carve out meanings in a world that is meaningless.
Alienation and insecurity are fundamental conditions of life –

though they are experienced differently by individuals and groups – and the regular rehumanization of man is everyman's task.

Lyman and Scott are arguing here for a 'sociology of the absurd'. Yet it seems to me, that in this respect, they are not saying anything that has not been said before, particularly by those sociologists who have long recognized the relational aspects of social thought. Although I am in sympathy with their commitment to intentionality, consciousness, and subjective meaning, as constituting the central focus of sociological inquiry, they do not in my view, meet Douglas's objection regarding 'over-concentration on contextual effects'.

In the contrasting of everyday life as experienced by common men with the concept of 'social structure' as used by sociologists, we are in danger of erecting a false dichotomy. This dichotomy also appears when we endeavour to establish the primacy of interactive processes as against normative and cultural definitions of the situation. All the models of interaction that we have discussed in this book are subject to the same stresses and strains. To construe social life as drama, as a game, as exchange, is to be guilty of an obsessive interest in the momentary, episodic and situational aspects of social relationships. Paradoxically, in spite of claims to the contrary, each one of these interaction models is intimately tied up with general models of society. The dramatic metaphor lends itself to the view of society as a network of interlocking roles, the game model is linked to a model of social conflict, the exchange model is easily assimilated into modern systems theory. Hence, it is probable that problems intrinsic to 'everyday life' are not only contextual but transcend the 'immediately given'. As yet we do not have the means to translate the mundane to the level of macro-processes.

When I say that we are in danger of erecting a false dichotomy, I am not saying that structure and interaction are fundamentally the same kind of social phenomenon. All I am saying is that the experience of power, deprivation, poverty, discrimination, tragedy, etc., is not only confined to the immediacy of episodic interaction. There is no way we can handle social revolution as an essay in 'impression-management', although for those involved, it is primarily the phenomenological present that has any sort of significance. In a concentration camp, the accounts and definitions of the situation which inform the inmates' everyday behaviour, is, from their point of view, the only social reality. Yet this reality does not exist independently of the structure of power relationships manifested in the concentration camp. What we have to ask

o

is whether, at both levels, we can speak of interpenetration of structural and phenomenological factors. The concentration camp guard does not only function as a tool of a political ideology, he also has constructed a complex set of mundane, everyday typifications which enable him to make sense of his own conduct as well as that of the inmates.

Furthermore, at the institutional level, we cannot only treat the functionary's behaviour as if it belonged to a different kind of social universe. If some men are victims, other men are executioners. Victims and executioners confront each other, not merely as role-players with structured expectations of the others' probable performance, but also as men who are capable of both physical and psychic suffering. We too easily assume that the prototype of the functionary or bureaucrat is always cast in the mould of an Eichman.

References

Introduction

1 BARNEY G. GLASER and ANSELM L. STRAUSS, *The Discovery of Grounded Theory*, London: Weidenfeld & Nicolson, 1967.

2 ABRAHAM KAPLAN, *The Conduct of Inquiry*, San Francisco: Chandler, 1964, p. 258.

3 HAROLD FALLDING, *The Sociological Task*, Englewood Cliffs: Prentice-Hall, 1968, p. 46.

4 B. BERELSON and G. A. STEINER, *Human Behaviour: An Inventory of Scientific Findings*, New York: Harcourt, Brace & World, 1964.

5 CHARLES D. BOLTON, 'Is sociology a behavioural science?', *Pacific Sociological Review*, Spring 1963, pp. 3–9.

6 WALTER BUCKLEY, *Sociology and Modern Systems Theory*, Englewood Cliffs: Prentice-Hall, 1967, pp. 23–36.

7 GEORGE C. HOMANS, *The Nature of Social Science*, New York: Harcourt, Brace & World, 1967.

8 PETER BERGER, *An Invitation to Sociology*, London: Penguin, 1968.

9 MAX WEBER, *The Methodology of the Social Sciences*, Chicago: Free Press, 1949.

10 PETER WINCH, *The Idea of a Social Science*, London: Routledge & Kegan Paul, 1958, p. 113.

11 L. M. LACHMAN, *The Legacy of Max Weber*, London: Heinemann, 1970, p. 18.

12 ALFRED J. SCHUTZ, 'Common sense and scientific interpretation of human action', *Philosophy and Phenomenological Research*, 14, 1953, pp. 1–38.

13 WARREN DUNHAM, 'Sociology: natural science or intellectual commitment', in *Human Nature and Collective Behaviour*, ed. Tamotso Shibutani, Englewood Cliffs: Prentice-Hall, 1970, pp. 33–4.

14 ROBERT W. FRIEDRICHS, *A Sociology of Sociology*, New York: Free Press; London: Collier-Macmillan, 1970, p. 108.

15 PETER BERGER, *The Social Reality of Religion*, London: Faber, 1969, pp. 3–28.

REFERENCES

16 ROBERT W. FRIEDRICHS, op. cit., p. 151.
17 HERBERT BLUMER, *Symbolic Interactionism*, Englewood Cliffs:
   Prentice-Hall, 1969, pp. 37–8.
18 MAX WEBER, op. cit.
19 WALTER WALLACE, *Sociological Theory*, London: Heinemann, 1969,
   pp. 1–59.
20 GEORGE C. HOMANS, *Social Behaviour: Its Elementary Forms*,
   London: Routledge & Kegan Paul, 1961.
21 KENNETH BURKE, *A Grammar of Motives*, University of California
   Press, 1969.
22 HUGH D. DUNCAN, *Communication and Social Order*, New York:
   Bedminster Press, 1962.
23 Ibid.
24 CHARLES HAMPDEN-TURNER, *Radical Man*, Cambridge, Mass.:
   Schenkman, 1970, p. 27.
25 DENNIS H. WRONG, 'The oversocialized conception of man in
   modern sociology', *American Sociological Review*, 26, 1961.
26 NORMAN K. DENZIN, *The Research Act in Sociology*, London:
   Butterworths, 1970, p. 25.
27 JOHN R. SEELEY, 'Social science? Some probative problems', in
   Sociology on Trial, ed. Maurice Stein and Arthur Vidich,
   Englewood Cliffs: Prentice-Hall, 1963, p. 58.
28 ALVIN W. GOULDNER, *The Coming Crisis of Western Sociology*,
   London: Heinemann, 1971.

1   The concept of interaction

1 T. M. NEWCOMBE, R. H. TURNER, P. E. CONVERSE, *Social Psychology*,
   London: Routledge & Kegan Paul, 1965, pp. v–vi.
2 G. SIMMEL, *The Sociology of Georg Simmel*, trs. and Introduction
   by K. H. Wolff, New York: Free Press, 1964, pp. 122–3.
3 H. BECKER, *Social Interaction, A Dictionary of the Social Sciences*,
   ed. J. Gould and W. L. Kolb, London: Tavistock, 1964.
4 T. PARSONS, 'Order as a sociological problem', in *The Concept of
   Order*, ed. P. G. Kuntz, University of Washington Press, 1968, p. 38.
5 A. GOULDNER, 'The norm of reciprocity: a preliminary statement',
   American Sociological Review, 25, 1960, pp. 161–79.
6 Ibid.
7 M. MAUSS, *The Gift*, London: Cohen & West, 1954.
8 C. LÉVI-STRAUSS, *The Elementary Structures of Kinship*, London:
   Eyre & Spottiswoode, 1969, p. 59.
9 Ibid., p. 59.
10 G. H. MEAD, *Mind, Self and Society*, University of Chicago Press,
   1967.
11 B. MALINOWSKI, *Argonauts of the Western Pacific*, Routledge, 1922.
12 T. PARSONS, *The Social System*, London: Routledge & Kegan
   Paul, 1952, pp. 60–5.
13 Ibid.
14 G. SIMMEL, op. cit., p. 44.

15 Ibid., p. 408.
16 T. ABEL, *The Foundation of Sociological Theory*, New York: Random House, 1970, pp. 89–90.
17 G. C. HOMANS, *Social Behaviour: Its Elementary Forms*, London: Routledge & Kegan Paul, 1961, p. 381.
18 H. D. DUNCAN, *Communication and Social Order*, New York: Bedminster Press, 1962, p. 30.

2 Non-symbolic interaction

1 G. H. MEAD, *Mind, Self and Society*, University of Chicago Press, 1967.
2 E. BECKER, *The Birth and Death of Meaning*, New York: Free Press, 1962, p. 17.
3 Ibid., p. 18.
4 T. M. NEWCOMB, R. H. TURNER, P. E. CONVERSE, *Social Psychology*, London: Routledge & Kegan Paul, 1965, p. 189.
5 P. A. SOROKIN, *Sociological Theories of Today*, 1966, New York: Harper & Row, pp. 528–52.
6 G. C. HOMANS, *The Human Group*, London: Routledge & Kegan Paul, 1951.
7 P. A. SOROKIN, *Social and Cultural Dynamics*, New York: Bedminster Press, 1962.
8 G. C. HOMANS, 'A life of synthesis', in *Sociological Self Images*, ed. I. L. Horowitz, Oxford & New York: Pergamon Press, 1969, pp. 26–7.
9 A. BANDURA and R. H. WALTERS, *Social Learning and Personality Development*, New York: Holt, Rinehart & Winston, 1963.
10 B. F. SKINNER, *Science and Human Behaviour*, New York: Free Press, 1965.
11 V. PARETO, *Selected Writings*, ed. S. E. Finer, London: Pall Mall Press, 1966.
12 G. C. HOMANS, *The Nature of Social Science*, New York: Harcourt, Brace & World, 1967, p. 45.
13 G. C. HOMANS, 'Fundamental social processes', in *Sociology*, ed. N. J. Smelser, New York: John Wiley, p. 41.

3 Emotional identification and the grammar of sociation

1 A. MONTAGUE, *The Direction of Human Development*, London: Watts, 1957.
2 C. WRIGHT MILLS, 'Situated actions and vocabularies of motive', *American Sociological Review*, 5, December 1949.
3 G. LENSKI, *Power and Privilege: A Theory of Stratification*, New York: McGraw-Hill, 1966, pp. 26–7.
4 Ibid., p. 29.
5 M. SCHELER, *The Nature of Sympathy*, London: Routledge & Kegan Paul, 1954, pp. 8–9.

6 W. MCDOUGALL, *An Outline of Social Psychology*, London: Methuen, 1923.

7 C. KIRKPATRICK, *The Family as Process and Institution*, New York: Ronald, 1955.

8 S. SCHACTER and J. SINGER, 'Cognitive, social and psychological determinants of emotional states', *Psychological Review*, 1962.

9 M. NATANSON, *The Journeying Self*, Reading, Mass.: Addison-Wesley, 1970.

10 G. W. ALLPORT, *Pattern and Growth in Personality*, New York: Holt, Rinehart & Winston, 1961, p. 114.

11 V. E. FRANKL, *The Doctor and the Soul*, New York: Knopf, 1955, p. 169.

12 C. R. ROGERS, *On Becoming a Person*, Boston: Houghton Miffin, 1961.

13 A. H. MASLOW, *Motivation and Personality*, New York: Harper, 1954.

14 G. H. MEAD, *Mind, Self and Society*, University of Chicago Press, 1967, pp. 135–226.

15 G. W. ALLPORT, op. cit., p. 560.

16 J. BUCKLEW, 'The subjective tradition in phenomenological psychology', *Phil. Sc.*, 22, pp. 289–99.

4 The grammar of symbolic sociation (1) acts, scenes and agents

Pp. 81–93 are partly based on my article, 'System, structures and consciousness: the social psychology of meaning', in *The Rules of the Game*, ed. T. Shanin, London: Tavistock, 1972, pp. 320–46.

1 G. P. STONE and H. A. FARBERMAN (eds), *Social Psychology Through Symbolic Interaction*, Waltham, Mass.: Ginn-Blaisdell, 1970, p. 1.

2 G. H. MEAD, *Mind, Self and Society*, University of Chicago Press, 1967, p. 78.

3 E. A. WEINSTEIN, 'The development of interpersonal competence', in *Handbook of Socialization Theory and Research*, ed. D. A. Goslin, Chicago: Rand McNally, 1969, p. 753.

4 K. BURKE, *A Grammar of Motives*, University of California Press, 1969.

5 H. D. DUNCAN, *Communication and Social Order*, New York: Bedminster Press, 1962, p. 145.

6 M. WEBER, *The Methodology of the Social Sciences*, ed. E. A. Shils and H. A. Finch, New York: Free Press, 1949.

7 E. GOFFMAN, *The Presentation of Self in Everyday Life*, Garden City: Doubleday, 1959.

8 H. GARFINKEL, *Studies in Ethnomethodology*, Englewood Cliffs: Prentice-Hall, 1967.

9 K. BURKE, op. cit.

10 K. LEWIN, *Field Theory in Social Science*, ed. D. Cartwright, London: Tavistock, 1951.

11 H. A. MURRAY, *Exploration in Personality*, New York: Oxford University Press, 1938.

12 K. BURKE, 'Dramatism', in *The International Encyclopedia of the Social Sciences*, ed. D. Sills, vol. 7, Macmillan, 1968, p. 446.
13 Ibid.

5 The grammar of symbolic sociation (2) purposes and agencies

Pp. 81–93 are partly based on my article, 'System, structures and consciousness: the social psychology of meaning', in *The Rules of the Game*, ed. T. Shanin, London: Tavistock, 1972, pp. 320–46.

1 C. WRIGHT MILLS, 'Situated actions and vocabularies of motive', *American Sociological Review*, 5, December 1949, pp. 912–13.
2 D. C. MCCLELLAND, *The Achieving Society*, Princeton: Van Nostrand, 1961.
3 H. GARFINKEL, *Studies in Ethnomethodology*, Englewood Cliffs: Prentice-Hall, 1967.
4 H. BLUMER, *Symbolic Interactionism*, Englewood Cliffs: Prentice-Hall, 1969.
5 R. N. FOOT, 'Identification as the basis for a theory of motivation', *American Sociological Review*, 16, February 1951, pp. 14–21.
6 T. PARSONS, *The Social System*, London: Routledge & Kegan Paul, 1952.
7 O. G. BRIM JNR and S. WHEELER, *Socialization after Childhood: Two Essays*, New York: John Wiley, 1966.
8 G. KELLY, *The Psychology of Personal Constructs*, New York: Norton, 1955.
9 F. C. BARTLETT, *Remembering*, Cambridge University Press, 1932.
10 S. FREUD, *The Interpretation of Dreams*, London: Hogarth, 1953.
11 C. LÉVI-STRAUSS, *Structural Anthropology*, New York: Basic Books, 1963.
12 E. A. WEINSTEIN, 'The development of interpersonal competence', in *Handbook of Socialization Theory and Research*, ed. D. A. Goslin, Chicago: Rand McNally, 1969, p. 755.
13 Ibid.
14 Ibid., p. 756.
15 K. E. BOULDING, *The Image*, University of Michigan Press, 1961.
16 G. A. MILLER, E. GALANTER, K. H. PRIBRAM, *Plans and the Structure of Behaviour*, New York: Holt, Rinehart & Winston, 1960.
17 H. BLUMER, op. cit., p. 16.
18 C. H. COOLEY, *Social Organization*, New York: Scribner, 1909, p. 61.
19 W. E. BROCKRIEDE, 'Dimensions of the concept of rhetoric', *Quarterly Journal of Speech*, 54, 1968, pp. 1–12.
20 H. D. DUNCAN, *Symbols in Society*, New York: Oxford University Press, 1968, p. 130.
21 J. DOUGLAS, *Deviance and Respectability: The Social Construction of Moral Meanings*, New York: Basic Books, 1970, pp. 15–16.
22 Ibid.
23 G. H. MEAD, op. cit.
24 J. PIAGET, *Structuralism*, London: Routledge & Kegan Paul, 1971.
25 P. L. BERGER and T. LACHMAN, *The Social Construction of Reality*, London: Allen Lane, 1967.

26 E. GOFFMAN, 'Embarrassment and social organization', *American Journal of Sociology*, 62, 1956, pp. 264–71.

6 Interaction as drama

1 G. J. MCCALL and J. L. SIMMONS, *Identities and Interactions*, New York: Free Press, 1966, pp. 6–7.
2 E. GOFFMAN, *The Presentation of Self in Everyday Life*, Garden City: Doubleday, 1959.
3 G. D. BERREMAN, 'Behind many masks', Monograph No. 4, Society for Applied Anthropology, 1962, p. 11.
4 H. D. DUNCAN, *Communication and Social Order*, New York: Bedminster Press, 1962, p. 126.

7 Interaction as game and exchange

1 J. PIAGET, *The Moral Judgment of the Child*, London, Kegan Paul, 1932.
2 G. H. MEAD, *Mind, Self and Society*, University of Chicago Press, 1967.
3 M. NICHOLSON, *Conflict Analysis*, London: English Universities Press, 1970, pp. 322–3.
4 H. GARFINKEL, *Studies in Ethnomethodology*, Englewood Cliffs: Prentice-Hall, 1967.
5 T. PARSONS, *The Social System*, Chicago: Free Press, 1951.
6 A. CICOUREL, *Method and Measurement in Sociology*, New York: Free Press, 1964, pp. 204–5.
7 Ibid., pp. 205–6.
8 H. GARFINKEL, op. cit.
9 A. F. C. WALLACE, *Culture and Personality*, New York: Random House, 1961.
10 E. GOFFMAN, *Strategic Interaction*, Oxford: Blackwell, 1970, p. 85.
11 R. D. LAING, H. PHILLIPSON, A. R. LEE, *Interpersonal Perception*, London: Tavistock, 1966.
12 S. M. JOURARD, *The Transparent Self*, Princeton: Van Nostrand, 1964.
13 Ibid., p. 24.
14 G. C. HOMANS, *Social Behaviour*, London: Routledge & Kegan Paul, 1961.
15 P. M. BLAU, *Exchange and Power in Social Life*, New York: John Wiley, 1967.
16 J. W. THIBAULT and H. H. KELLEY, *The Social Psychology of Groups*, New York: John Wiley, 1959.
17 H. P. RICKMAN, *Understanding and the Human Sciences*, Heinemann, 1967.
18 R. A. NISBET, *The Social Bond*, New York: Alfred A. Knopf, 1970, p. 65.
19 P. M. BLAU, op. cit., p. 112.
20 J. W. THIBAULT and H. H. KELLEY, op. cit.

21 G. J. MCCALL and J. L. SIMMONS, *Identities and Interactions*, New York: Free Press, 1966, p. 163.

8   Interaction as the negotiation of identity

1 E. GOFFMAN, *The Presentation of Self in Everyday Life*, Garden City: Doubleday, 1959.
2 Ibid.
3 G. J. MCCALL and J. L. SIMMONS, *Identities and Interactions*, New York: Free Press, 1966, p. 67.
4 Ibid.
5 E. A. WEINSTEIN and P. DEUTSCHBERGER, 'Tasks, bargains and identities', in *Social Forces*, 42, May 1964, pp. 451–6.
6 E. GOFFMAN, *Encounters*, Indianapolis: Bobbs-Merrill, 1961.
7 P. BERGER, *An Invitation to Sociology*, London: Penguin, 1968.
8 O. E. KLAPP, *Collective Search for Identity*, New York: Holt, Rinehart & Winston, 1969.
9 G. P. STONE, 'Appearance and the self', in *Human Behaviour and Social Processes*, ed. A. M. Rose, London: Routledge & Kegan Paul, 1962.
10 E. GOFFMAN, *Stigma*, London: Penguin, 1968.
11 D. MATZA, *Becoming Deviant*, Englewood Cliffs: Prentice-Hall, 1969, pp. 180–1.
12 G. J. MCCALL and J. L. SIMMONS, op. cit.
13 G. H. MEAD, *Mind, Self and Society*, University of Chicago Press, 1967.
14 T. PARSONS, 'The position of identity in the general theory of action', in *The Self In Social Interaction*, ed. C. Gordon and K. J. Gergen, New York: John Wiley, 1968, p. 14.

9   Interaction, selves and social fragmentation

1 H. GERTH and C. WRIGHT MILLS, *Character and Social Structure*, London: Routledge & Kegan Paul, 1954, p. 11.
2 Ibid.
3 M. YINGER, *Toward a Field Theory of Behaviour*, New York: McGraw-Hill, 1965.
4 T. PARSONS, *Social Structure and Personality*, New York: Free Press, 1964.
5 M. YINGER, op. cit.
6 A. F. C. WALLACE, *Culture and Personality*, New York: Random House, 1961, p. 42.
7 H. FINGARETTE, *Self Deception*, London: Routledge & Kegan Paul, 1969, pp. 72–3.
8 D. HUME, *A Treatise of Human Nature*, Oxford: Clarendon Press, 1955, p. 252.
9 R. MERTON, *Bureaucratic Structure and Personality in Social Theory and Social Structure*, New York: Free Press, 1957, pp. 195–206.
10 E. F. BORGATTA, 'Role playing specification personality and performance', *Sociometry*, September 1961, pp. 218–33.

REFERENCES

11 R. F. BALES, *Interaction Process Analysis*, Reading, Mass.: Addison-Wesley, 1950.
12 J. C. DIGGORY, *Self-Evaluation*, New York: John Wiley, 1966, p. 4.
13 G. W. ALLPORT, *Becoming*, New Haven: Yale University Press, 1955.
14 W. JAMES, *Psychology: The Briefer Course*, New York: Holt, 1910, pp. 200–3.
15 G. H. MEAD, *The Social Psychology of George Herbert Mead*, ed. Anselm Strauss, University of Chicago Press, 1956, p. 217.
16 A. W. GOULDNER, *The Coming Crisis of Western Sociology*, London: Heinemann, 1971, p. 495.
17 K. MARX, *Karl Marx, Early Writings*, ed. T. B. Bottomore, New York, 1964.

10   Reservations

1 M. NATANSON, *The Journeying Self*, Reading, Mass.: Addison-Wesley, 1970, p. 64.
2 H. GARFINKEL, *Studies in Ethnomethodology*, Englewood Cliffs: Prentice-Hall, 1967.
3 D. L. PHILLIPS, *Knowledge From What*, Chicago: Rand McNally, 1971, p. 55.
4 B. L. WHORF, *Language, Thought and Reality*, New York: John Wiley, 1956.
5 H. D. DUNCAN, *Communication and Social Order*, New York: Bedminster Press, 1962.
6 B. HARREL, 'Symbols, perception and meaning', in *Sociological Theory: Inquiries and Paradigms*, ed. L. Gross, New York: Harper & Row, 1967, pp. 122–3.
7 Ibid., p. 126.
8 G. SIMMEL, *The Sociology of Georg Simmel*, Chicago: Free Press, 1950, p. 309.
9 A. F. C. WALLACE, *Culture and Personality*, New York: Random House, 1961, pp. 39–40.
10 Ibid., p. 40.
11 A. ETZIONI, *The Active Society*, New York: Free Press, 1971.
12 J. D. DOUGLAS (ed.), *Understanding Everyday Life*, London: Routledge & Kegan Paul, 1971, p. 42.
13 S. M. LYMAN and M. B. SCOTT, *A Sociology of the Absurd*, New York: Appleton-Century-Crofts, 1970, p. 1.

Index

International Library of
Sociology

Edited by
John Rex
University of Warwick

Founded by
Karl Mannheim
as The International Library of Sociology
and Social Reconstruction

*This Catalogue also contains other Social Science
series published by Routledge*

Routledge & Kegan Paul London and Boston

68-74 Carter Lane London EC4V 5EL
9 Park Street Boston Mass 02108

Contents

● *Books so marked are available in paperback*
All books are in Metric Demy 8vo format (216 × 138mm approx.)

GENERAL SOCIOLOGY

Belshaw, Cyril. The Conditions of Social Performance. *An Exploratory Theory. 144 pp.*

Brown, Robert. Explanation in Social Science. *208 pp.*

Cain, Maureen E. Society and the Policeman's Role. *About 300 pp.*

Gibson, Quentin. The Logic of Social Enquiry. *240 pp.*

Homans, George C. Sentiments and Activities: *Essays in Social Science. 336 pp.*

Isajiw, Wsevold W. Causation and Functionalism in Sociology. *165 pp.*

Johnson, Harry M. Sociology: *a Systematic Introduction. Foreword by Robert K. Merton. 710 pp.*

Mannheim, Karl. Essays on Sociology and Social Psychology. *Edited by Paul Keckskemeti. With Editorial Note by Adolph Lowe. 344 pp.*

Systematic Sociology: *An Introduction to the Study of Society. Edited by J. S. Erös and Professor W. A. C. Stewart. 220 pp.*

Martindale, Don. The Nature and Types of Sociological Theory. *292 pp.*

● **Maus, Heinz.** A Short History of Sociology. *234 pp.*

Mey, Harald. Field-Theory. *A Study of its Application in the Social Sciences. 352 pp.*

Myrdal, Gunnar. Value in Social Theory: *A Collection of Essays on Methodology. Edited by Paul Streeten. 332 pp.*

Ogburn, William F., and **Nimkoff, Meyer F.** A Handbook of Sociology. *Preface by Karl Mannheim. 656 pp. 46 figures. 35 tables.*

Parsons, Talcott, and **Smelser, Neil J.** Economy and Society: *A Study in the Integration of Economic and Social Theory. 362 pp.*

● **Rex, John.** Key Problems of Sociological Theory. *220 pp.*

Stark, Werner. The Fundamental Forms of Social Thought. *280 pp.*

FOREIGN CLASSICS OF SOCIOLOGY

● **Durkheim, Emile.** Suicide. *A Study in Sociology. Edited and with an Introduction by George Simpson. 404 pp.*

Professional Ethics and Civic Morals. *Translated by Cornelia Brookfield. 288 pp.*

● **Gerth, H. H.,** and **Mills, C. Wright.** From Max Weber: *Essays in Sociology. 502 pp.*

Tönnies, Ferdinand. Community and Association. *(Gemeinschaft und Gesellschaft.) Translated and Supplemented by Charles P. Loomis. Foreword by Pitirim A. Sorokin. 334 pp.*

SOCIAL STRUCTURE

Andreski, Stanislav. Military Organization and Society. *Foreword by Professor A. R. Radcliffe-Brown. 226 pp. 1 folder.*

● **Cole, G. D. H.** Studies in Class Structure. *220 p.*

Coontz, Sydney H. Population Theories and the Economic Interpretation. *202 pp.*

Coser, Lewis. The Functions of Social Conflict. *204 pp.*

Dickie-Clark, H. F. Marginal Situation: *A Sociological Study of a Coloured Group. 240 pp. 11 tables.*

Glass, D. V. (Ed.). Social Mobility in Britain. *Contributions by J. Berent, T. Bottomore, R. C. Chambers, J. Floud, D. V. Glass, J. R. Hall, H. T. Himmelweit, R. K. Kelsall, F. M. Martin, C. A. Moser, R. Mukherjee, and W. Ziegel. 420 pp.*

Glaser, Barney, and **Strauss, Anselm L.** Status Passage. *A Formal Theory. 208 pp.*

Jones, Garth N. Planned Organizational Change: *An Exploratory Study Using an Empirical Approach. 268 pp.*

Kelsall, R. K. Higher Civil Servants in Britain: *From 1870 to the Present Day. 268 pp. 31 tables.*

König, René. The Community. *232 pp. Illustrated.*

● **Lawton, Denis.** Social Class, Language and Education. *192 pp.*

McLeish, John. The Theory of Social Change: *Four Views Considered. 128 pp.*

Marsh, David C. The Changing Social Structure in England and Wales, 1871-1961. *272 pp.*

Mouzelis, Nicos. Organization and Bureaucracy. *An Analysis of Modern Theories. 240 pp.*

Mulkay, M. J. Functionalism, Exchange and Theoretical Strategy. *272 pp.*

Ossowski, Stanislaw. Class Structure in the Social Consciousness. *210 pp.*

SOCIOLOGY AND POLITICS

Crick, Bernard. The American Science of Politics: *Its Origins and Conditions. 284 pp.*

Hertz, Frederick. Nationality in History and Politics: *A Psychology and Sociology of National Sentiment and Nationalism. 432 pp.*

Kornhauser, William. The Politics of Mass Society. *272 pp. 20 tables.*

Laidler, Harry W. History of Socialism. *Social-Economic Movements: An Historical and Comparative Survey of Socialism, Communism, Co-operation, Utopianism; and other Systems of Reform and Reconstruction. 992 pp.*

Mannheim, Karl. Freedom, Power and Democratic Planning. *Edited by Hans Gerth and Ernest K. Bramstedt. 424 pp.*

Mansur, Fatma. Process of Independence. *Foreword by A. H. Hanson. 208 pp.*

Martin, David A. Pacificism: *an Historical and Sociological Study. 262 pp.*

Myrdal, Gunnar. The Political Element in the Development of Economic Theory. *Translated from the German by Paul Streeten. 282 pp.*

Verney, Douglas V. The Analysis of Political Systems. *264 pp.*

Wootton, Graham. Workers, Unions and the State. *188 pp.*

FOREIGN AFFAIRS: THEIR SOCIAL, POLITICAL AND ECONOMIC FOUNDATIONS

Bonné, Alfred. State and Economics in the Middle East: *A Society in Transition. 482 pp.*

Studies in Economic Development: *with special reference to Conditions in the Under-developed Areas of Western Asia and India. 322 pp. 84 tables.*

Mayer, J. P. Political Thought in France from the Revolution to the Fifth Republic. *164 pp.*

CRIMINOLOGY

Ancel, Marc. Social Defence: *A Modern Approach to Criminal Problems. Foreword by Leon Radzinowicz. 240 pp.*

Cloward, Richard A., and **Ohlin, Lloyd E.** Delinquency and Opportunity: *A Theory of Delinquent Gangs. 248 pp.*

Downes, David M. The Delinquent Solution. *A Study in Subcultural Theory. 296 pp.*

Dunlop, A. B., and **McCabe, S.** Young Men in Detention Centres. *192 pp.*

Friedlander, Kate. The Psycho-Analytical Approach to Juvenile Delinquency: *Theory, Case Studies, Treatment. 320 pp.*

Glueck, Sheldon, and **Eleanor.** Family Environment and Delinquency. *With the statistical assistance of Rose W. Kneznek. 340 pp.*

Lopez-Rey, Manuel. Crime. *An Analytical Appraisal. 288 pp.*

Mannheim, Hermann. Comparative Criminology: *a Text Book. Two volumes. 442 pp. and 380 pp.*

Morris, Terence. The Criminal Area: *A Study in Social Ecology. Foreword by Hermann Mannheim. 232 pp. 25 tables. 4 maps.*

Trasler, Gordon. The Explanation of Criminality. *144 pp.*

SOCIAL PSYCHOLOGY

Bagley, Christopher. The Social Psychology of the Child with Epilepsy. *320 pp.*

Barbu, Zevedei. Problems of Historical Psychology. *248 pp.*

Blackburn, Julian. Psychology and the Social Pattern. *184 pp.*

● **Fleming, C. M.** Adolescence: *Its Social Psychology: With an Introduction to recent findings from the fields of Anthropology, Physiology, Medicine, Psychometrics and Sociometry. 288 pp.*

● The Social Psychology of Education: *An Introduction and Guide to Its Study. 136 pp.*

Homans, George C. The Human Group. *Foreword by Bernard DeVoto. Introduction by Robert K. Merton. 526 pp.*

Social Behaviour: *its Elementary Forms. 416 pp.*

5

Klein, Josephine. The Study of Groups. *226 pp. 31 figures. 5 tables.*

Linton, Ralph. The Cultural Background of Personality. *132 pp.*

Mayo, Elton. The Social Problems of an Industrial Civilization. *With an appendix on the Political Problem. 180 pp.*

Ottaway, A. K. C. Learning Through Group Experience. *176 pp.*

Ridder, J. C. de. The Personality of the Urban African in South Africa. *A Thematic Apperception Test Study. 196 pp. 12 plates.*

● **Rose, Arnold M.** (Ed.). Human Behaviour and Social Processes: *an Interactionist Approach. Contributions by Arnold M. Rose, Ralph H. Turner, Anselm Strauss, Everett C. Hughes, E. Franklin Frazier, Howard S. Becker, et al. 696 pp.*

Smelser, Neil J. Theory of Collective Behaviour. *448 pp.*

Stephenson, Geoffrey M. The Development of Conscience. *128 pp.*

Young, Kimball. Handbook of Social Psychology. *658 pp. 16 figures. 10 tables.*

SOCIOLOGY OF THE FAMILY

Banks, J. A. Prosperity and Parenthood: *A Study of Family Planning among The Victorian Middle Classes. 262 pp.*

Bell, Colin R. Middle Class Families: *Social and Geographical Mobility. 224 pp.*

Burton, Lindy. Vulnerable Children. *272 pp.*

Gavron, Hannah. The Captive Wife: *Conflicts of Household Mothers. 190 pp.*

George, Victor, and **Wilding, Paul.** Motherless Families. *220 pp.*

Klein, Josephine. Samples from English Cultures.
   1. Three Preliminary Studies and Aspects of Adult Life in England. *447 pp.*
   2. Child-Rearing Practices and Index. *247 pp.*

Klein, Viola. Britain's Married Women Workers. *180 pp.*
   The Feminine Character. *History of an Ideology. 244 pp.*

McWhinnie, Alexina M. Adopted Children. *How They Grow Up. 304 pp.*

Myrdal, Alva, and **Klein, Viola.** Women's Two Roles: *Home and Work. 238 pp. 27 tables.*

Parsons, Talcott, and **Bales, Robert F.** Family: *Socialization and Interaction Process. In collaboration with James Olds, Morris Zelditch and Philip E. Slater. 456 pp. 50 figures and tables.*

SOCIAL SERVICES

Bastide, Roger. The Sociology of Mental Disorder. *Translated from the French by Jean McNeil. 264 pp.*

Carlebach, Julius. Caring For Children in Trouble. *266 pp.*

Forder, R. A. (Ed.). Penelope Hall's Social Services of Modern England. *352 pp.*

George, Victor. Foster Care. *Theory and Practice. 234 pp.*
   Social Security: *Beveridge and After. 258 pp.*

● **Goetschius, George W.** Working with Community Groups. *256 pp.*

Goetschius, George W., and **Tash, Joan.** Working with Unattached Youth. *416 pp.*

Hall, M. P., and **Howes, I. V.** The Church in Social Work. *A Study of Moral Welfare Work undertaken by the Church of England. 320 pp.*

Heywood, Jean S. Children in Care: *the Development of the Service for the Deprived Child. 264 pp.*

Hoenig, J., and **Hamilton, Marian W.** The De-Segration of the Mentally Ill. *284 pp.*

Jones, Kathleen. Lunacy, Law and Conscience, *1744-1845: the Social History of the Care of the Insane. 268 pp.*

Mental Health and Social Policy, 1845-1959. *264 pp.*

King, Roy D., Raynes, Norma V., and **Tizard, Jack.** Patterns of Residential Care. *356 pp.*

Leigh, John. Young People and Leisure. *256 pp.*

Morris, Pauline. Put Away: *A Sociological Study of Institutions for the Mentally Retarded. 364 pp.*

Nokes, P. L. The Professional Task in Welfare Practice. *152 pp.*

Timms, Noel. Psychiatric Social Work in Great Britain (1939-1962). *280 pp.*

● Social Casework: *Principles and Practice. 256 pp.*

Trasler, Gordon. In Place of Parents: *A Study in Foster Care. 272 pp.*

Young, A. F., and **Ashton, E. T.** British Social Work in the Nineteenth Century. *288 pp.*

Young, A. F. Social Services in British Industry. *272 pp.*

SOCIOLOGY OF EDUCATION

Banks, Olive. Parity and Prestige in English Secondary Education: a Study in Educational Sociology. *272 pp.*

Bentwich, Joseph. Education in Israel. *224 pp. 8 pp. plates.*

● **Blyth, W. A. L.** English Primary Education. *A Sociological Description.*
1. Schools. *232 pp.*
2. Background. *168 pp.*

Collier, K. G. The Social Purposes of Education: *Personal and Social Values in Education. 268 pp.*

Dale, R. R., and **Griffith, S.** Down Stream: *Failure in the Grammar School. 108 pp.*

Dore, R. P. Education in Tokugawa Japan. *356 pp. 9 pp. plates*

Evans, K. M. Sociometry and Education. *158 pp.*

Foster, P. J. Education and Social Change in Ghana. *336 pp. 3 maps.*

Fraser, W. R. Education and Society in Modern France. *150 pp.*

Grace, Gerald R. Role Conflict and the Teacher. *About 200 pp.*

Hans, Nicholas. New Trends in Education in the Eighteenth Century. *278 pp. 19 tables.*

● Comparative Education: *A Study of Educational Factors and Traditions. 360 pp.*

Hargreaves, David. Interpersonal Relations and Education. *432 pp.*
● Social Relations in a Secondary School. *240 pp.*
Holmes, Brian. Problems in Education. *A Comparative Approach. 336 pp.*
King, Ronald. Values and Involvement in a Grammar School. *164 pp.*
● **Mannheim, Karl,** and **Stewart, W. A. C.** An Introduction to the Sociology of Education. *206 pp.*
Morris, Raymond N. The Sixth Form and College Entrance. *231 pp.*
● **Musgrove, F.** Youth and the Social Order. *176 pp.*
● **Ottaway, A. K. C.** Education and Society: *An Introduction to the Sociology of Education. With an Introduction by W. O. Lester Smith. 212 pp.*
Peers, Robert. Adult Education: *A Comparative Study. 398 pp.*
Pritchard, D. G. Education and the Handicapped: *1760 to 1960. 258 pp.*
Richardson, Helen. Adolescent Girls in Approved Schools. *308 pp.*
Simon, Brian, and **Joan** (Eds.). Educational Psychology in the U.S.S.R. *Introduction by Brian and Joan Simon. Translation by Joan Simon. Papers by D. N. Bogoiavlenski and N. A. Menchinskaia, D. B. Elkonin, E. A. Fleshner, Z. I. Kalmykova, G. S. Kostiuk, V. A. Krutetski, A. N. Leontiev, A. R. Luria, E. A. Milerian, R. G. Natadze, B. M. Teplov, L. S. Vygotski, L. V. Zankov. 296 pp.*
Stratta, Erica. The Education of Borstal Boys. *A Study of their Educational Experiences prior to, and during Borstal Training. 256 pp.*

SOCIOLOGY OF CULTURE

Eppel, E. M., and **M.** Adolescents and Morality: *A Study of some Moral Values and Dilemmas of Working Adolescents in the Context of a changing Climate of Opinion. Foreword by W. J. H. Sprott. 268 pp. 39 tables.*
● **Fromm, Erich.** The Fear of Freedom. *286 pp.*
The Sane Society. *400 pp.*
● **Mannheim, Karl.** Diagnosis of Our Time: *Wartime Essays of a Sociologist. 208 pp.*
Essays on the Sociology of Culture. *Edited by Ernst Mannheim in co-operation with Paul Kecskemeti. Editorial Note by Adolph Lowe. 280 pp.*
Weber, Alfred. Farewell to European History: *or The Conquest of Nihilism. Translated from the German by R. F. C. Hull. 224 pp.*

SOCIOLOGY OF RELIGION

Argyle, Michael. Religious Behaviour. *224 pp. 8 figures. 41 tables.*
Nelson, G. K. Spiritualism and Society. *313 pp.*

Stark, Werner. The Sociology of Religion. *A Study of Christendom.*
  Volume I. *Established Religion. 248 pp.*
  Volume II. *Sectarian Religion. 368 pp.*
  Volume III. *The Universal Church. 464 pp.*
  Volume IV. *Types of Religious Man. 352 pp.*
  Volume V. *Types of Religious Culture. 464 pp.*
Watt, W. Montgomery. Islam and the Integration of Society. *320 pp.*

SOCIOLOGY OF ART AND LITERATURE

Beljame, Alexandre. Men of Letters and the English Public in the Eighteenth
  Century: *1660-1744, Dryden, Addison, Pope. Edited with an Introduction
  and Notes by Bonamy Dobrée. Translated by E. O. Lorimer. 532 pp.*
Jarvie, Ian C. Towards a Sociology of the Cinema. *A Comparative Essay
  on the Structure and Functioning of a Major Entertainment Industry.
  405 pp.*
Rust, Frances S. Dance in Society. *An Analysis of the Relationships between
  the Social Dance and Society in England from the Middle Ages to the
  Present Day. 256 pp. 8 pp. of plates.*
Schücking, L. L. The Sociology of Literary Taste. *112 pp.*
Silbermann, Alphons. The Sociology of Music. *Translated from the German
  by Corbet Stewart. 222 pp.*

SOCIOLOGY OF KNOWLEDGE

Mannheim, Karl. Essays on the Sociology of Knowledge. *Edited by Paul
  Kecskemeti. Editorial note by Adolph Lowe. 353 pp.*
Stark, Werner. The Sociology of Knowledge: *An Essay in Aid of a Deeper
  Understanding of the History of Ideas. 384 pp.*

URBAN SOCIOLOGY

Ashworth, William. The Genesis of Modern British Town Planning: *A Study
  in Economic and Social History of the Nineteenth and Twentieth Centuries.
  288 pp.*
Cullingworth, J. B. Housing Needs and Planning Policy: *A Restatement of
  the Problems of Housing Need and 'Overspill' in England and Wales.
  232 pp. 44 tables. 8 maps.*
Dickinson, Robert E. City and Region: *A Geographical Interpretation.
  608 pp. 125 figures.*
  The West European City: *A Geographical Interpretation. 600 pp. 129 maps.
  29 plates.*
● The City Region in Western Europe. *320 pp. Maps.*

Humphreys, Alexander J. New Dubliners: *Urbanization and the Irish Family. Foreword by George C. Homans. 304 pp.*

Jackson, Brian. Working Class Community: *Some General Notions raised by a Series of Studies in Northern England. 192 pp.*

Jennings, Hilda. Societies in the Making: *a Study of Development and Re-development within a County Borough. Foreword by D. A. Clark. 286 pp.*

Kerr, Madeline. The People of Ship Street. *240 pp.*

● **Mann, P. H.** An Approach to Urban Sociology. *240 pp.*

Morris, R. N., and **Mogey, J.** The Sociology of Housing. *Studies at Berinsfield. 232 pp. 4 pp. plates.*

Rosser, C., and **Harris, C.** The Family and Social Change. *A Study of Family and Kinship in a South Wales Town. 352 pp. 8 maps.*

RURAL SOCIOLOGY

Chambers, R. J. H. Settlement Schemes in Africa: *A Selective Study. 268 pp.*

Haswell, M. R. The Economics of Development in Village India. *120 pp.*

Littlejohn, James. Westrigg: *the Sociology of a Cheviot Parish. 172 pp. 5 figures.*

Williams, W. M. The Country Craftsman: *A Study of Some Rural Crafts and the Rural Industries Organization in England. 248 pp. 9 figures. (Dartington Hall Studies in Rural Sociology.)*

The Sociology of an English Village: *Gosforth. 272 pp. 12 figures. 13 tables.*

SOCIOLOGY OF INDUSTRY AND DISTRIBUTION

Anderson, Nels. Work and Leisure. *280 pp.*

● **Blau, Peter M.,** and **Scott, W. Richard.** Formal Organizations: *a Comparative approach. Introduction and Additional Bibliography by J. H. Smith. 326 pp.*

Eldridge, J. E. T. Industrial Disputes. *Essays in the Sociology of Industrial Relations. 288 pp.*

Hetzler, Stanley. Technological Growth and Social Change. *Achieving Modernization. 269 pp.*

Hollowell, Peter G. The Lorry Driver. *272 pp.*

Jefferys, Margot, *with the assistance of Winifred Moss.* Mobility in the Labour Market: *Employment Changes in Battersea and Dagenham. Preface by Barbara Wootton. 186 pp. 51 tables.*

Millerson, Geoffrey. The Qualifying Associations: *a Study in Professionalization. 320 pp.*

Smelser, Neil J. Social Change in the Industrial Revolution: *An Application of Theory to the Lancashire Cotton Industry, 1770-1840. 468 pp. 12 figures. 14 tables.*

Williams, Gertrude. Recruitment to Skilled Trades. *240 pp.*

Young, A. F. Industrial Injuries Insurance: *an Examination of British Policy.* *192 pp.*

ANTHROPOLOGY

Ammar, Hamed. Growing up in an Egyptian Village: *Silwa, Province of Aswan. 336 pp.*

Brandel-Syrier, Mia. Reeftown Elite. *A Study of Social Mobility in a Modern African Community on the Reef. 376 pp.*

Crook, David, and **Isabel.** Revolution in a Chinese Village: *Ten Mile Inn. 230 pp. 8 plates. 1 map.*
The First Years of Yangyi Commune. *302 pp. 12 plates.*

Dickie-Clark, H. F. The Marginal Situation. *A Sociological Study of a Coloured Group. 236 pp.*

Dube, S. C. Indian Village. *Foreword by Morris Edward Opler. 276 pp. 4 plates.*
India's Changing Villages: *Human Factors in Community Development. 260 pp. 8 plates. 1 map.*

Firth, Raymond. Malay Fishermen. *Their Peasant Economy. 420 pp. 17 pp. plates.*

Gulliver, P. H. Social Control in an African Society: a Study of the Arusha, Agricultural Masai of Northern Tanganyika. *320 pp. 8 plates. 10 figures.*

Ishwaran, K. Shivapur. *A South Indian Village. 216 pp.*
Tradition and Economy in Village India: *An Interactionist Approach. Foreword by Conrad Arensburg. 176 pp.*

Jarvie, Ian C. The Revolution in Anthropology. *268 pp.*

Jarvie, Ian C., and **Agassi, Joseph.** Hong Kong. *A Society in Transition. 396 pp. Illustrated with plates and maps.*

Little, Kenneth L. Mende of Sierra Leone. *308 pp. and folder.*
Negroes in Britain. *With a New Introduction and Contemporary Study by Leonard Bloom. 320 pp.*

Lowie, Robert H. Social Organization. *494 pp.*

Mayer, Adrian C. Caste and Kinship in Central India: *A Village and its Region. 328 pp. 16 plates. 15 figures. 16 tables.*

Smith, Raymond T. The Negro Family in British Guiana: *Family Structure and Social Status in the Villages. With a Foreword by Meyer Fortes. 314 pp. 8 plates. 1 figure. 4 maps.*

DOCUMENTARY

Meek, Dorothea L. (Ed.). Soviet Youth: *Some Achievements and Problems. Excerpts from the Soviet Press, translated by the editor. 280 pp.*

Schlesinger, Rudolf (Ed.). Changing Attitudes in Soviet Russia.
2. *The Nationalities Problem and Soviet Administration. Selected Readings on the Development of Soviet Nationalities Policies. Introduced by the editor. Translated by W. W. Gottlieb. 324 pp.*

SOCIOLOGY AND PHILOSOPHY

Barnsley, John H. The Social Reality of Ethics. *A Comparative Analysis of Moral Codes. 448 pp.*

Douglas, Jack D. (Ed.). Understanding Everyday Life. *Toward the Reconstruction of Sociological Knowledge. Contributions by Alan F. Blum. Aaron W. Cicourel, Norman K. Denzin, Jack D. Douglas, John Heeren, Peter McHugh, Peter K. Manning, Melvin Power, Matthew Speier, Roy Turner, D. Lawrence Wieder, Thomas P. Wilson and Don H. Zimmerman. 358 pp.*

Jarvie, Ian C. Concepts and Society. *216 pp.*

Roche, Maurice. Phenomenology, Language and the Social Sciences. *About 400 pp.*

Sklair, Leslie. The Sociology of Progress. *320 pp.*

International Library of Social Policy

General Editor Kathleen Janes

Jones, Kathleen. Mental Health Services. *A history, 1744-1971. About 500 pp.*

Thomas, J. E. The English Prison Officer since 1850: *A Study in Conflict. 258 pp.*

Primary Socialization, Language and Education

General Editor Basil Bernstein

Bernstein, Basil. Class, Codes and Control. *2 volumes.*
  1. *Theoretical Studies Towards a Sociology of Language. 254 pp.*
  2. *Applied Studies Towards a Sociology of Language. About 400 pp.*

Brandis, Walter, and **Henderson, Dorothy.** Social Class, Language and Communication. *288 pp.*

Cook, Jenny. Socialization and Social Control. *About 300 pp.*

Gahagan, D. M., and **G. A.** Talk Reform. *Exploration in Language for Infant School Children. 160 pp.*

Robinson, W. P., and **Rackstraw, Susan, D. A.** A Question of Answers. *2 volumes. 192 pp. and 180 pp.*

Turner, Geoffrey, J., and **Mohan, Bernard, A.** A Linguistic Description and Computer Programme for Children's Speech. *208 pp.*

Reports of the Institute of Community Studies and the Institute of Social Studies in Medical Care

Cartwright, Ann. Human Relations and Hospital Care. *272 pp.*
  Parents and Family Planning Services. *306 pp.*
  Patients and their Doctors. *A Study of General Practice. 304 pp.*
Dunnell, Karen, and **Cartwright, Ann.** Medicine Takers, Prescribers and Hoarders. *About 140 pp.*
● **Jackson, Brian.** Streaming: *an Education System in Miniature. 168 pp.*
Jackson, Brian, and **Marsden, Dennis.** Education and the Working Class: *Some General Themes raised by a Study of 88 Working-class Children in a Northern Industrial City. 268 pp. 2 folders.*
Marris, Peter. Widows and their Families. *Foreword by Dr. John Bowlby. 184 pp. 18 tables. Statistical Summary.*
  Family and Social Change in an African City. *A Study of Rehousing in Lagos. 196 pp. 1 map. 4 plates. 53 tables.*
  The Experience of Higher Education. *232 pp. 27 tables.*
Marris, Peter, and **Rein, Martin.** Dilemmas of Social Reform. *Poverty and Community Action in the United States. 256 pp.*
Marris, Peter, and **Somerset, Anthony.** African Businessmen. *A Study of Entrepreneurship and Development in Kenya. 256 pp.*
Runciman, W. G. Relative Deprivation and Social Justice. *A Study of Attitudes to Social Inequality in Twentieth Century England. 352 pp.*
Townsend, Peter. The Family Life of Old People: *An Inquiry in East London. Foreword by J. H. Sheldon. 300 pp. 3 figures. 63 tables.*
Willmott, Peter. Adolescent Boys in East London. *230 pp.*
  The Evolution of a Community: *a study of Dagenham after forty years. 168 pp. 2 maps.*
Willmott, Peter, and **Young, Michael.** Family and Class in a London Suburb. *202 pp. 47 tables.*
Young, Michael. Innovation and Research in Education. *192 pp.*
● **Young, Michael,** and **McGeeney, Patrick.** Learning Begins at Home. *A Study of a Junior School and its Parents. 128 pp.*
Young, Michael, and **Willmott, Peter.** Family and Kinship in East London. *Foreword by Richard M. Titmuss. 252 pp. 39 tables.*

Medicine, Illness and Society
General Editor   W. M. Williams

Robinson, David. The Process of Becoming Ill.
Stacey, Margaret. *et al.* Hospitals, Children and Their Families. *The Report of a Pilot Study. 202 pp.*

Routledge Social Science Journals

The British Journal of Sociology. *Edited by Terence P. Morris. Vol. 1, No. 1, March 1950 and Quarterly. Roy. 8vo. Back numbers available. An international journal with articles on all aspects of sociology.*

Economy and Society. *Vol. 1, No. 1. February 1972 and Quarterly. Metric Roy. 8vo. A journal for all social scientists covering sociology, philosophy, anthropology, economics and history.*

Printed in Great Britain by Lewis Reprints Limited
Brown Knight & Truscott Group, London and Tonbridge   21972